21 Great Track Plans for Compact Layouts

by
Ken Hoganson

From the pages of *O Gauge Railroading* magazine

Cover Photo: Mel Garelick
Design and Layout: Rich Melvin

Print ISBN: 978-1-7361500-1-6
E-Book ISBN: 978-1-7361500-2-3

LIONEL LLC © and Lionel® brand names and logos used with permission.
AtlasO® brand names and logos used with permission.

©2021 ALL RIGHTS RESERVED
OGR Publishing, Inc., 1310 Eastside Centre Ct., Suite 6
Mountain Home, AR 72653
www.ogaugerr.com

An Introduction by Editor-in-Chief Allan Miller

Ken Hoganson's creativity first graced the pages of *O Gauge Railroading* magazine in Run 275, our January 2015 issue, with an article titled "Twice the Fun." Subsequently, he began providing a variety of track plans for the magazine on a fairly regular basis. Most of these O gauge layouts were designed for small to medium-size spaces using Lionel FasTrack or the Atlas O track system.

In Run 304, the February/March 2019 issue, Ken presented a track plan titled, "The Triple-R Railroad: O Gauge in a Small Space" and that kicked off what became a truly regular series of interesting and fun-filled track plans that have been published in every issue of *OGR* to date (and hopefully well into the future).

Early in 2021, I was browsing through the *O Gauge Railroading* Master Article Index that *OGR* Publisher Emeritus Rich Melvin had just compiled; and on a let-me-give-it-a-test whim, I decided to type **Ken Hoganson** into the search box. Lo and behold, up came a long string of layout-planning articles by Ken! This triggered a light bulb (LED, of course, consistent with energy saving) in my aging mind, and it dawned on me that a book comprised of the full range of Ken's track plans might be of great use to beginners in our great hobby as well as those hobbyists who already have a good bit of experience and are interested in exploring something a bit different.

Discussions with my magazine partners, Publisher Alan Arnold and Associate Editor Ed Boyle, and including Rich and Ken, resulted in a decision to offer the entire O gauge community an opportunity to benefit from Ken Hoganson's experience and creativity.

This book also includes a track plan not published in the magazine, along with two special sections devoted to thorough discussions of the Lionel FasTrack system and the Atlas O track system. Those two sections alone are, in my view, worth the price of the book.

It has been my pleasure to serve as Ken's editor at *OGR* over the over the past seven-plus years; and I am grateful for his contributions to enhancing what surely is the world's greatest, most diverse, and most creative hobby. And as a final word: if you decide to construct a layout with one of the track plans presented here, please be sure to document the process with words and pictures. Then consider submitting an article to *OGR* so you, too, can be a part of sharing our great hobby.

Allan Miller
Editor-in-Chief
O Gauge Railroading magazine
www.ogaugerr.com

About the Author

Ken Hoganson is a Professor of Computer Science and a textbook author. He grew up in Fargo, North Dakota (yes, *that* Fargo), watching Great Northern, Northern Pacific, and Milwaukee Road trains run through his home town. As a young man, he was an avid outdoor adventurer, swimmer, and long-distance runner.

Ken's career has spanned a multitude of vocations including pool manager and lifeguard, blackjack dealer, assembly-line worker, and security guard. After his initial education, he served in the U.S. Army running computer systems, finishing his military service as a captain. Ken earned his Ph.D. in Computer Science at Auburn University.

Ken has built layouts in Z, N, HO, and O scale, and ran an outdoor G scale layout in his backyard for a few years. He jumped into O gauge with the birth of his son, as a fun activity they could share. He is currently working on his first 5x12 S scale layout using Lionel's S-FasTrack.

Ken is avidly following SpaceX's adventures with their new Starship rocket in Boca Chica, Texas.

Ken's children are grown, and he lives with his wife and three cats in a small town in Georgia, just North of Atlanta.

At Work

At Play

TABLE of CONTENTS

Layout Planning with Lionel FasTrack	5
Layout Planning with Atlas O Track	17
An Intro-to-O Layout	25
Just a Bit Beyond the Basic	27
Planning the North Ridge Railroad	31
Something Old, Something New	35
Track Combo for the Valley City Northern	39
The Triple-R Railroad	45
John Allen's "Timesaver" in O Gauge	49
Action on the Peach Grove Line	51
Pumping Iron on the DM&IR	55
A 3-Rail Gorre & Daphetid	61
Model the Nickel Plate Road	67
Lionel's 56"x 86" Train Table	71
Lionel FasTrack Layout for a Spare Room	75
Railroad Action at Bellows Falls, Vermont	79
A Room Full of Operating Fun	83
Summit Canyon RR on a Shelf	91
Anaconda Mining Railroad	95
The Easy-A Railroad	99
The Great Valley Western RR in 4x8	103
The Southern & Pacific Railroad	107
Twice the Fun on the Cisco RR	111

Layout Planning with Lionel FasTrack

Lionel's FasTrack with its integrated plastic, molded roadbed is a popular and widely available track system. Lionel packages this track in their O gauge train sets, so FasTrack has wide exposure to hobbyists as well as the casual train runner and excited kids. Lionel offers classic Christmas sets and the very popular Polar Express train set with add-ons and expansion possibilities with FasTrack.

The FasTrack system has good electrical conductivity and snaps together tightly for excellent alignment of track sections. FasTrack curves are offered in diameters ranging from 31" (O31) to 96" (O96), measured at the center rail diameter in 12" increments from O36 (36" diameter) to O48, O60, O72, O84, and O96, which is the widest (Figure A). Curved sections are offered in varying degrees of curvature, which can be important in designing layouts and fitting curves (Table 1). You can create different combinations of curvature.

to run without concern of sideswiping or overhang of cars and locomotives. The wide spacing also allows you to get your hands and fingers on track and equipment between the tracks. The wide 6" center-rail spacing looks too wide for yard tracks, which are often quite close together, and that limits the number of yard tracks in a given space. Later on in this chapter I will show you a few *tricks* to make tighter yards.

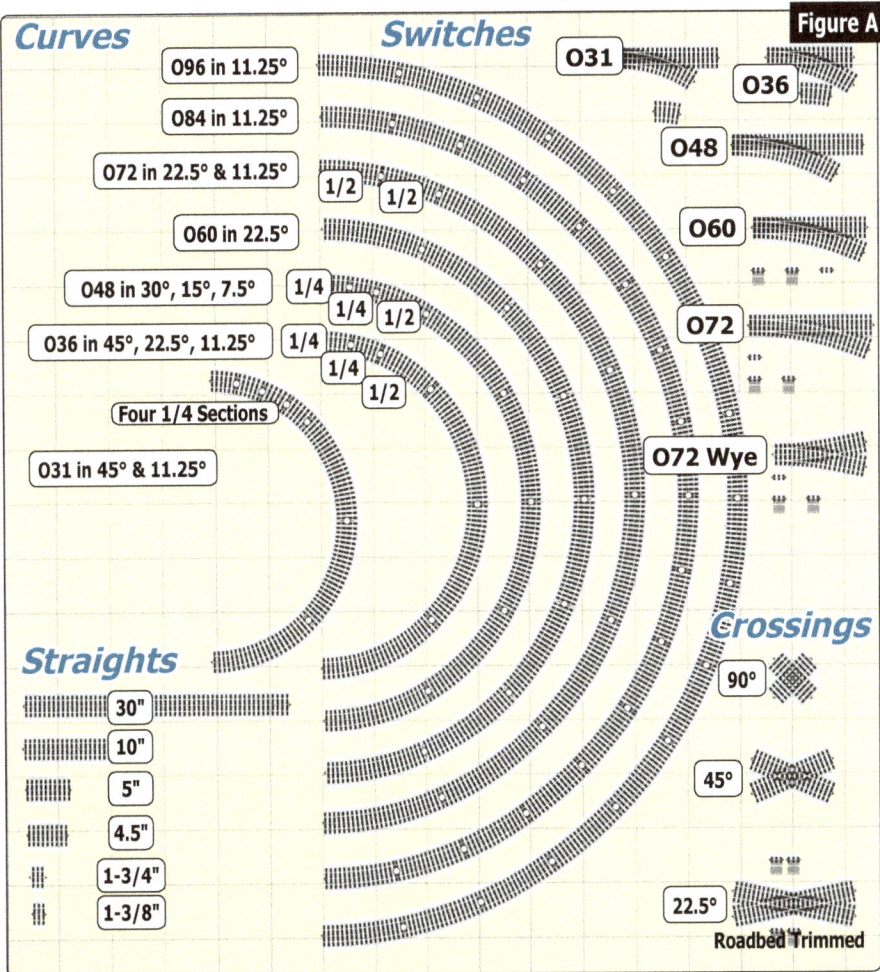

FasTrack Curves — Table 1
Sections by Degrees

DIAM	FULL	HALF	QTR
O31	45°	n/a	11.25°
O36	45°	22.5°	11.25°
O48	30°	15°	7.5°
O60	22.5°	n/a	n/a
O72	22.5°	11.25°	n/a
O84	11.25°	n/a	n/a
O96	11.25°	n/a	11.25°

Parallel curved diameter track with a 12" spacing has a 6" center-rail clearance between trains running on parallel tracks. This is a wide spacing that allows for trains

Integrated Plastic Roadbed

The plastic FasTrack roadbed is 3-3/8" wide. The roadbed extends 3/8" beyond the edge of the ties (Photo 1), so FasTrack roadbed builds in a bit of often-useful clearance between the trains and the edge of the table.

FasTrack Switches

Switches are available in curve diameters from O31 to O72, but they are not offered in O84 or O96 (Figure A). The switches are excellent, and the switch points are held securely in the correct position. Switches are available with manual operation or remote/command-control operation. O31 and O36 switches are packaged with a quarter section of track to fill in a complete curve section. O31, O36, and O48 switches are drop-in replacements for curved sections of track without changing the curve alignment. But O60 and O72 switches include small 1-3/8" fitter track sections, so they are not drop-in replacements for curves without a little modification.

The switches are actually a bit tighter in diameter than the equivalent curved track sections due to the short straight length just before the points. When it's possible, you should consider using a switch of the next wider diameter for smoother operation.

FasTrack Straight Sections

A wide selection of straight sections is offered, ranging from 1-3/8" to 30" long. One note of caution: the smallest straight section difference that can be covered is 1/8" (Table 2), which means that some care and a bit of trial and error may be needed to make good section joints everywhere, and this can be a time-consuming and frustrating process.

The difference in lengths of the two small sections—1-3/8" and 1-3/4"—is 3/8", while the difference between the next size up of 4-1/2" and 5" is, logically, 1/2". But other spans can be created with combinations of small straight sections. For example, three 1-3/8" sections together make a straight of 4-1/8". Four 1-3/8" sections combined make a length of 5-1/2". A 1-3/8" section with two 1-3/4" sections makes a combined length of 4-7/8", a difference of 1/8" to the next size up of 5", which is the smallest difference possible with FasTrack. Combining small sections to make precise-length straights can add to the section count and the total cost of a layout. In general, a smaller section count is better in terms of both cost and electrical conductivity across fewer joints. Table 2 shows the combinations of sections to give you all the possible lengths in a minimum number of track sections.

FasTrack Straight Lengths Combinations — Table 2

Length	Difference	1-3/8"	1-3/4"	4-1/2"	5"	10"	# Pieces
1-3/8		1					1
1-3/4	3/8		1				1
2-3/4	1	2					2
3-1/8	3/8	1	1				2
3-1/2	3/8		2				2
4-1/8	5/8	3					3
4-1/2	3/8			1			1
4-7/8	3/8	1	2				3
5	1/8				1		1
5-1/4	1/4		3				3
5-1/2	1/4	4					4
5-7/8	3/8	1		1			2
6-1/4	3/8		1	1			2
6-3/8	1/8	1			1		2
6-5/8	1/4	1	3				4
6-3/4	1/8		1		1		2
6-7/8	1/8	5					5
7	1/8		4				4
7-1/4	1/4	2		1			3
7-5/8	3/8	1	1	1			3
7-3/4	1/8	2			1		3
8	1/4		2	1			3
8-1/8	1/8	1	1		1		3
8-1/4	1/8	6					6
8-3/8	1/8	1	4				5
8-1/2	1/8		2		1		3
8-5/8	1/8	3		1			4
8-3/4	1/8		5				5
9	1/4			2			2
9-1/8	1/8	3			1		4
9-3/8	1/4	1	2	1			4
9-1/2	1/8			1	1		2
9-5/8	1/8	7					7
9-3/4	1/8		3	1			4
9-7/8	1/8	1	2		1		4
10	1/8					1	1

Finding Closing Solutions with FasTrack

Because FasTrack snaps together so tightly and precisely, track plans allow little room for *fudging*. For example, Lionel traditional tubular track has solid pins between track sections that allow for track joints to stretch a bit. Trains can span the stretched track joints by running on the pins, with just a *click-clack* as they cross the rail joints. A long alignment of multiple track sections can distribute a gap to spread the difference, so it is not very noticeable.

Due to the unforgiving tight tolerances and the holding strength of FasTrack joints, and in light of the 1/8" minimum section lengths (refer to Table 2), layout planning with FasTrack can take time and may require multiple attempts in order to make a plan with good section joints. Figure B shows a process of trial and error to make a good closing joint with O36 FasTrack.

- The first try is close, but not close enough, even with the 1-3/4" section.

- The second try is better, using two 1-3/8" sections, but the alignment is still off and will not close.

- The solution required a bit of creativity. I used quarter sections of O36 and added 22.5 degrees of O48 curvature, comprised of an O48 quarter section (7.5 degree) and a O48 half section (15 degree). That made it work.

With experience, finding good alignment-fitting solutions will get easier but will still take some trial and error, along with time and effort. But some alignments may still not close, even after trying multiple arrangements. If you find yourself facing one of these situations, consider FasTrack modifications, which can be part of the closing solution.

Modifying FasTrack Sections

It is possible to make custom-length FasTrack sections by cutting out a middle length of a larger piece, preserving the section end connections, and then combining the two end pieces together. It is, however, difficult to achieve a precise fit, and it is difficult to align the two cut sections precisely with a clean joint. Note that the plans presented here do not use custom-length FasTrack sections.

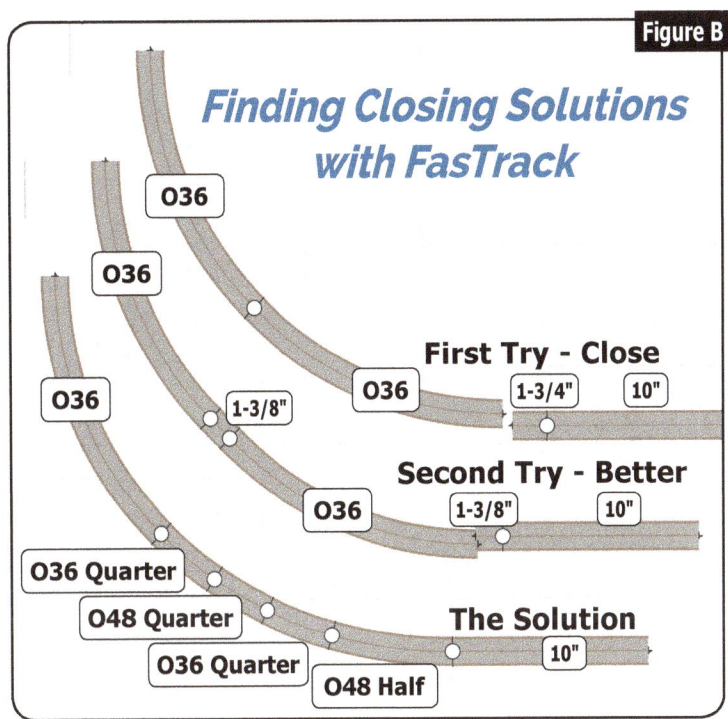

Figure B

Stretching FasTrack Joints

FasTrack will not compress and will not tolerate much of an angle difference in making a joint, so all the plans presented here are perfect in curvature alignment.

However, FasTrack section joints can be stretched a bit. The section joints pull tightly together, but by trimming the ball of each section that fits into the socket on both sections to be joined, a bit of stretch can be achieved—up to 1/16". This leaves a gap in the roadbed across the joint, which can be filled with a filler cut from a plastic sheet in a matching gray color. You can find these sheets at hobby stores in an assortment of precise thicknesses. Paper of various thicknesses could also be used. The inserted filler can be glued to the end of one of the sections to be joined. Multiple section joints in a length of track can be stretched to make a variety of track lengths in between the lengths shown in Table 1, which would not be possible otherwise.

Photo 2 illustrates a joint stretched by about 1/32" with plastic glued between two sections (shown in yellow for clarity). The plastic balls were first trimmed flat on one side with a hobby knife so they would not hold as tightly in the sockets and thus allow the stretch (Photo 3). Photo 4 shows the back of the joint, with the two trimmed balls fitting perfectly and tightly together. The plans presented here do not rely on stretching FasTrack joints this way, but this easy technique can be used if your plans have a bit of a joint that is noticeable when actually constructed on the table.

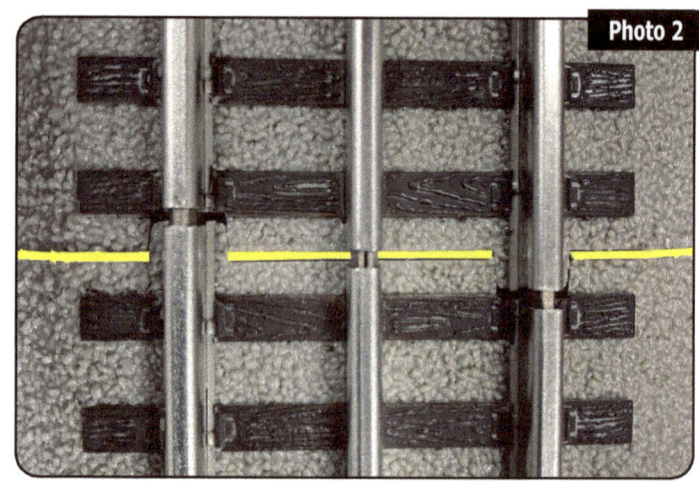

The technique of trimming the balls of ball-socket FasTrack section joints can be put to another use: to make a track section that is easier to separate and then reconnect when a layout module or section is intended to disconnect. The balls of a FasTrack section that span a module or section joint can be trimmed, as well as the balls on the receiving track section.

FasTrack Manufacturing Variance

Different manufacturing runs will, at times, introduce a small variance in the length of the plastic roadbed in some sections, measured as much as 1/32". That seems like a very small variance, but as Table 1 shows, in order to make needed specific lengths of FasTrack, multiple track sections need to be combined. If four sections with a 1/32" variance are used together, the total variance may quadruple to 1/8", which is sufficient to cause ill-fitting track arrangements. Fortunately, the above technique of stretching FasTrack joints can come to your rescue.

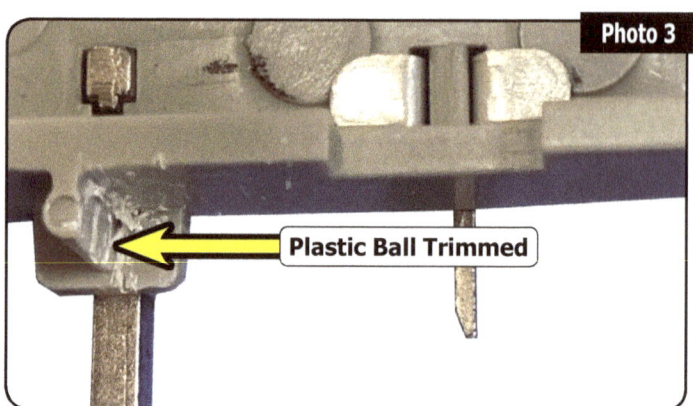

O60 and O72 Switch 1-3/8" Fitter Omission

FasTrack O60 and O72 switches are not drop-in replacements for O60 and O72 curves due to the lack of 1-3/8" fitter sections. However, if the switches are to be connected with a curve section of track, you can trim a piece of the roadbed on a curved section so it will mate with a switch without a 1-3/8" fitter piece.

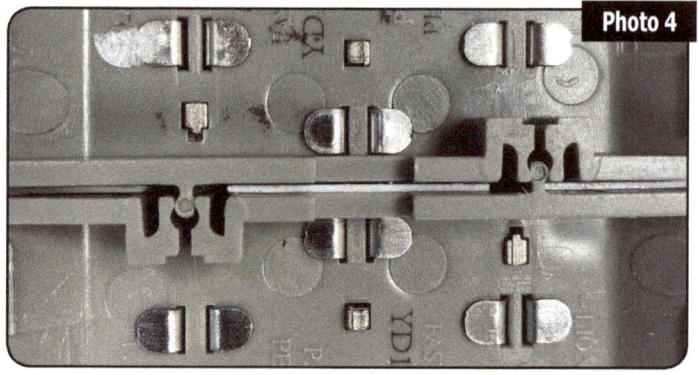

Photo 5 shows an O60 switch mating with an O60 section of track curving in the opposite direction. Note that this creates an S curve between the orientation of the curves of the switch and curved track section. S curves are generally to be avoided as they tend to cause more dynamic forces on the car trucks navigating the S curve. The trucks on the cars, when coupled together, are not entirely free to swivel with the curvature of the track, thereby threatening more derailments at speed as they cross the joint of the S curve. Solutions to this problem are to insert a straight section of track between opposing direction curves, and/or to use the next wider diameter curved sections at that point. The layout plans presented here do not use tight S curves.

The omission of O60 and O72 switch fitters results in mild S curves that do not cause problems for most O gauge equipment. If running very long equipment requiring O72 minimum curves, it might be prudent to do some testing in advance. Three of the plans presented here do use this technique to trim a curved roadbed section. They are the Cisco Railroad, the Valley City Northern, and the Nickel Plate layouts. The trimmed sections are clearly marked.

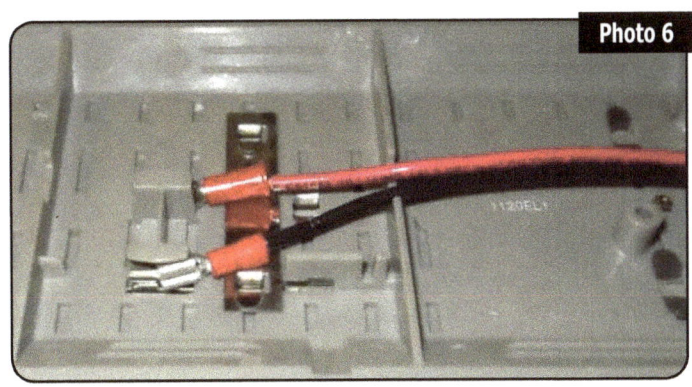

Supplying Power to FasTrack Sections

FasTrack has good electrical connectivity, and the tight fit between sections helps to ensure that strong connectivity and low resistance to the flow of current does not vary over time with a permanent layout. Lionel provides a FasTrack terminal section to connect power (and a FasTrack section to tap track power for accessories), but FasTrack full curves and 10" and 30" straight sections provide connection tabs beneath for power connections (Photo 6).

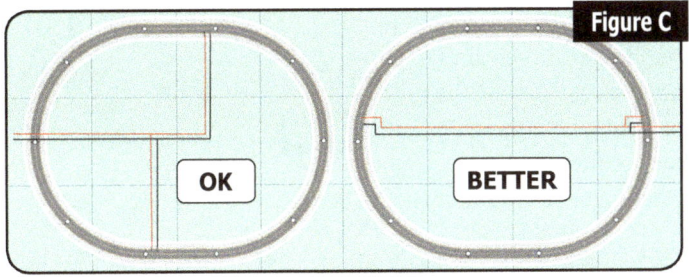

When running trains under conventional control, you may notice that trains will slow down as they enter curves due to increased rolling resistance through the curves. You can mitigate this slow-down problem by applying electrical connections to each curve of a layout oval or other shape (Figure C). As a general rule, it's better to have two power connections for each electrical block of the layout unless the sections are very short or are tracks. Longer blocks may need three or more power connections, but for the layouts presented here, two power connections for each block is the maximum needed; and for small layouts, a single power connection per electrical blocks is fine.

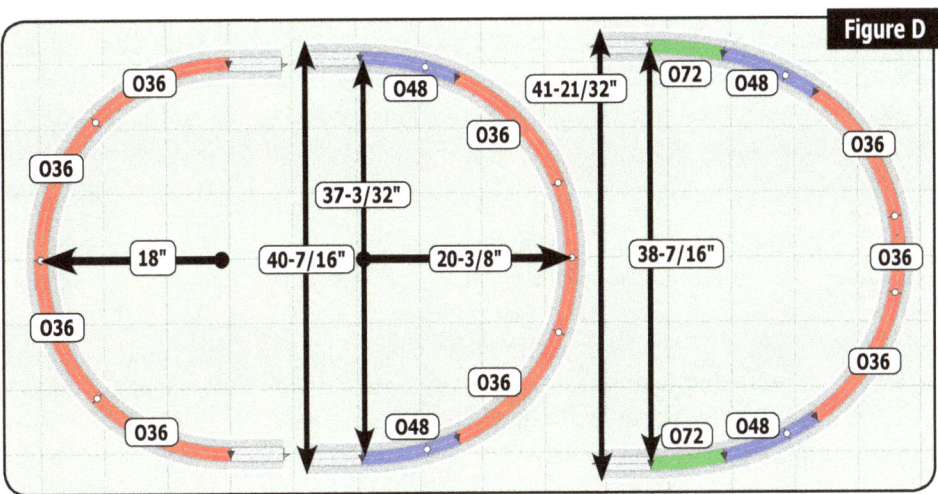

Easements and Compound Curves

Easements are gradual introductions to a curve, with a wider diameter curve leading into the tighter curve. On prototype railroads, easements are intended to reduce the dynamic stresses of locomotives and cars entering a section of curved track. For model trains, easements are not required, but they do smooth the operation of a train into a curved section. But perhaps more importantly, easements will also ease your vision into a curve. The human eye is not generally well trained to estimate how tight a curve is when comparing it against a section of straight track. So an easement will make curves appear more gradual and more realistic when compared to what we see with real trains.

The center diagram in Figure D shows an easement of O48 FasTrack leading into an O36 curve. The first easement of O48 with O36 shows that using an easement does not dramatically widen a curved section. In this case, we have a 36" diameter curve without the easement, and a 37-3/32" diameter curve with the easement. Easements have a larger effect on the length of the turn rather than the width. In this example the curve length goes from 18" without the easement to 20-3/8" with the easement, adding 2-3/8" to the length of the curve.

The right side of Figure D shows an easement of two diameters leading into an O36 curve: an 11.25° section of O72 followed by a 22.5° section of O48. Even with this larger compound easement, the overall curve diameter only increases from 36" to 37-7/16". You should use easements where the space and layout geometry allows for them.

Compound curves are curves that create a track diameter that is not offered in the FasTrack system. You can create a wider curve by simply inserting some sections of straight track to open up the curve. This works and is easy enough to do, but we see the change from curve to straight and then back to curve again, and the locomotives and cars appear to jog as they go around the curves. A better solution is to use compound curves to achieve a wider diameter.

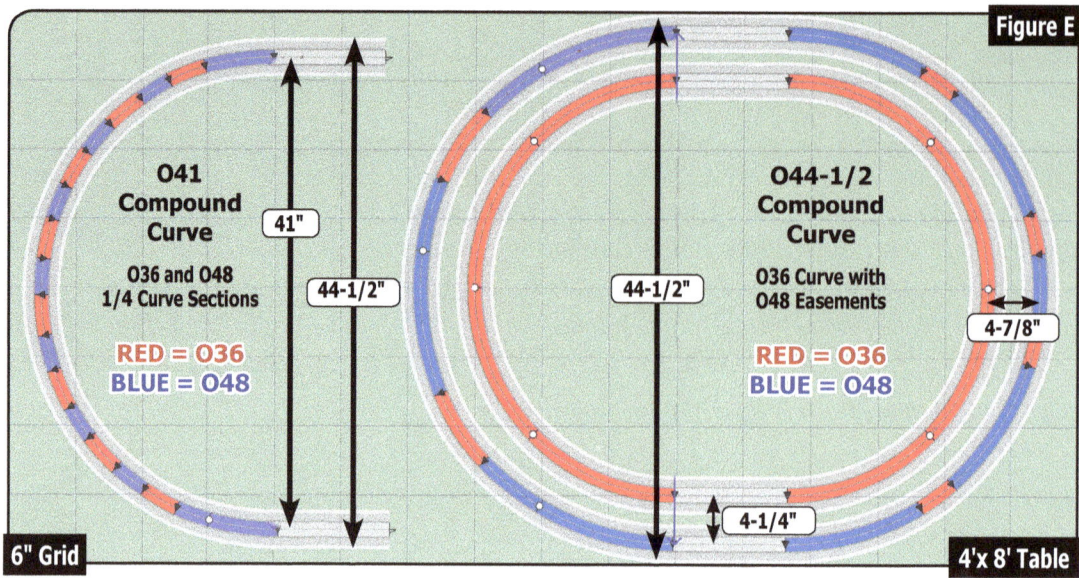

The left side diagram in Figure E shows an O41-diameter curve assembled with alternating O36 quarter sections and O48 quarter sections. These small changes in track diameter across small sections of track are not readily apparent to the eye, and trains will roll smoothly through these curves without a noticeable jerking. However, the higher cost of assembling all these small sections can be frustrating.

The O44-1/2" diameter compound curve shown in the center of Figure E is also important and useful for three reasons. First, it is a wider circle that still fits on a 4'x 8' table. The track will run right to the edges, including the roadbed. An outside frame of 3/4"-thick 1x4s will provide enough clearance from the wall when the layout is positioned against a wall or in a corner.

The right side diagram in Figure E is an even better design for O44-1/2". The O36 curves are distributed around the curve, using quarter-sections of O36. You will not detect the small change in curvature across these small sections visually, and the trains will appear to proceed smoothly through the curve. Nine sections of track are needed to create a half-circle with this arrangement.

Figure E also shows that an O44-1/2" diameter curve will enclose an O36 loop. That means you can enjoy two loops of track and run two trains on a 4x8 table, without having to use the smaller O31 diameter track.

The O44-1/2" diameter will handle most equipment that requires O42 diameter, with the small sections of O36 not causing a problem for most equipment Even so, I suggest that you test your O42 equipment beforehand. Lionel and some other manufacturers do offer some equipment requiring O42 as the minimum curve diameter.

The O44-1/2" compound curve has a minimum center-rail spacing of 4-1/4", which is a bit tighter than Atlas O's convention of 4-1/2" center-rail clearance. This has been tested with many cars and locomotives, including Lionel's Scale SD60M on the outside loop without sideswiping of equipment. You must be careful to arrange the two curves so they are evenly spaced.

Photo 7 shows the outside O44-1/2" diameter track running Menard's Double-Stack Intermodal cars, while on the inside O36 track is Lionel's GE ET44C4 Lion-Chief locomotive. Spacing is tight but notice that the locomotive does not overhang the roadbed on the outside of the curve, while the double-stack has a considerable amount of overhang. Conventional O gauge semi-scale and traditional trains will not have an overhang problem that causes sideswiping, but I suggest you check and test your specific rolling stock and locomotives.

Building Crossovers with FasTrack

Single crossovers are used to connect two lines together so trains can switch tracks or to create a passing track. But they also introduce an S curve, which can potentially cause problems, depending on how tight the S curve is. Figure F shows crossovers with switches of O36, O48, O60, and O72. The amount of curvature in the switches decreases as the diameter increases. The O60 and O72 crossovers have a very gradual S curve that will not be a problem for O gauge locomotives and rolling stock. The O36, O60, and O72 crossovers result in 6" parallel track centers, while the O48 crossover has a 6-1/2" parallel track center.

Building a crossover on a curve can avoid the S curve problem entirely. Figure G shows two crossovers; the upper crossover uses two O36 switches to connect parallel O36 and O48 curves. The center rail spacing of the horizontal parallel tracks is at 5-3/4".

The lower diagram in Figure G shows two O60 switches used to make a crossover maintaining the 6" center rail spacing of O36 and O48 curves.

Double crossovers are useful track arrangements that can allow trains to switch from one line to another, in either direction. FasTrack allows you to assemble a wide variety of double crossovers. Figure H shows several designs using O72 switches and O72 and O84 curves. Some of these designs require the use of the roadbed-trimming technique to make a closer crossover of a smaller width. Four of the double crossovers shown need a bit of stretching for a good fit using the *joint stretch* technique I described above, and I have indicated which joints need to be stretched. The bottom three double crossovers use curved approach tracks, which may be useful in some layout configurations.

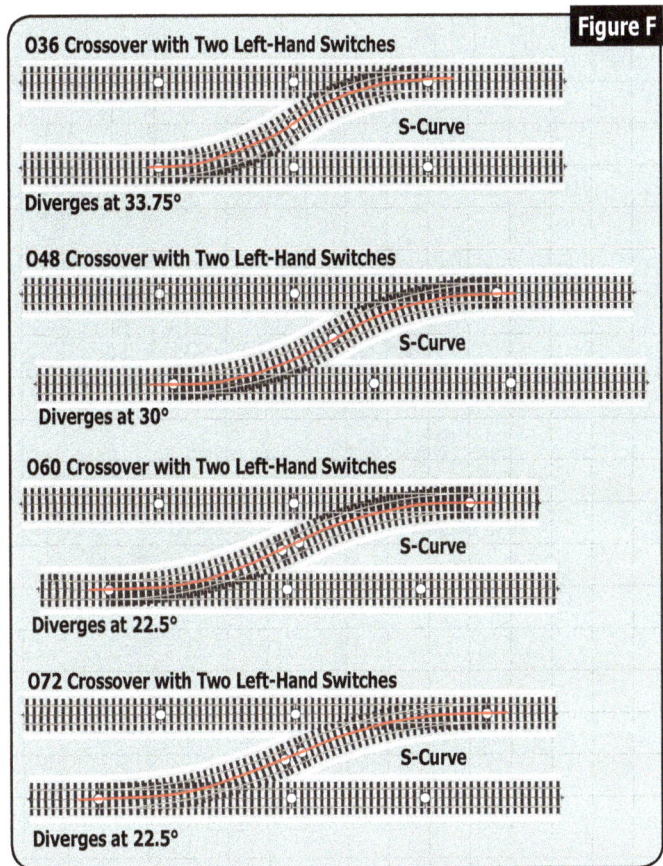

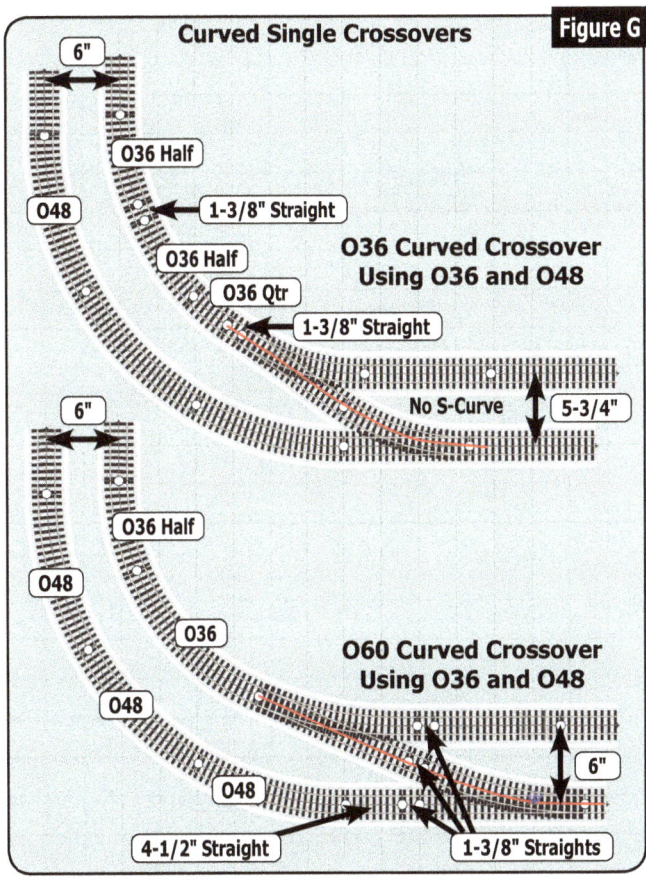

Layout Planning with Lionel FasTrack

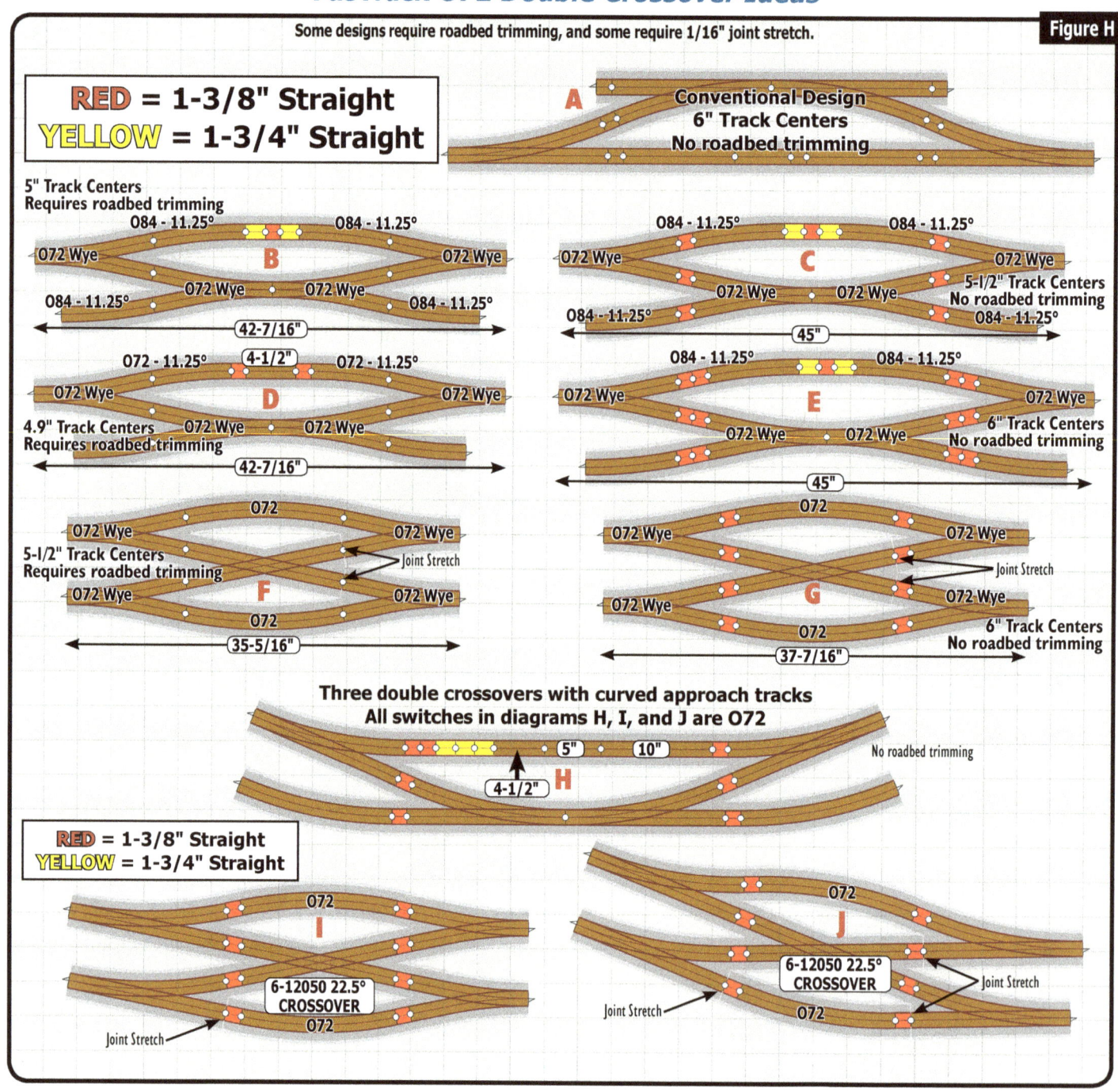

FasTrack O72 Double Crossover Ideas

Figure H

Designing Yards with FasTrack

Yards are a great thing to have if your layout space allows. They are a place where you can store your cars and locomotives on the layout for convenience and to have them displayed. Yards also allow you to do a bit of prototypical switching, such as breaking down and making up trains in the yard, then taking them out on the main line.

Figure I shows three sample yard arrangements. Yard A is a conventional O36 yard design, with 6" spacing between yard tracks. Yards B and C orient the yards at an angle, to achieve a tighter spacing of yard tracks, which is more efficient in building yards in a tighter space. Yard C shows the use of O60 switches, which diverge at 22.5 degrees off the straight (tangent), which leads to a longer yard, but one that is easier to switch with the gentler curvature.

The layout diagrams below show how yards can be included in even the smallest layouts.

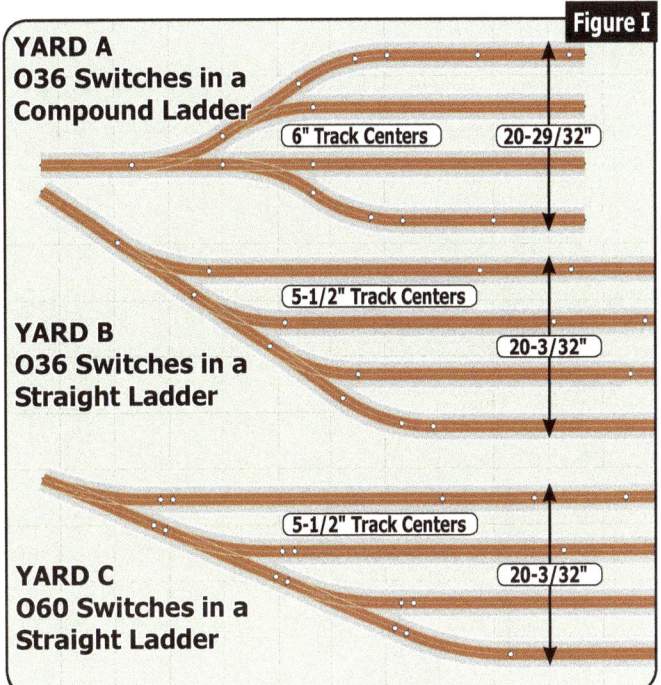

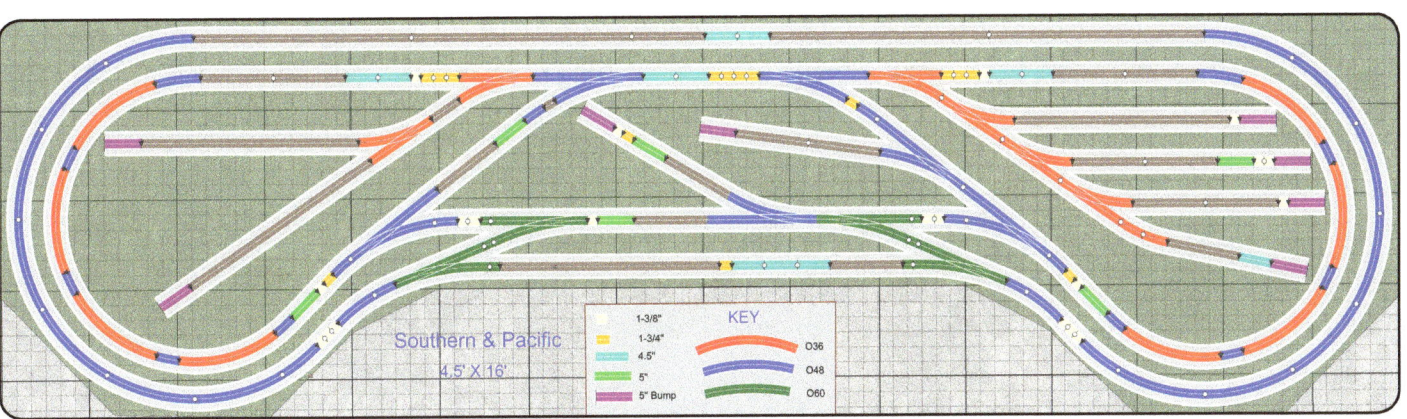

The Southern & Pacific Railroad

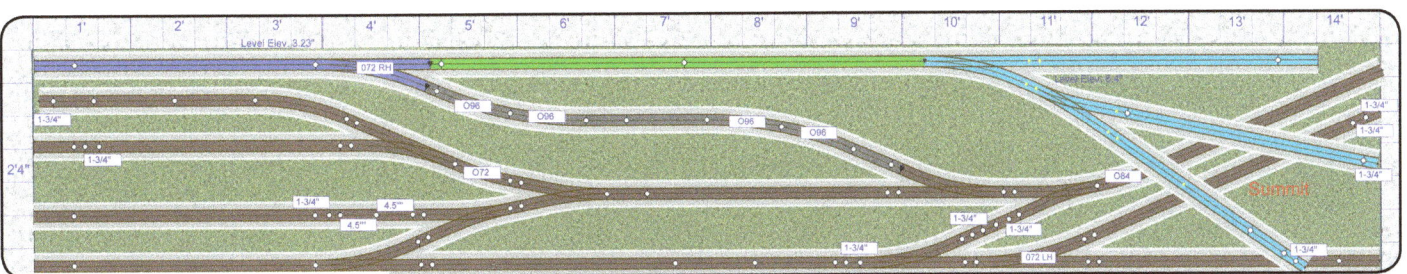

The Summit Canyon Railroad

Layout Planning with Lionel FasTrack Page 13

Example Yard 1: Using O60 Switches

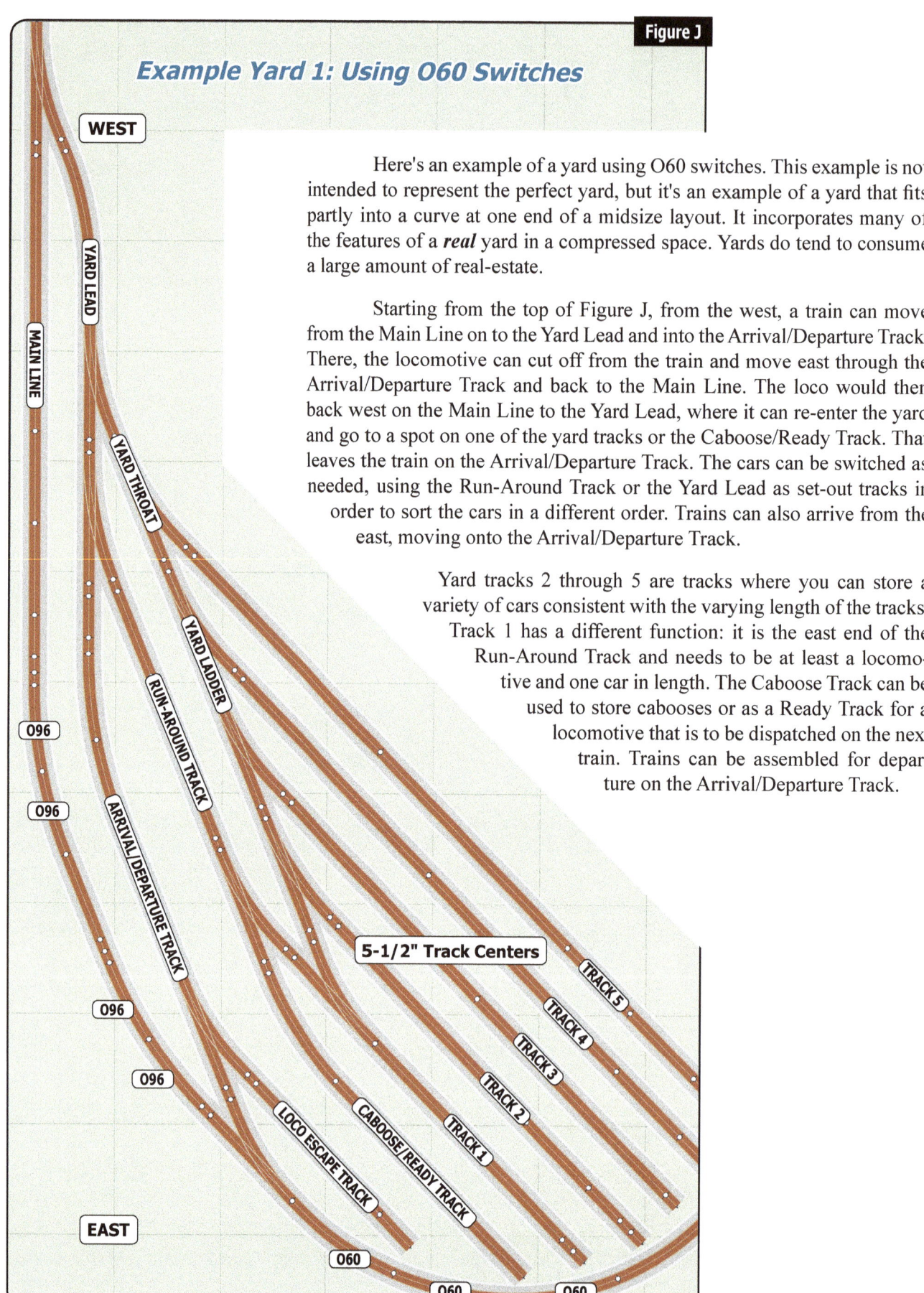

Figure J

Here's an example of a yard using O60 switches. This example is not intended to represent the perfect yard, but it's an example of a yard that fits partly into a curve at one end of a midsize layout. It incorporates many of the features of a *real* yard in a compressed space. Yards do tend to consume a large amount of real-estate.

Starting from the top of Figure J, from the west, a train can move from the Main Line on to the Yard Lead and into the Arrival/Departure Track. There, the locomotive can cut off from the train and move east through the Arrival/Departure Track and back to the Main Line. The loco would then back west on the Main Line to the Yard Lead, where it can re-enter the yard and go to a spot on one of the yard tracks or the Caboose/Ready Track. That leaves the train on the Arrival/Departure Track. The cars can be switched as needed, using the Run-Around Track or the Yard Lead as set-out tracks in order to sort the cars in a different order. Trains can also arrive from the east, moving onto the Arrival/Departure Track.

Yard tracks 2 through 5 are tracks where you can store a variety of cars consistent with the varying length of the tracks. Track 1 has a different function: it is the east end of the Run-Around Track and needs to be at least a locomotive and one car in length. The Caboose Track can be used to store cabooses or as a Ready Track for a locomotive that is to be dispatched on the next train. Trains can be assembled for departure on the Arrival/Departure Track.

Layout Planning with Lionel FasTrack

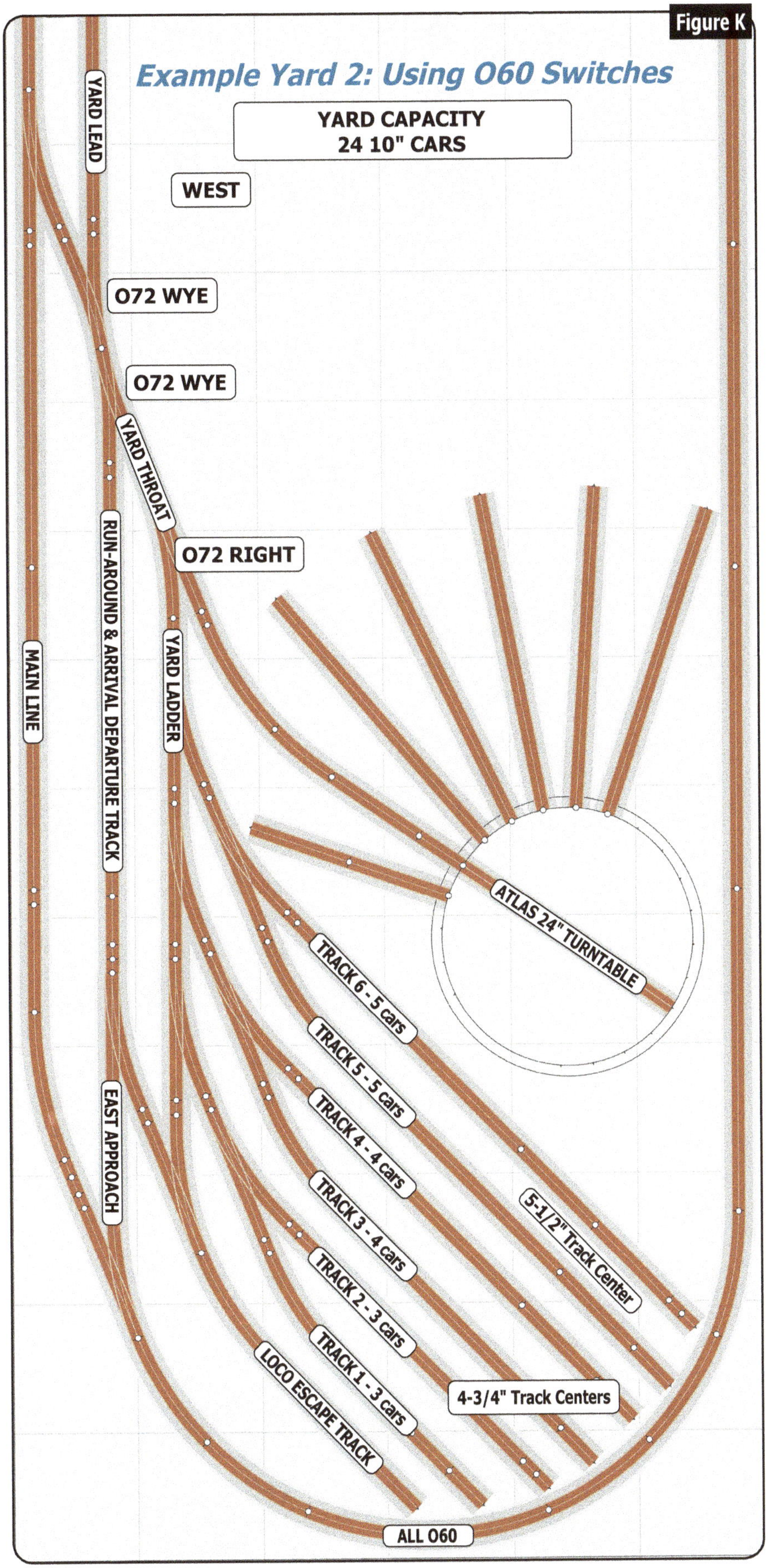

Example Yard 2: Using O60 Switches

Figure K

**YARD CAPACITY
24 10" CARS**

(Diagram labels: WEST, YARD LEAD, O72 WYE, O72 WYE, YARD THROAT, O72 RIGHT, RUN-AROUND & ARRIVAL DEPARTURE TRACK, MAIN LINE, YARD LADDER, EAST APPROACH, TRACK 6 - 5 cars, TRACK 5 - 5 cars, TRACK 4 - 4 cars, TRACK 3 - 4 cars, TRACK 2 - 3 cars, TRACK 1 - 3 cars, LOCO ESCAPE TRACK, ATLAS 24" TURNTABLE, 5-1/2" Track Center, 4-3/4" Track Centers, ALL O60)

Example Yard 2 in Figure K is compressed to fit in a small space, with some compromises. The Run-Around track is combined with the Arrival/Departure Track to save space, at the cost of some flexibility. The plan fits in a 6' wide space and incorporates an Atlas O 24" turntable with five 30" turntable tracks.

Lionel offers a 5" transition track, item no. 6-12040 (Photo 8), that will allow FasTrack to mate with traditional O gauge track. Atlas offers joiners to mate with traditional track, so the two track systems can be used together.

Photo 8 — 6-12040 TRANSITION PIECE

The three yard ladder switches each lead into a second switch for a total of six ladder switches and six yard tracks. This yard can be approached from either east or west. The extended yard lead to the west provides the headroom you need for switching cuts of cars. The capacity is twenty-four 10" cars. Lengthening the yard at the east end would allow yard tracks 1 through 6 to be lengthened.

The yard is designed with no S curves, with one exception: there is an S curve from the yard lead through the O72 Y switches at the yard throat, to the O72 switch. Shoving cuts of cars into the yard from the yard lead will cross this S curve, but this is a gradual O72 curve with a 1-3/8" section placed between the switches.

Layout Planning with Lionel FasTrack

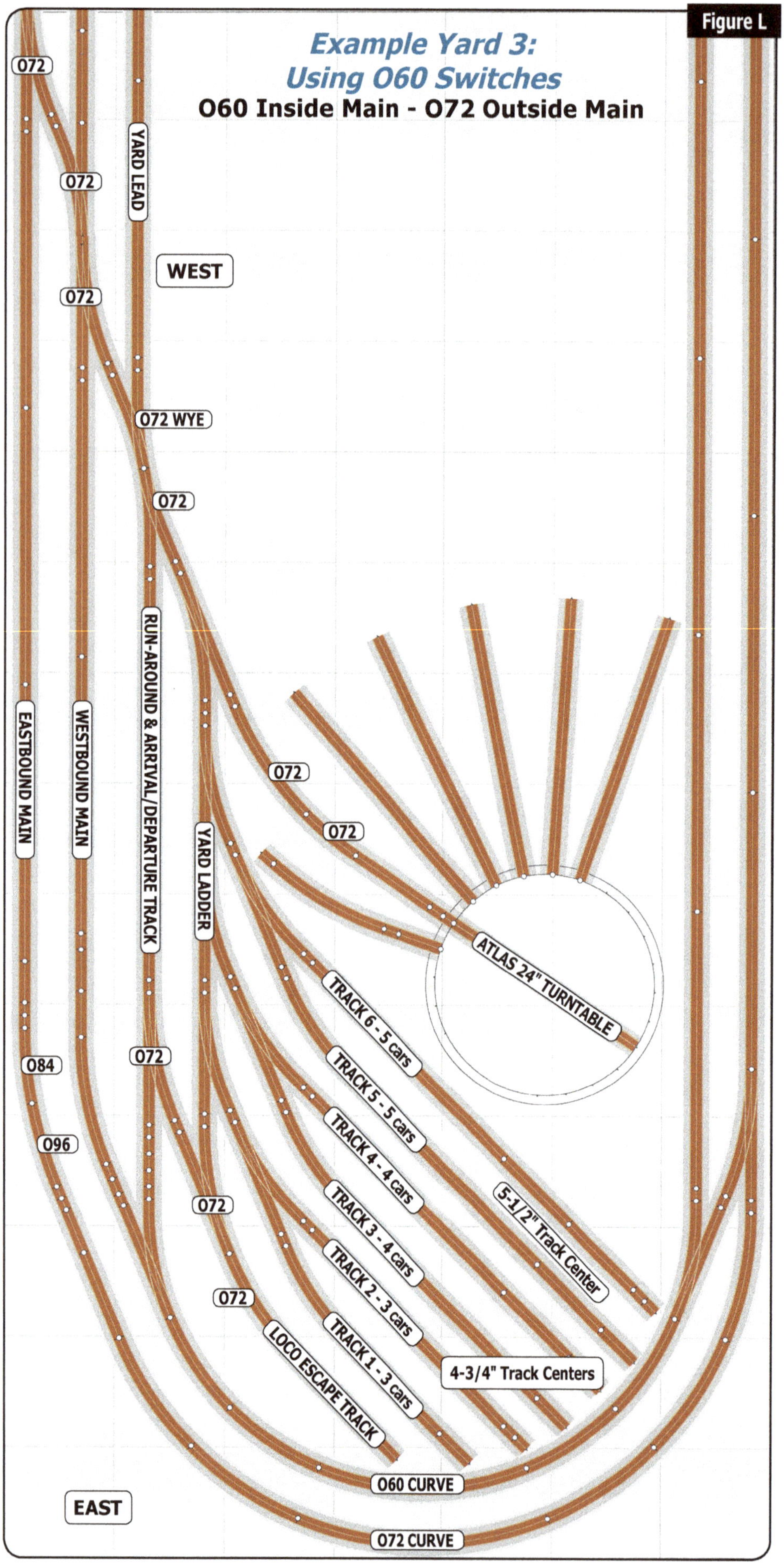

Example Yard 3: Using O60 Switches
O60 Inside Main - O72 Outside Main

Figure L

Example Yard 3 (Figure L) adds an O72 outside main line around the O60 main of Figure K and modifies the yard for O72 access. This yard can be accessed by O72 trains from the west approach. O72 locomotives can also reach the turntable. The Run-Around and Arrival/Departure Tracks are accessible by O72 locomotives. The Loco Escape Track is O72. The Loco Escape Track can also be used as a set-out track when switching cars in the yard. The straight alignment of the yard ladder can be accessed by O72 locomotives.

In closing, Lionel's O-Gauge FasTrack is an outstanding track system for O gauge layouts. It has great flexibility, and the integrated roadbed allows good-looking trackwork to be laid quickly and easily. FasTrack switches are outstanding and reliable, with features that include optional remote operation, and even command-control operation. Remote/Command switches are non-derailing, meaning they automatically switch to accommodate trains approaching from the divergent or tangent route. A wide variety of excellent plans can be designed with FasTrack, which is why it is so popular for building outstanding layouts!

Happy Railroading!

Layout Planning with Atlas O Track

Atlas O's 21st Century O gauge track is a popular and widely-available track system with thick ties and strong rails. It's also usable outdoors since the plastic ties are formulated to reduce breakdown from the sun's ultra-violet rays. In addition to a wide assortment of curved sections, the Atlas O system also includes Flex-Track that can be bent to fit almost any curve. Atlas O switches are available with and without remote control. A 24" turntable is also available at a reasonable cost, and it works very well. The curves in the Atlas track system have 4-1/2" center rail spacing.

Atlas O curves are offered in diameters ranging from 27" (O27) to 108" (O108), measured at the center rail diameter, in 9" increments of spacing, with 4-1/2" center-rail spacing (see Table 1). Parallel curved tracks with 4-1/2" center rail spacing is wide enough so that trains can run without side-swiping or overhang of cars and locomotives.

Switches are available in every curve diameter from O36 to O72, plus Atlas offers No. 5 and No. 7.5 switches. The switches are well made, with positive switching of the points to assure they are held in the correct position. Switches are available with manual operation or remote/command-control operation. All Atlas O switches are drop-in replacements for curved sections of track without changing the curve alignment.

The Atlas curved switch is a fascinating option, with a curve through the switch at O72, and a tighter curve at O54. This switch can solve a number of tight layout problems if the O54 inside route diameter is acceptable. In practice, the curved switch is not likely to be of use on smaller layouts due to is size, length, and the wide O72 diameter.

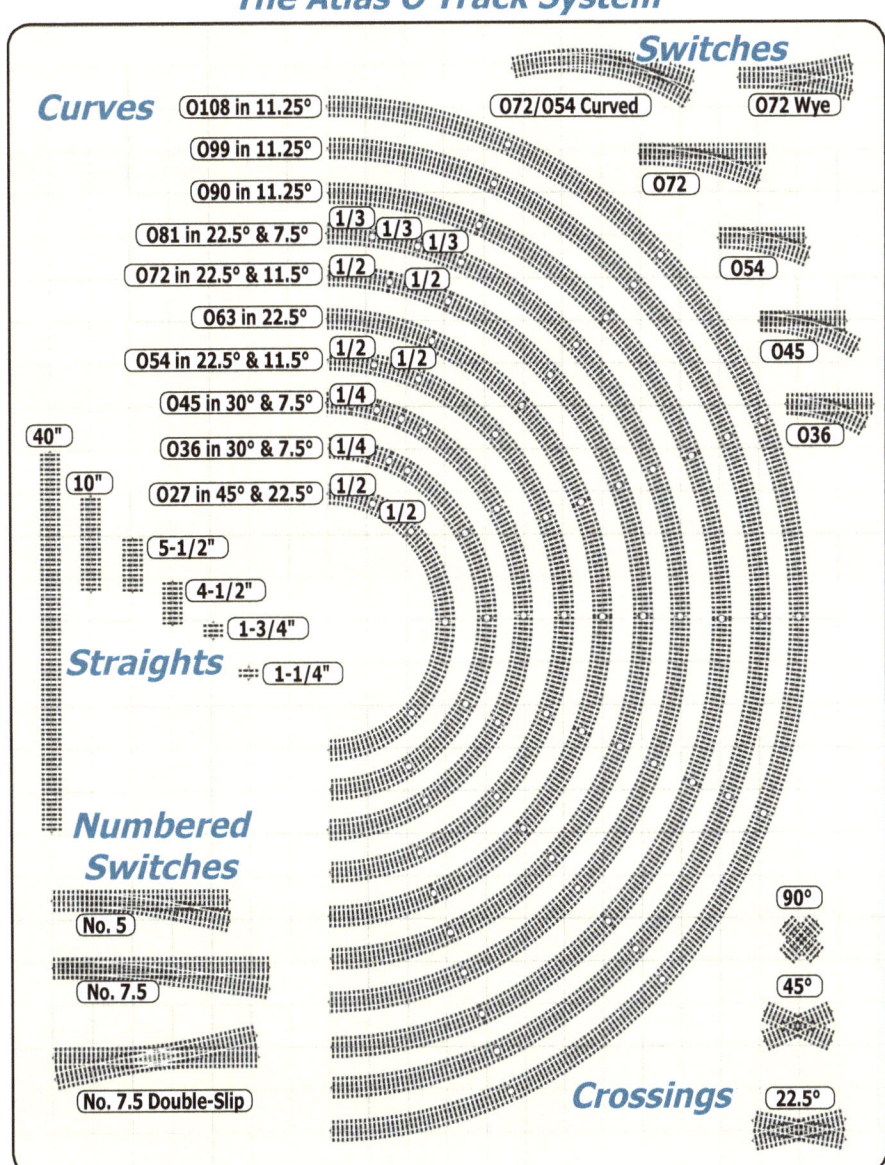

Table 1
Atlas O Curved Track
Sections by Degrees

	FULL	HALF	QTR
O27	45°	22.5°	n/a
O36	30°	n/a	7.5°
O45	30°	n/a	7.5°
O54	22.5°	11.25°	n/a
O63	22.5°	n/a	n/a
O72	22.5°	11.25°	n/a
O81	22.5°	n/a	7.5°
O90	22.5°	n/a	n/a
O99	22.5°	n/a	n/a
O108	22.5°	n/a	n/a

Atlas O's numbered switches allow very gradual divergence from the straight route that is closer to prototype practice. This results in beautiful trackwork and alignments that trains glide through gracefully. However these numbered switches are not for the beginner, as they may require additional power feeds and power routing in order to accommodate a wide range of locomotives.

The double-slip switch is unique. It allows trains entering from either direction to select either diverging track at the exit from the switch. It is like two switches mashed together, but the angled line through the switch is also straight, which is something that cannot be achieved with two separate switches. This is potentially a very useful switch, but may require some special attention to get it working well. Consequently, this is not a switch I would recommend for the beginner.

Atlas O's Remote Switches can be wired to be non-derailing; the switch will detect if a train is approaching from either diverging direction, and will switch the switch for that direction, so the trains sail on through.

Straight track sections are available from 1-1/4" to 40" long. With Atlas track, the smallest straight section difference that can be covered is 1/4", which means that some care and trial-and-error may be needed to make good section joints everywhere (see Table 2). This can be a time-consuming and somewhat frustrating process. The difference in lengths of the two smallest sections — 1-1/4" and 1-3/4" — is 1/2", while the difference between the next size up of 4-1/2" and 5-1/2" is obviously 1". Other lengths can be created with combinations of small straight sections. For instance, three 1-1/4" sections together make a straight of 3-3/4". Four 1-1/4" sections combined makes a length of 5". A 1-1/4" section with two 1-3/4" sections makes a combined length of 4-3/4", a difference of 1/4" to the next smaller length of a 4.5" straight, which is the smallest difference possible. Combining small sections to make precise-length straights can add to the section count and total cost of a layout. In general, a smaller section count is better in terms of both cost and electrical conductivity across multiple joints.

Table 2
Atlas O Straight Section Combinations

Length	Difference	1-1/4	1-3/4	4-1/2	5-1/2	10	Pieces
1-1/4		1					1
1-3/4	1/2		1				1
2-1/2	3/4	2					2
3	1/2	1	1				2
3-1/2	1/2		2				2
3-3/4	1/4	3					3
4-1/4	1/2	2	1				3
4-1/2	1/4			1			1
4-3/4	1/4	1	2				3
5	1/4	4					4
5/1-4	1/4		3				3
5-1/2	1/4				1		1
5-3/4	1/4	1		1			2
6	1/4	2	2				4
6/1-4	1/4		1	1			2
6-1/2	1/4	1	3				4
6-3/4	1/4	1			1		2
7	1/4	2		1			3
7/1-4	1/4	3	2				5
7-1/2	1/4	1	1		1		3
7-3/4	1/4	2	3				5
8	1/4	2			1		3
8/1-4	1/4	3		1			4
8-1/2	1/4	1	1		1		3
8-3/4	1/4	2	1	1			4
9	1/4			2			2
9/1-4	1/4	3			1		4
9-1/2	1/4	4		1			5
9-3/4	1/4	2	1		1		3
10	1/4					1	1

You can use Atlas flexible track (Flex-Track) to make curves of any diameter and to make connections between track alignments that don't quite line up. This track is reasonably easy to use with careful bending and shaping of the curve, trimming the longer rail that results, and filing the end of the rail to allow the joiner to slide on easily. Atlas O track can also be cut into custom lengths of any length between 1-1/4" and 40". Because the Atlas track does not have a plastic roadbed like FasTrack, cutting Flex-Track into custom lengths is easy to do, and it adds great flexibility to the track system.

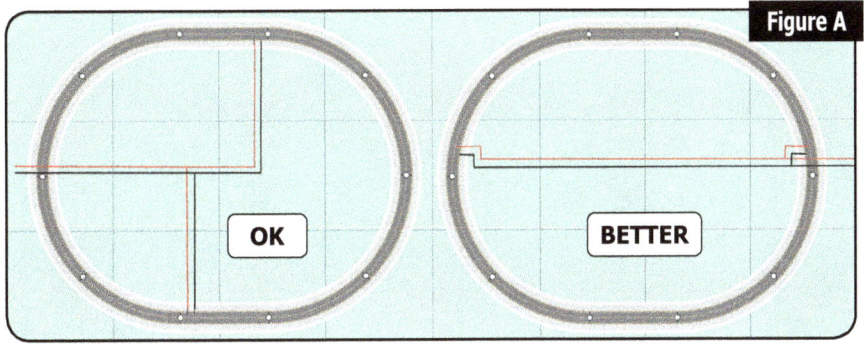

Supplying Power to Atlas O Sections

Atlas O track has good electrical connectivity, using rail joiners with a bump on the inside to help maintain a tight electrical contact point with the rail. Terminal sections of straight track are available to provide power to the rails, but you can choose also to use the Atlas rail-joiners that have feeder wires soldered to them.

As with FasTrack, you may notice that trains will slow down a bit as they enter curves due to increased rolling resistance through the curves. If you put your electrical connections on each curve of a layout oval or other shape (see Fig. A), that will cure the slow-down problem. As a general rule, it is better to have two power connections for each electrical block of the layout, unless the sections are very short. Longer blocks may need three or more power connections, but for the layouts presented here, two power connections for each block is generally the maximum needed. For small layouts, a single power connection per electrical block is fine.

Easements, Compound Curves, and Crossovers

Easements are gradual introductions to a curve, with a wider diameter curve leading into the tighter curve. On prototype railroads, easements are intended to reduce the dynamic stresses of locomotives and cars entering a section of curved track. For model trains, easements are not really necessary, but they do smooth a train's progression into a curved section. More importantly, easements will ease your visual transition into a curve. An eased curve will make your curves appear to be more gradual than they actually are, and thus a bit closer to what we see with real trains.

Figure B shows an easement of O54 leading into an O36 curve. When we look at this easement carefully, you'll see that using an easement does not dramatically widen the curve. We have a 36" diameter curve without the easement, and a 37-3/8" diameter curve with the easement, a small difference of 1-3/8". Easements do have a slightly larger effect on the length of the curve rather than the width. In this example the curve went from 18" without the easement to 21-1/2" with the easement, thus adding 3-1/2" to the length. You should use easements in your curves when your layout space and geometry allows for them.

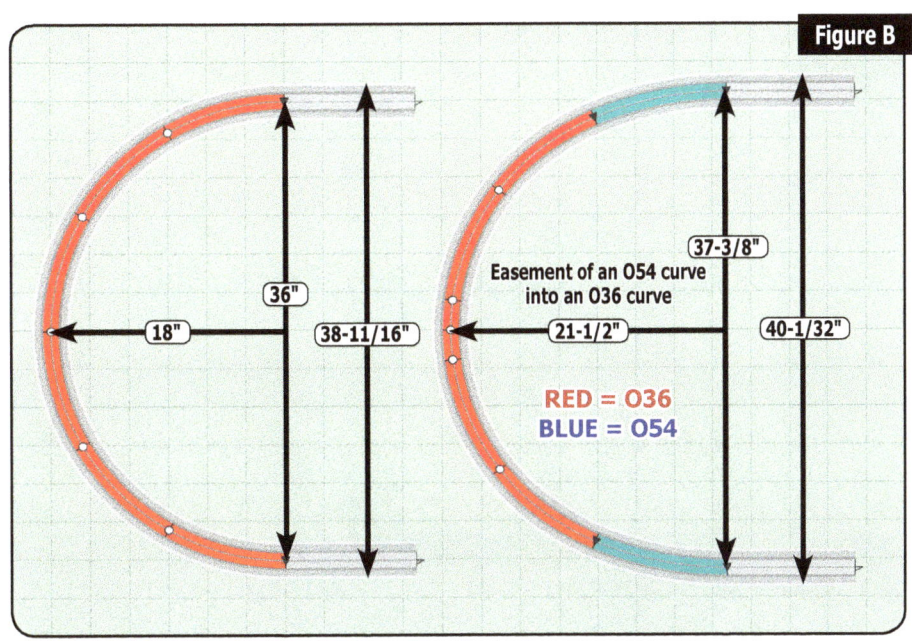

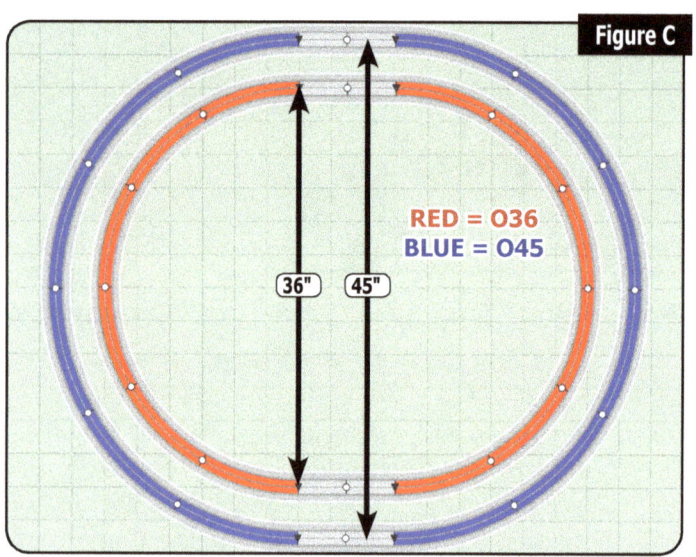

**O36/O45 Nested Loops fit within a 4-foot table
4-1/2" Track Centers**

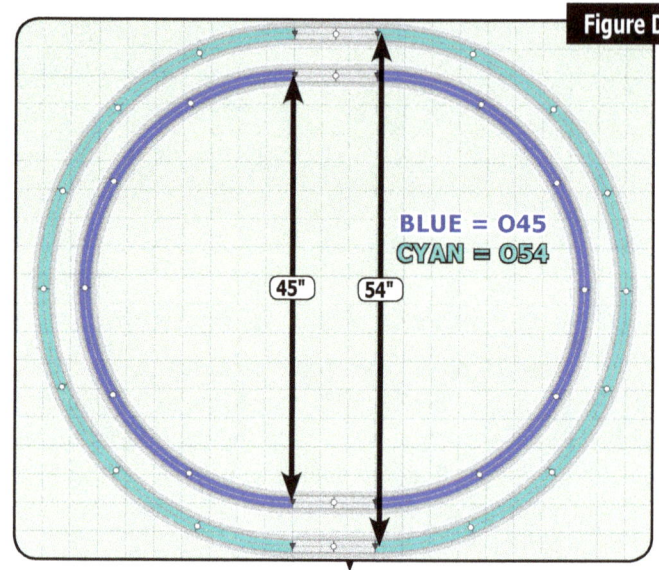

**O45/O54 Nested Loops fit within a 5-foot table
4-1/2" Track Centers**

O42 as a Minimum Curve Diameter

Two diameters of Atlas O track can fit within a 4' width. This allows two loops to be placed on a 4x8 layout surface. The O45 outside diameter allows O42 equipment to operate flawlessly (Figure C). Expanding the table to a 5'x 9' surface allows two (or even three) loops of track to run within that space (Figure D). O54 is a fairly common rolling-stock and locomotive requirement, so an O54 loop is a good and flexible option. These features are very convenient for building a wider array of layouts within standard 4x8 or 5x9 layout sizes. Similarly, an O54/O63 pair of loops will run all O54 equipment. An O72/O81 pair of turns will run all O72-minimum equipment.

Double Crossovers

Double-Crossovers are useful track arrangements that can allow trains to switch from one track to another, traveling in either direction. Atlas O allows you to assemble a variety of double-crossover designs, and they can be spaced tightly together. Figure E on the next page shows a variety of double-crossover designs using O72 switches and O72 curves.

The bottom three double crossovers use curved approach tracks, which you may find useful in some layout configurations. I used Atlas O Flex-Track in crossovers F and G. They are examples crossovers where a fixed diameter curve of the correct diameter is not available, but using Flex-Track here makes everything fit perfectly.

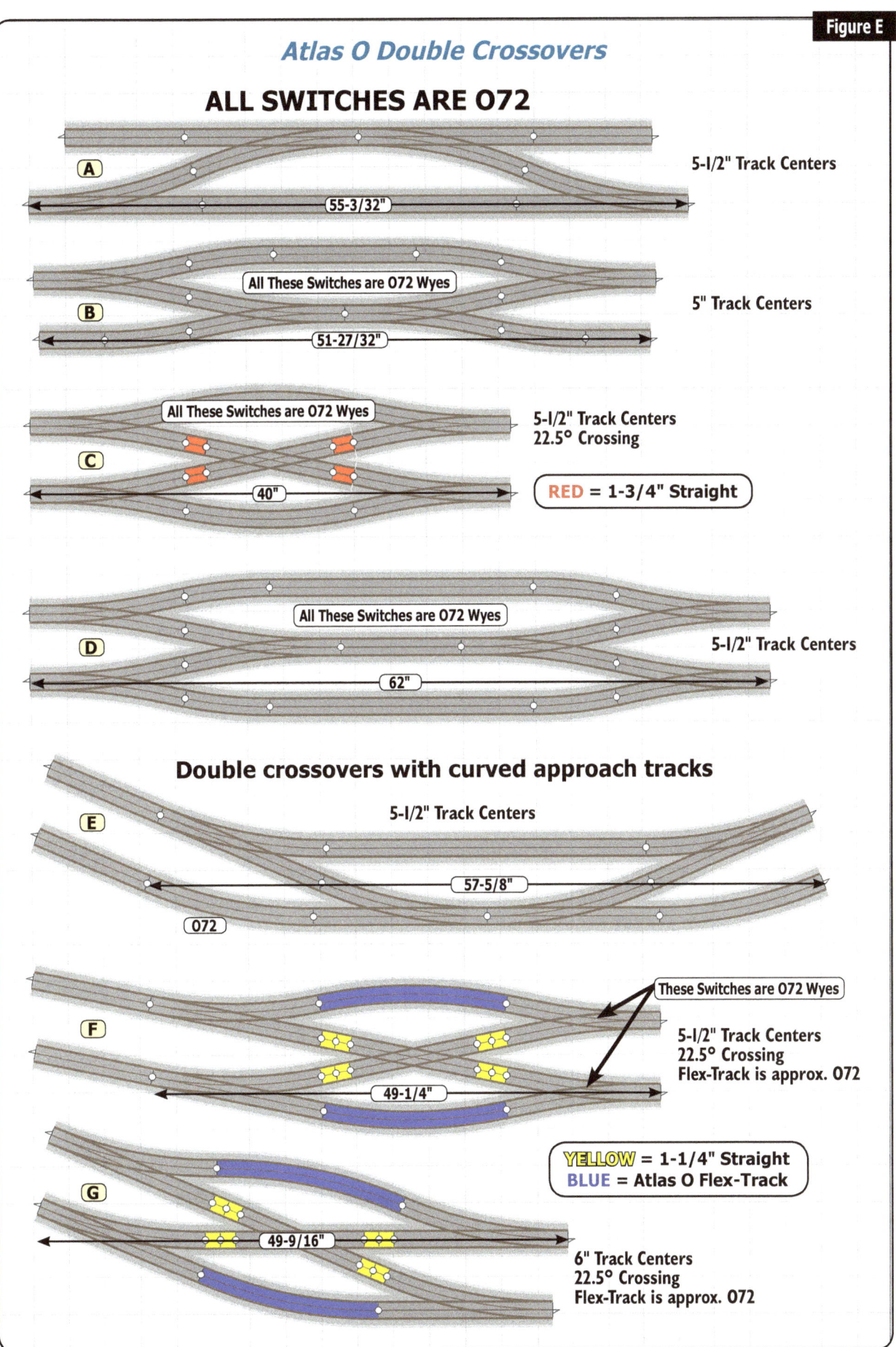

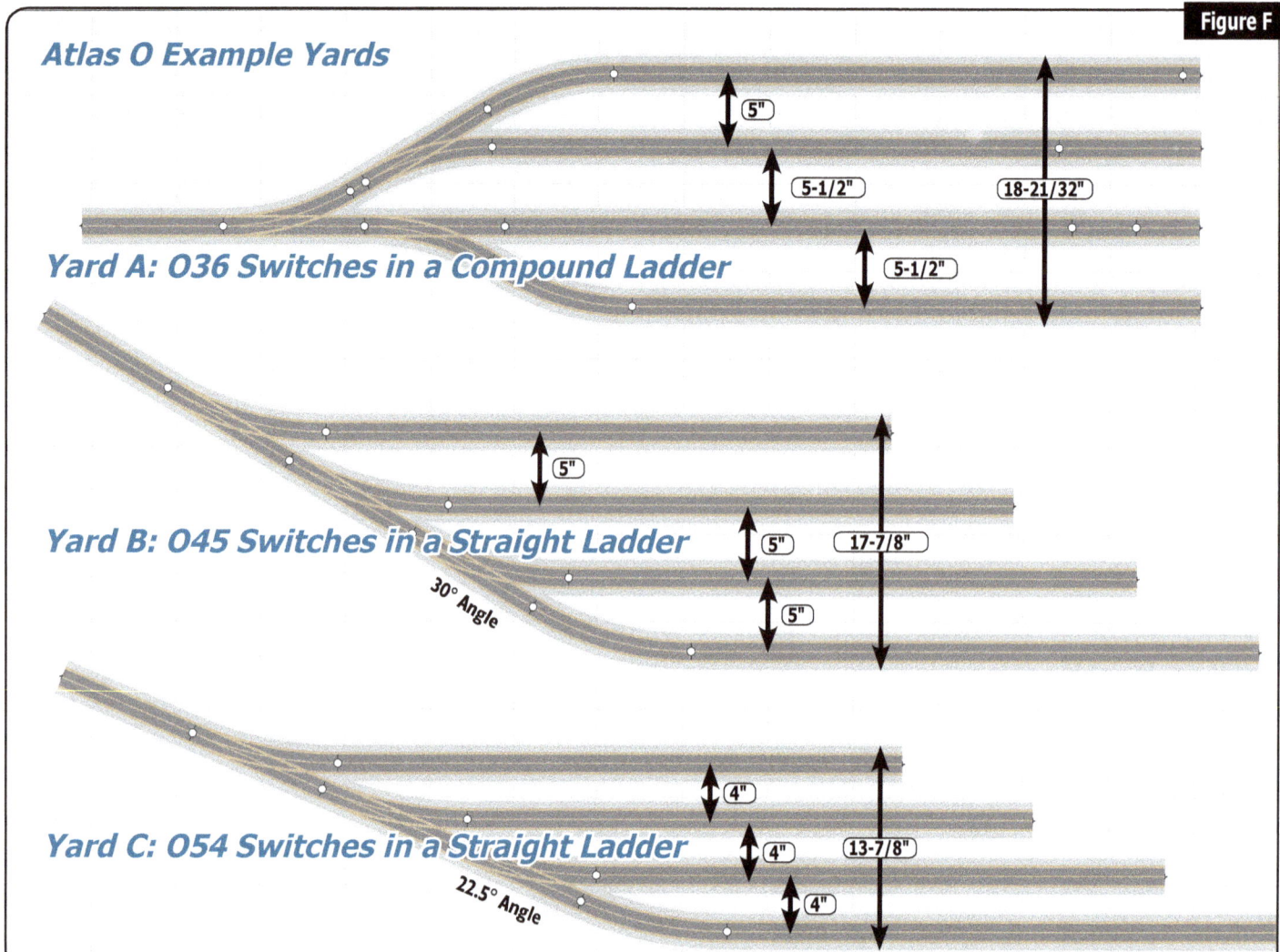

Figure F

Designing Yards with Atlas O

If you have room for a yard, even a small one, you should plan to build one. A yard provides a place to store cars and locomotives on the layout. It also allows you to do a bit of prototypical switching, breaking-down and making-up trains to run on the main line. In fact, switching cars in a well-designed yard can provide hours of fun.

Figure F illustrates three possible yard arrangements. Yard A is a conventional O36 yard design, with 5-1/2" spacing between yard tracks. Yards B and C set the yards at a more shallow angle to achieve a tighter spacing between the yard tracks. This is a more efficient use of space when building yards that must fit in a small area. Yard B is set at 30 degrees from horizontal using O45 switches with a 5" center rail spacing. Yard C shows the use of O54 switches, which diverge at 22.5 degrees off the straight (tangent) route. This results in a longer yard that is easier to switch due to the more gentle curvature. The center-rail spacing is only 4", which is fine for straight tracks. The O54 yard is a nice, compact yard with the potential for adding even more yard tracks.

Atlas O Yard Using O54 Switches

Figure G

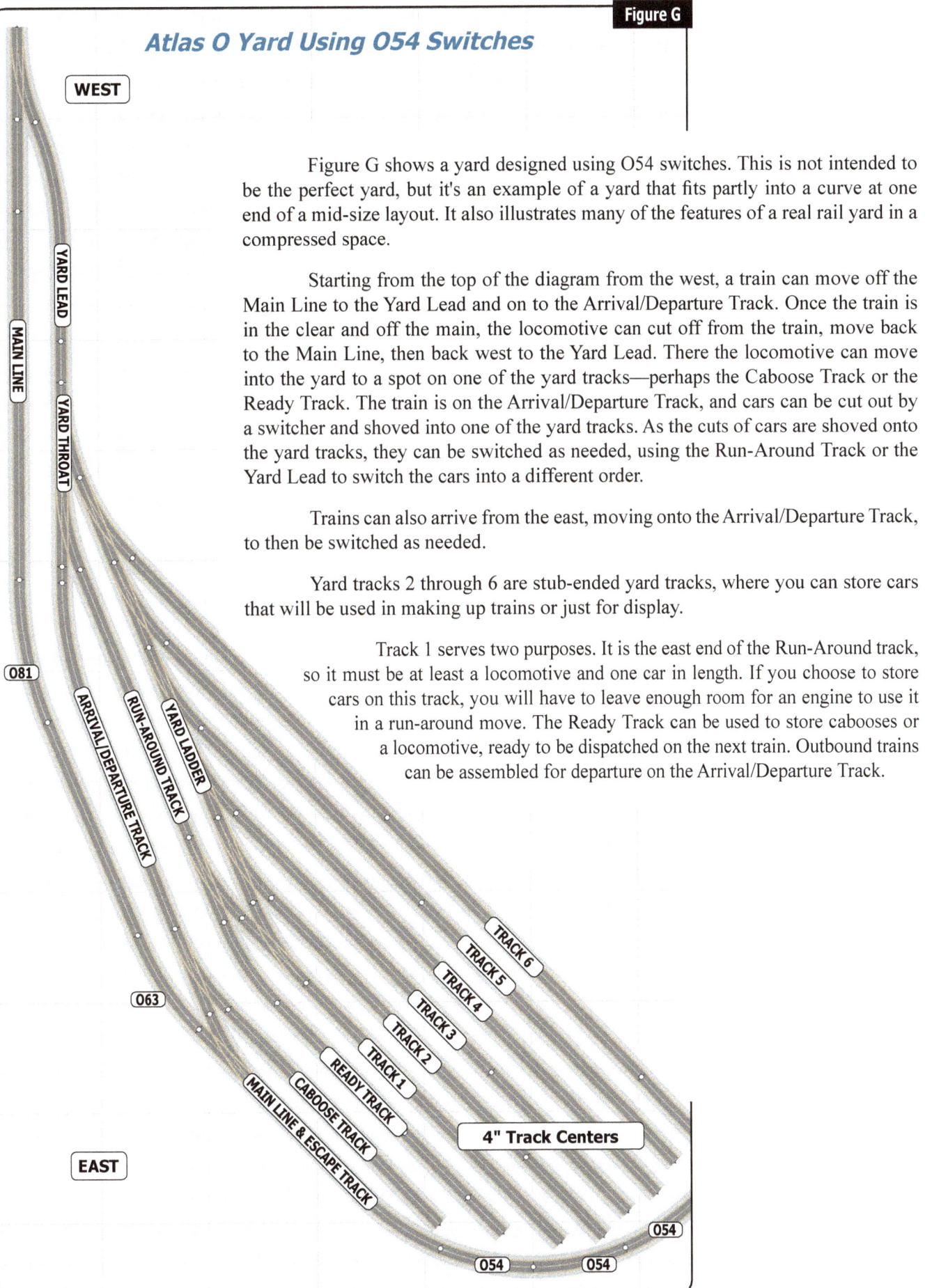

Figure G shows a yard designed using O54 switches. This is not intended to be the perfect yard, but it's an example of a yard that fits partly into a curve at one end of a mid-size layout. It also illustrates many of the features of a real rail yard in a compressed space.

Starting from the top of the diagram from the west, a train can move off the Main Line to the Yard Lead and on to the Arrival/Departure Track. Once the train is in the clear and off the main, the locomotive can cut off from the train, move back to the Main Line, then back west to the Yard Lead. There the locomotive can move into the yard to a spot on one of the yard tracks—perhaps the Caboose Track or the Ready Track. The train is on the Arrival/Departure Track, and cars can be cut out by a switcher and shoved into one of the yard tracks. As the cuts of cars are shoved onto the yard tracks, they can be switched as needed, using the Run-Around Track or the Yard Lead to switch the cars into a different order.

Trains can also arrive from the east, moving onto the Arrival/Departure Track, to then be switched as needed.

Yard tracks 2 through 6 are stub-ended yard tracks, where you can store cars that will be used in making up trains or just for display.

Track 1 serves two purposes. It is the east end of the Run-Around track, so it must be at least a locomotive and one car in length. If you choose to store cars on this track, you will have to leave enough room for an engine to use it in a run-around move. The Ready Track can be used to store cabooses or a locomotive, ready to be dispatched on the next train. Outbound trains can be assembled for departure on the Arrival/Departure Track.

Layout Planning with Atlas O Track

Working with Atlas No. 5 Switches

Switch alignment A shows that the divergence of a No. 5 switch is equal to a 12.5° curve. The broadest 12.5° curve offered by Atlas is O72, which results in a tight center rail spacing of only 3". Adding a 4-1/2" straight length between the switch and the 12.5° curve will increase the center rail spacing to 4".

Switch alignment B shows a conventional double crossover with center-rail spacing of 4-1/2", matching the 4-1/2" difference of Atlas O sectional curves.

Switch alignment C shows a double crossover with a passing track in the center of the triple-track. That center track can be used in either direction from either main and can double as a passing track for either main line.

Switch alignment D shows six No. 5 switches set into a crossover with curved approach tracks. This alignment could be used the end of a layout table where the track naturally begins a curve. By using the switches integrated with the curves, the tracks between the switches can be longer by 13-3/16" for a longer passing siding by more than a car length. The broad diverging angle of the No. 5 switches acts as an easement at the start of each curve. Flex-Track might be needed in the curve to properly close it up, due to the 12.5° easement effect of the No. 5 switches. However if you want an O72 curve at that location, you may not need to use any Flex-Track.

Switch alignment E shows a yard using No. 5 switches. They provide nice, tight, 4" track centers. If you want 4-1/2" between the tracks, insert a 1-1/4" straight on the diverging route of the switch, as shown.

In closing, Atlas O offers a great O gauge track system. It has a wide selection of curves, straights, fixed radius switches, plus their numbered switches to choose from. They also have a 24" turntable as part of this track system. Atlas O Flex-Track makes the system even more usable. And when you ballast Atlas O track, it looks fantastic!

Happy Railroading!

Using Atlas O No. 5 Switches

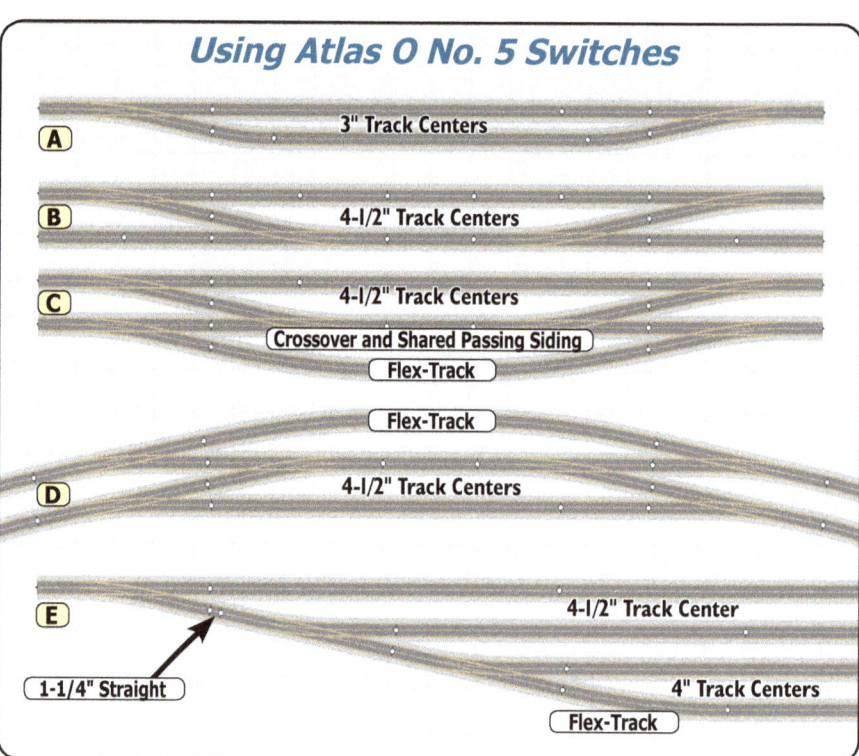

What's a Numbered Switch?

Numbered switches are a bit different from the fixed diameter switches typically used on three-rail, O gauge layouts. The switch number refers to a unit of distance, not a curve diameter or radius. For example, in a No. 5 switch, for every 5 units of length along the switch, the diverging route moves away from the tangent route by 1 unit. The diverging angle is determined by the switch number. Higher numbers yield longer switches and more gradual diverging route angles. On a model train layout, numbered switches provide tighter yard track spacing than fixed diameter switches.

Real railroads use numbered switches everywhere. They range from short No. 6 switches used in yards, to the long, graceful, No. 20 switches used in high speed, 79-mph main line crossovers.

Atlas O offers both No. 5 and No. 7.5 switches

Atlas Numbered Switches

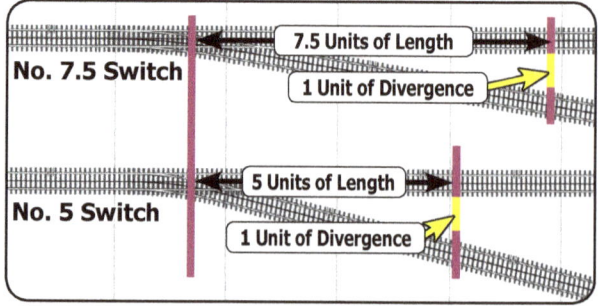

An Intro-to-O Layout
The Reading & Western in 4'x 8'

This O gauge layout would be a fine introduction to the world of O gauge railroading. It features Lionel's FasTrack, with an O31 figure-8 nestled inside an O36 loop. There are two industry tracks and two 90-degree crossings, with the potential for lots of train-running interest and excitement for two engineers. Scenery is simple and basic, so you can get to running trains right away.

Track Plan

This track plan uses O31 for the inside figure-8, with O36 minimum for the rest of the layout, including switches. The sharp O31 curves use O36 easements to lead into the curves, while the O36 curves use O48 curved sections as easements. There are two O60 switches used with O48 sections to make the crossovers, which connect the figure-8 and outside loop for easy switching of trains between routes. One half-section of O72 is located in the center area of the layout.

Scenery

Scenery is simple and easy for this introductory layout plan. The terrain is flat except for a slight, tree-covered hill in the upper left corner. Otherwise, there are trees scattered about, a couple of roads, and a dirt area around the yard tower in the center, by the crossings.

Structures

The layout shown includes a variety of structures:

- Lionel Animated Freight Station
- Lionel Barrel Loader
- Lionel Yard Tower andWwater Tower
- Menards Station
- Menards Morton Salt Factory
- Mernards Hobby Shop
- OGR Ameri-Towne No. 442 Acme Machine Shop

The water tank and a shed, or a whistle-stop station could come from any manufacturer, and a small shack would be an easy scratchbuild project.

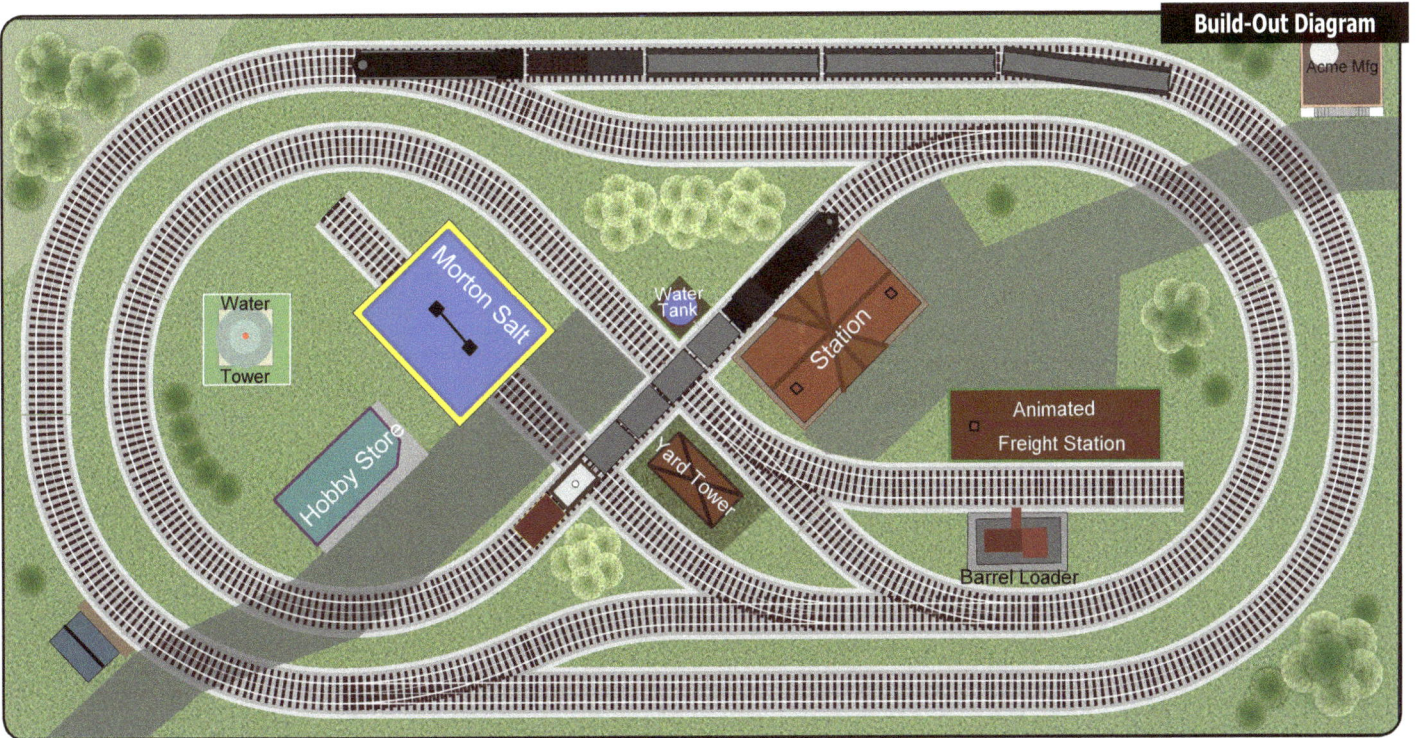

Build-Out Diagram

An Intro-to-O Layout — Page 25

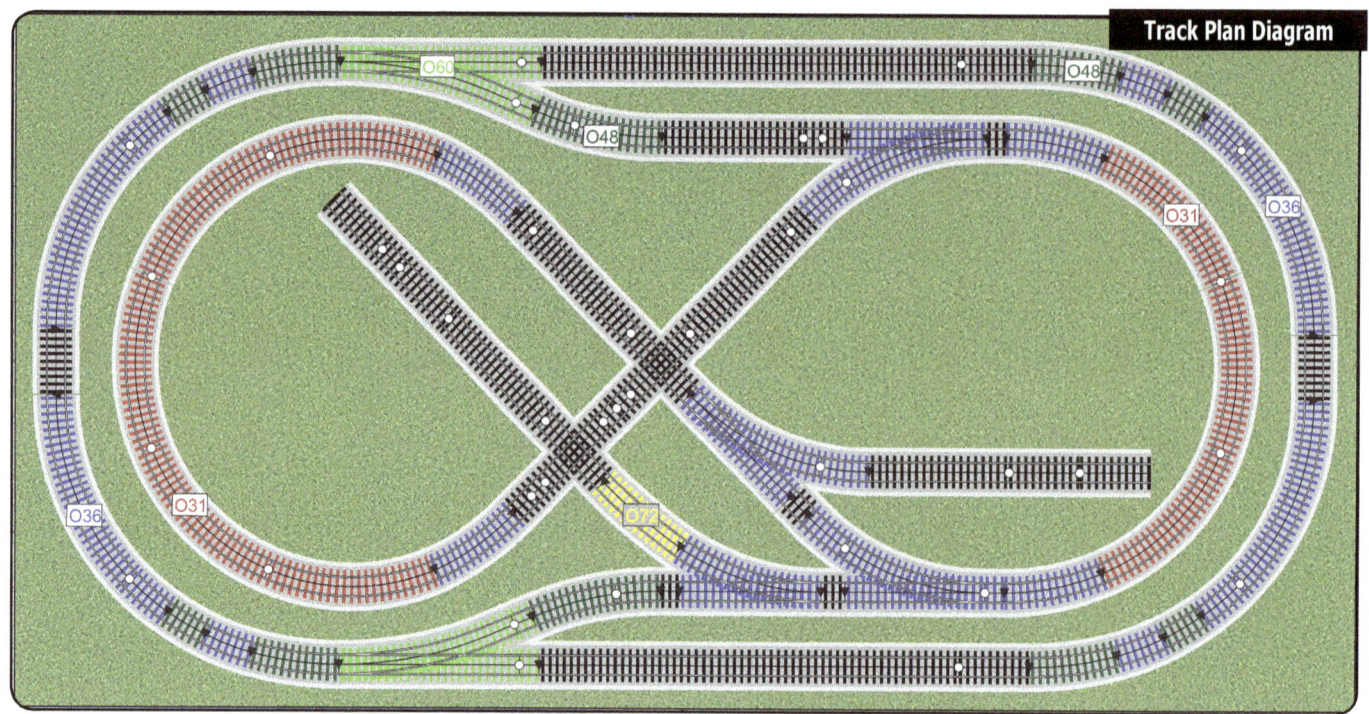

Track Plan Diagram

Construction and Track Plan Diagram

Construction is easy, consisting of a single 4x8 sheet of plywood or 2"-thick foam sheet set on a table, mounted on a simple foundation, or set up on a couple of folding tables.

The Track Plan Diagram shows the different curvature FasTrack sections labeled and identified with different colors. The tightest O31 curves are shown in red, with the curves widening in different colors through O36, O48, O60 switches, and one half-section of O72.

Power and Wiring

A single transformer can power the layout with two trains; or if conventional control is desired, the figure-8 and the outside loop can be isolated and powered with two transformers. This is a good layout for LionChief trains that can handle O31 curves.

Trains

The layout as shown might feature Lionel's Polar Express Berkshire and three passenger cars, plus Lionel's Granite Run Quarry set with its saddle-tank locomotive, four short gondolas, a water car for putting out lineside fires started by cinders, and a shorty caboose. And of course, there are many other options that would include small steam or diesel motive power.

The Reading and Western is a simple 4x8 layout and track plan ideal for beginners, with easy construction and a whole lot of train running fun for two engineers.

Happy Railroading!

An Intro-to-O Layout Lionel FasTrack Bill of Materials

Straights		
6-12042	Straight 30"	2
6-12014	Straight 10"	5
6-12024	Straight 5"	4
6-12025	Straight 4-1/2"	2
6-12026	Straight 1-3/4"	7
6-12073	Straight 1-3/8"	7
6-12035	Lighted Bumper	2
6-12019	90° Crossing	2
Curves		
6-37103	O31 Curve, angle 45°	8
6-12015	O36 Curve, angle 45°	4
6-12022	O36 Curve, angle 22.5°	4
6-12023	O36 Curve, angle 11.25°	11
6-16834	O48 Curve, angle 15°	6
6-16835	O48 Curve, angle 7.5°	6
6-12055	O72 Curve, angle 11.25°	1
Switches		
6-12045 or 6-81947	O36 Left	2
6-12046 or 6-81946	O36 Right	2
6-12057 or 6-81951	O60 Left	1
6-12058 or 6-81950	O60 Right	1
Straight 1-3/8" roadbed, included with switches		4

Just a Bit Beyond the Basic
Build the South Fork & Western with Lionel FasTrack

The South Fork and Western Railroad layout is an interesting and slightly complex layout, with lots of cool train-running and scenery to enhance your train-watching. It can be built as shown as the full 5'x 9' layout, or it can be built as a smaller 4'4"x 8' layout, consisting of just the two inside loops. The accompanying Track Section Diagram highlights the inside layout as it would look. Or you can build the inside layout first on the full 5'x 9' table, and then expand the layout later to make the full-size 5'x 9' railroad. Then again, you might want to construct it in the opposite order. The track shown is Lionel FasTrack, with a minimum O36 curvature; and the outside loop is comprised of all O48 curves, which enables equipment requiring O42 curves to run there. Two or three trains can run the layout simultaneously.

Understanding the Track Plan

This layout can be built with Lionel FasTrack sections simply by following the Track Section Diagram. But to understand how the nested inside curves work, a bit of explanation is in order.

To fully understand this layout plan, start with the smaller 4'4"x8' inside layout, consisting of the two inside loops that are outlined on the Track Section Diagram.

This is an up-and-over pair of nested loops, and each loop has arms angled slightly at 3.75 degrees from the horizontal to maximize the length of the run up the grade. Basically, a full loop of track runs each way in order to keep the grade at a comfortable 3%. The track is level at the bridges above and below, but all the rest is on grade.

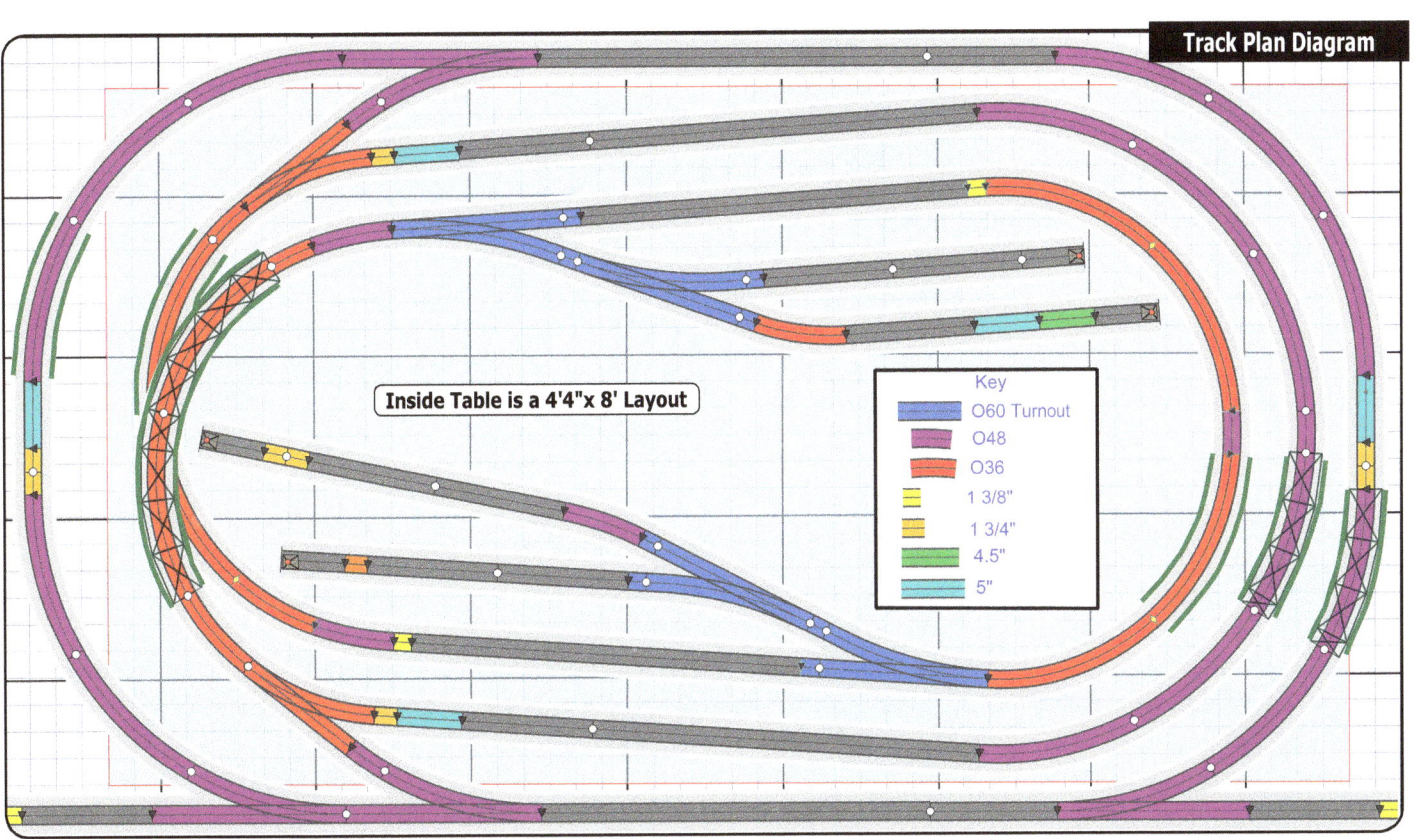

Just a Bit Beyond the Basic

South Fork & Western RR FasTrack Bill of Materials

	Straights	
6-12042	Straight 30"	6
6-12014	Straight 10"	13
6-12024	Straight 5"	5
6-12025	Straight 4½"	1
6-12026	Straight 1¾"	9
6-12073	Straight 1⅜"	4
6-12035	Lighted Bumper	4
	Curves	
6-12015	O36 Curve, angle 45°	8
6-12022	O36 Curve, angle 22.5°	3
6-12023	O36 Curve, angle 11.25°	2
6-12043	O48 Curve, angle 30°	16
6-16834	O48 Curve, angle 15°	3
6-16835	O48 Curve, angle 7.5°	4
	Switches	
6-12045 or 6-81947	O36 Left	1
6-12046 or 6-81946	O36 Right	1
6-12065 or 6-81949	O48 Left	2
6-12066 or 6-81948	O48 Right	2
6-12057 or 6-81951	O60 Left	2
6-12058 or 6-81950	O60 Right	2
Roadbed-trimmed 1⅜" sections included with the O60 switches		8

This small offsetting angle is created by an O48 1/4 section of 7.5 degrees, and that angle is then split between the two arms of each loop. You can see this quarter O48 track section in the Track Section Diagram at the middle of the right-side curve of each of the two angled inside loops.

The outside loop is just an O48 oval, which connects through crossover switches. Here's how the switch angles match the small offset angle of 3.75 degrees. The switches coming off the outside loop, plus one 1/4 curve section, make a total curve angle of 37.5 degrees (30+7.5). Then the connecting inside loop O36 switch is at 33.75 degrees, for a matching difference between the crossover switches of 3.75 degrees, thus keeping all angles and curves perfectly aligned.

One other point: note that the outside loop crossover switches are at different levels—one at the layout base height, and the other descending from the high bridge. So the entire outside loop connecting these two switches on the right-hand portion of the loop is also on a grade as well, again at 3%!

A comment about the left-side section of the outside oval: this section is actually optional. Deleting it saves two switches and eight inches in layout table length, making a shorter 5'x 8'4" layout. Most of the layout fun is still there, but it does lose the separate outside loop route so I would not recommend it. Nevertheless, it is reasonable to do if space is tight.

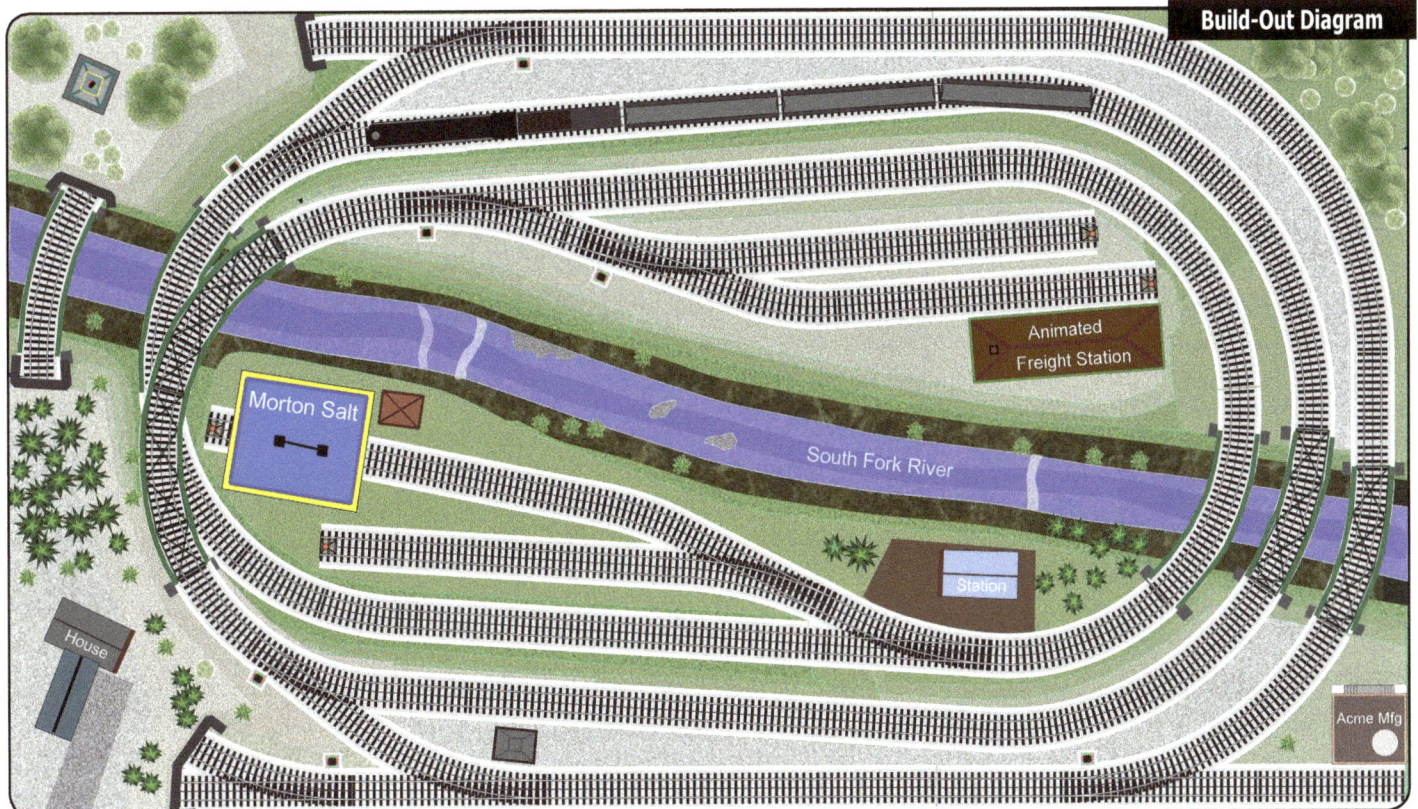

Build-Out Diagram

The section on the left side of the outside loop grade is steep, at a 5.5% grade, in order to connect with the two crossover switches, which are each at different elevations. A 5.5% grade is steep, but not too steep for Lionel traditional-type locomotives. But this should be kept in mind; and it might be advisable to restrict the outside loop to clockwise direction to take this steep grade downhill, with the uphill climb being made over the long half of the loop.

For operations with the outside loop and the nested two inside loops, clearly two trains can run without crossing paths, and perhaps three trains can run in the same direction if train speeds are aligned together, suggesting the use of command control that maintains a continuous train speed.

Layout Construction

The Track Plan Diagram shows the FasTrack sections needed, color-coded for the curves and small straight sections. The track runs pretty close against the limit of the train table's 4'4" width, so an outside frame of 1x3s or 2x4s will make a nice framework with 3/4" of additional outside clearance.

The track height across the layout varies just about everywhere. The nested inside loops are on 3% grades except on the upper and lower bridges. The pair of tracks on each side of the South Fork River are each on the level, but at different elevations as they come off higher and lower switches.

The consistent 3% grade standard is convenient to make it easier to build the elevations, but Woodland Scenics curveable foam inclines at 3% can make the entire grade-constructing project quite simple. Then there also is the 5.5% grade on the outside loop at the left side of the layout, which can be made with piers/supports cut to fit, or can be made with two stacked foam inclines, each of 3% for a total 6% grade.

The Woodland Scenics inclines are 3" wide, just short of the width of Lionel's FasTrack, so inside curve supports need to be added along the foam inclines to complete the full width. This is easy enough to do with some scrap foam and a hot glue gun.

In addition to the grades, there is a river about 1" below grade. And there are two high tunnels on the left side of the outside oval. The terrain has to be filled in everywhere.

Just a Bit Beyond the Basic

The changing elevation and terrain can make for a lovely scenic layout, but keep in mind that terrain work will involve some time and creativity. This, plus the continual grades, suggests that this layout might not be ideal for a modeler's first layout.

Operations and Structures

This small 5'x 9' layout is not intended to emulate prototypical railroad operations; it's about having fun with running traditional O gauge trains through some cool scenery. But two sets of tracks on opposite sides of the South Fork River can be created so rolling stock needs to be interchanged between the two.

The two O48 switches on the bottom of the track plan are optional and can either represent a connecting railroad to interchange cars with, or deleted, as desired.

The structures I used on the layout are:

- Lionel Animated Freight Station
- Lionel Rotating Beacon (on the tunnel upper left)
- Menards Morton Salt Tower
- OGR/Ameri-Towne No. 442 Acme Machine Shop

You can get the house and the small station from a variety of manufacturers, or you might consider building them yourself! The same applies to the small switch tower at the bottom crossover switch.

Power and Wiring

For conventional control, you can use two transformers to power the separate outside and double-loop inside circles. The two angled oval inside loops can each be a block, and the O48 outside loop can also be divided into two blocks, for a total of four conventional blocks.

LionChief or some other command control method makes the layout easier to wire and run and can maintain constant train speeds climbing or descending the grades. The switches can be remote, command, or manual, as you desire.

Conclusion

The South Fork and Western RR is a fun-filled and interesting scenic layout, but it is a bit complex given the grades and all the scenery work. But the effort can be highly rewarding, resulting in a beautiful and entertaining layout capable of operating two or three trains.

Happy Railroading!

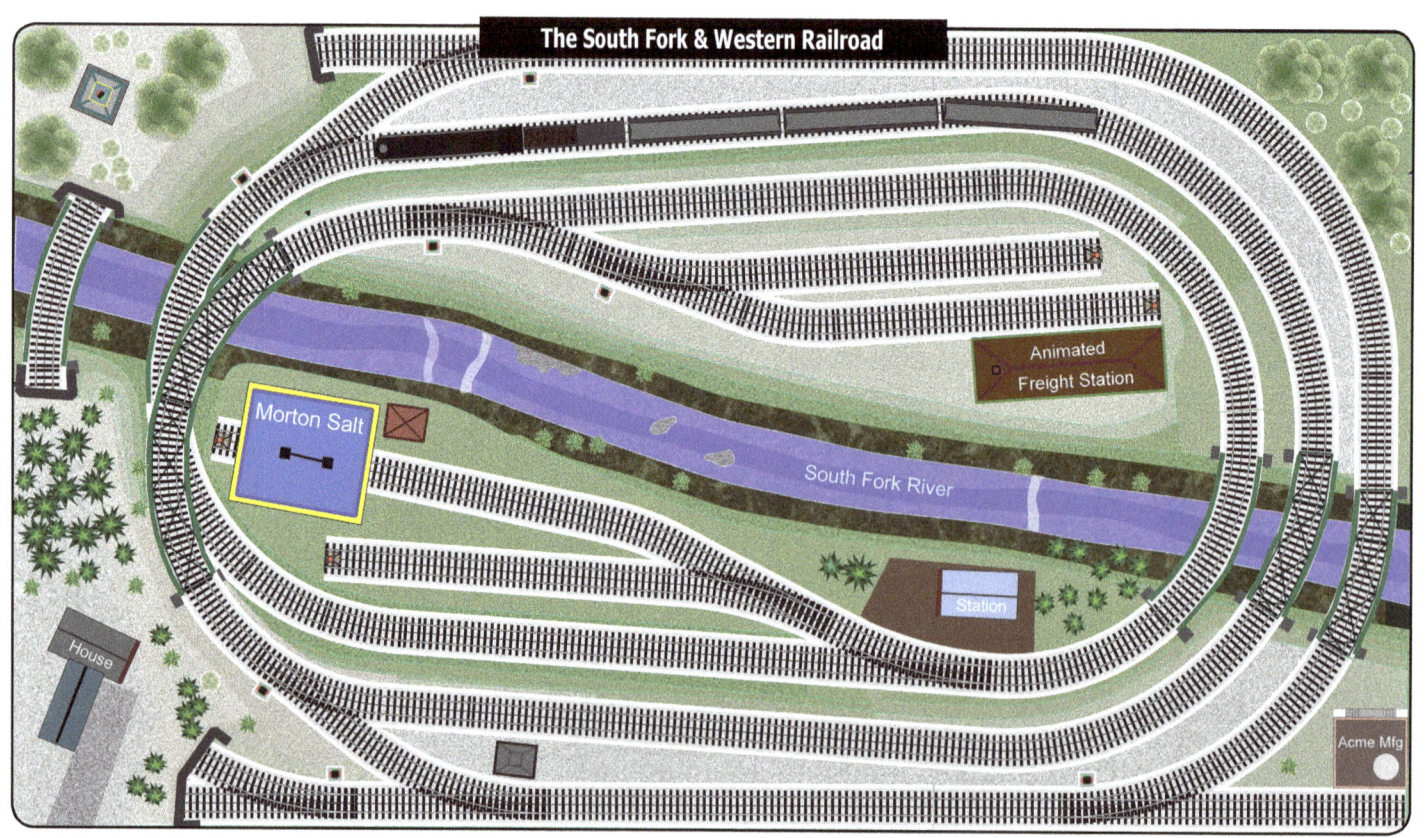

Planning the North Ridge Railroad

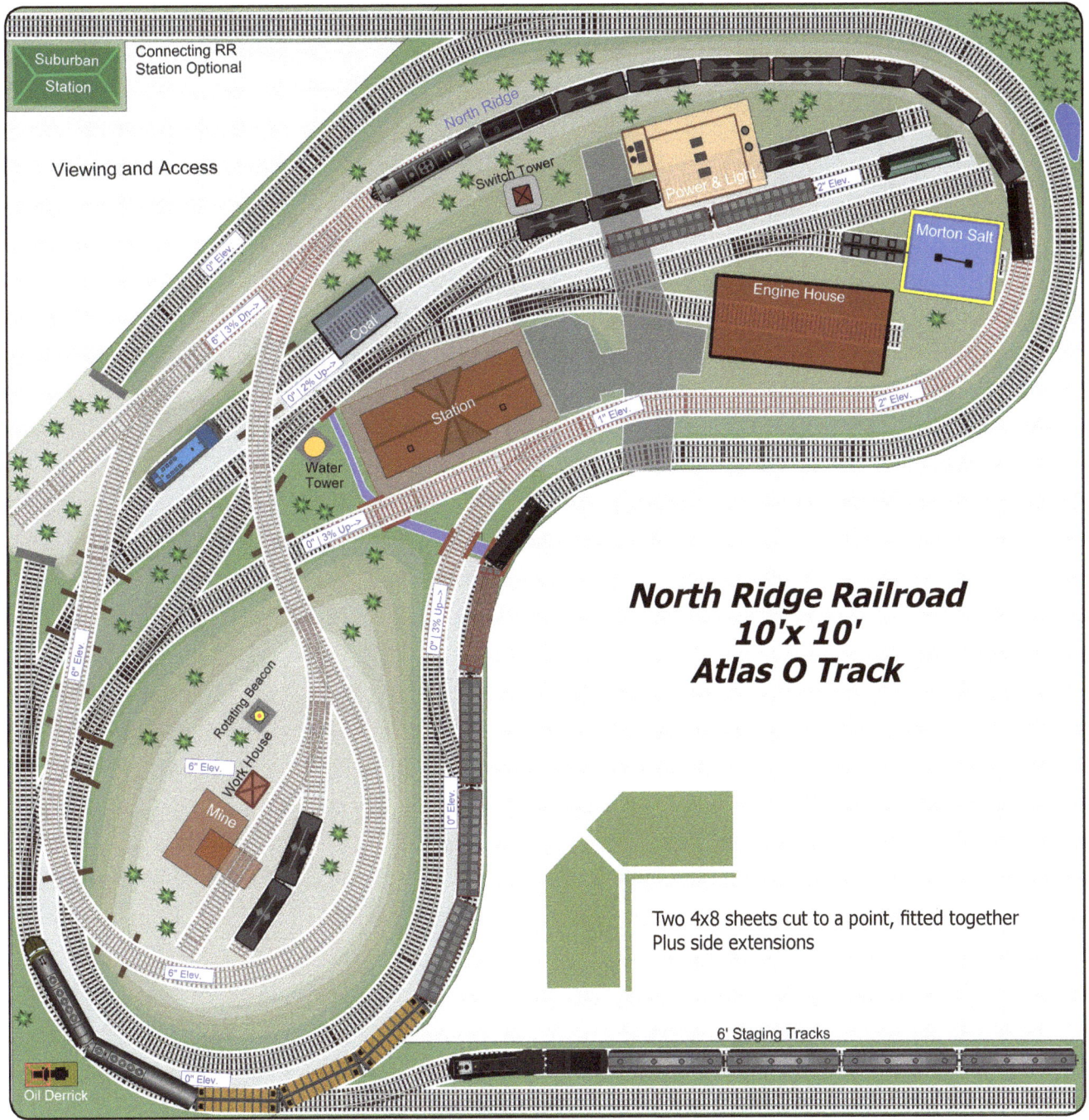

The North Ridge Railroad layout plan can 1192fit in a small 10'x 10' bedroom using Atlas O sectional track. This design is especially appropriate for traditional, LionChief, and LionScale locomotives and rolling stock.

The inside route is a mountain branch of O36 minimum curves comprised of two return loops and a long 3 percent grade climbing up North Ridge to 6" of elevation to reach a mine with two track tracks. The outside route is a level bent oval of O45 minimum curves. Both routes have wide-diameter track sections and easements into many of the curves. The layout also incorporates a small curving yard with a yard lead and runaround track.

The layout has two access areas for train operation, viewing, and layout access. Two trains can run continuously on the two main line routes or can work past each other on a grand tour route from the yard, around the outer loop, up the mine grade, back down and around, and returning to the yard. From the yard, trains can directly access each of the two main lines. Trains can be reversed on the return loops, and turning a locomotive from the yard can be accomplished with the connection from the yard to the inside return loop with locomotives reversing direction past the station.

Track Design

Layout minimum curves are O36 for the inside route with the two return loops and the climb up North Ridge to the mine and O45 for the outside bent-oval route. The switch standard is a minimum of O54 on the main lines with O36 allowed to service the mine tracks. Having a main line switch minimum diameter larger than the minimum curvature assures smooth and trouble-free train running, even at relatively high speeds.

An examination of the track sections needed, listed in Diagram B, shows that even with the O36 minimum curves inside route and the O45 minimum curves outside route, there is a great deal of wide and graceful fixed track section curvature included: 67.5 degrees of O108, 120 degrees of O81, 67.5 degrees of O72, and 169.75 degrees of O54. Even with the tight minimum curvature specified, these wider curves make for smooth and graceful layout operation where locomotives and consists will be a pleasure to watch.

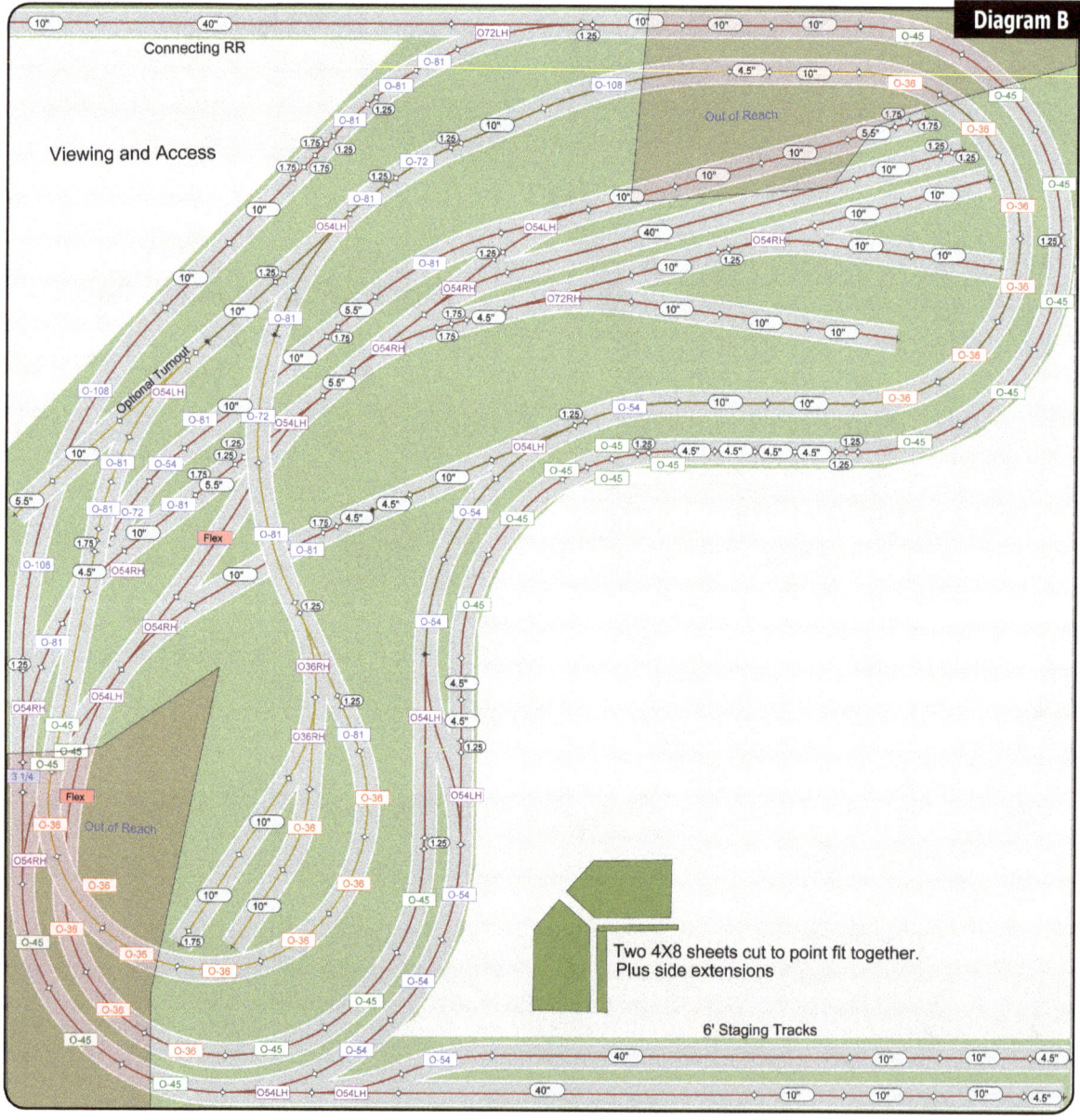

There are two sections of very gently curved Atlas flexible track: one of O82 and the other of O256 (almost straight). These will be easy to bend from a single 40" section of flexible track. There is also one custom-cut straight section of 3-1/4" that can be cut from a 4-1/2" straight or a leftover piece of flexible track. Be sure to smooth the cut rail ends so that rail joiners will slide on easily. A tie may need to be removed to accommodate rail joiners and sanded down to slide beneath the rail joiners of these track joints.

There are two sections of elevated track on trestles completing the mine loop. These are at 6" in height and can be supported on trestle bents or concrete pillars. You may even include thin girder bridges or other types of bridges. Optionally, raising the slope on the grade up the ridge from 3 percent to 4 percent raises the elevated height section to 8".

Northridge RR Bill of Materials
Bill of Materials

Curved Sections			Need
6016	Radius 54" (O108)	22.5°	3
6011	Radius 40-1/2" (O81)	22.5°	2
6012	Radius 40-1/2" (O81)	7.5°	10
6062	Radius 36" (O72)	22.5°	1
6063	Radius 36" (O72)	11.25°	2
6060	Radius 27" (O54)	22.5°	7
6061	Radius 27" (O54)	11.25°	1
6045	Radius 22-1/2" (O45)	30°	14
6046	Radius 22-1/2" (O45)	7.5°	6
6066	Radius 18" (O36)	30°	17
Straight Sections			
6058	Straight 40"		4
6050	Straight 10"		39
6053	Straight 5-1/2"		4
6051	Straight 4-1/2"		14
6052	Straight 1-3/4"		11
6015	Straight 1-1/4"		27
Flexible and Cut Straight Sections			
6056	3-1/4" (cut to length)		1
6056	flexible 14-17/32" (min. radius=41-1/32") (O82)		1
6056	flexible 16-7/8" (min. radius=128-3/16") (O256)		1
Switches			
6072	O72 Left		1
6073	O72 Right		1
6070	O54 Left		10
6071	O54 Right		7
6076	O36 Right		2

Benchwork, Construction, and Access

Layout benchwork is made up of two 4x8 1/2"-thick plywood sheets cut to a point at 45 degree angles to fit together. These can be supported using a 2x4 framework or other construction. The inside edge of each sheet has a narrow addition of less than 6" in order to accommodate the track curvature.

There are also two extensions: one for a junction with a connecting railroad and optional station and another two-track staging yard of 6' for each track.

The track section diagram also shows decent reach access to the layout with just two areas that are beyond an easy reach from any of the edges. Plan your construction so you can build these areas first and install the detailed scenery you may want in these areas. During construction and scenery building, these areas can be accessed by standing on a stool and lying on top of a rug or carpet fragment placed on an area with track that is close to an access point.

All but one of the switches, which can be operated remotely or by hand throws, are within a comfortable reach from the layout access areas.

A sound-absorbing material can be layered on top of the plywood surface. This material can be foam sheets, cork, Homasote, grass mats, or even felt. The Atlas track should be mounted on roadbed and ballasted during the scenery construction process. Either 1" or 2" thick foam sheets can be used to build the elevated sections. For example, the ends of the yard tracks are at 2" elevation, North Ridge climbs to a 6" elevation, the mine mountain is 6" high, and the outside O45 bent-oval main line is all level.

There is a tunnel located over the lower track where North Ridge continues to climb, which is located to the left beyond the layout. This tunnel is over O108 track sections and is fun to watch as trains enter and exit. Optionally, an O54 left-hand switch can be installed on the elevated loop to allow the mine run to continue across the tunnel and up the ridge beyond the layout edge.

With a door to the room leading into the main operations area, you can access the triangular viewing and access space in the upper left by scooting beneath the layout on a rolling chair or stool. Leave a pathway beneath the center of the layout clear of obstructions, such as supporting posts and storage, to facilitate easy transit. Benchwork constructed somewhat higher than the customary 42" or 48" will ease this access transition without bumped heads, banged knees, or bent backs and will leave room for more storage under the layout. It also places the layout surface at a higher viewing level and comes closer to the ground level position where most real railroad activity is viewed.

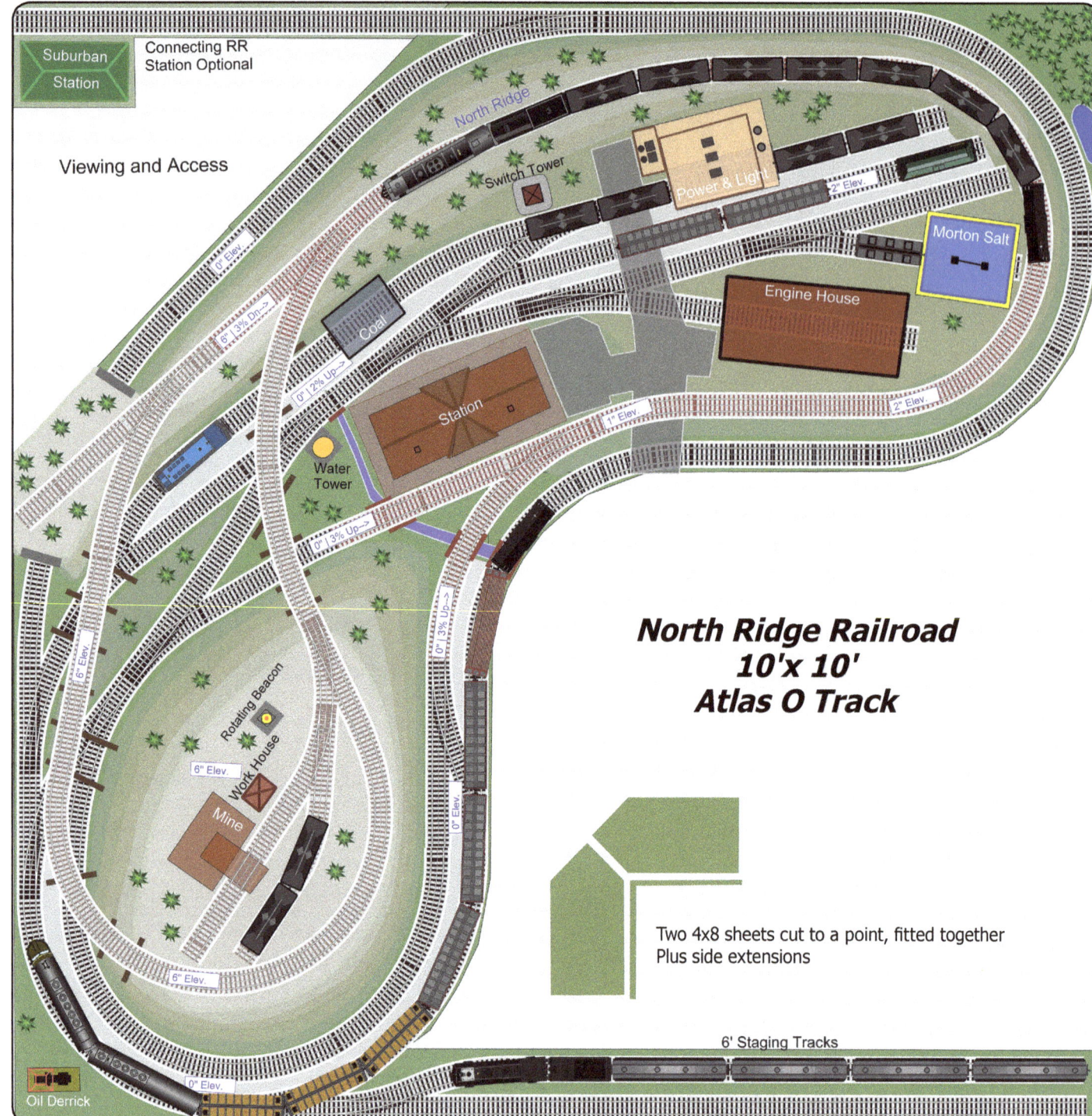

Structures and Operations

A variety of structures can be included with this track plan. Illustrated on the diagram are four of the large Menards lighted and detailed structures: power plant, Morton Salt tower, station, and engine shed. Three Lionel operating accessories, such as the coal loader, oil derrick, and rotating beacon, are included. Also shown are the Lionel suburban station, work house with sound, water tower, switch tower, and a scratchbuilt mine. Operating signals can also be added to protect the junctions and crossovers between the main lines.

The North Ridge RR layout should provide hours of enjoyment for one or two engineers, varying the routes, moving coal between the mine and power plant, switching in the yard, or just watching two trains roll through the track work, mountain scenery, and wide curves. Have you ever wondered how your trains might look operating on wide curves? Even this small layout has some wide track curves so you can watch your express passenger, freight, and mine run drag trains roll through wide O72, O81, and O108 curves and scenery.

Happy Railroading!

Something Old, Something New

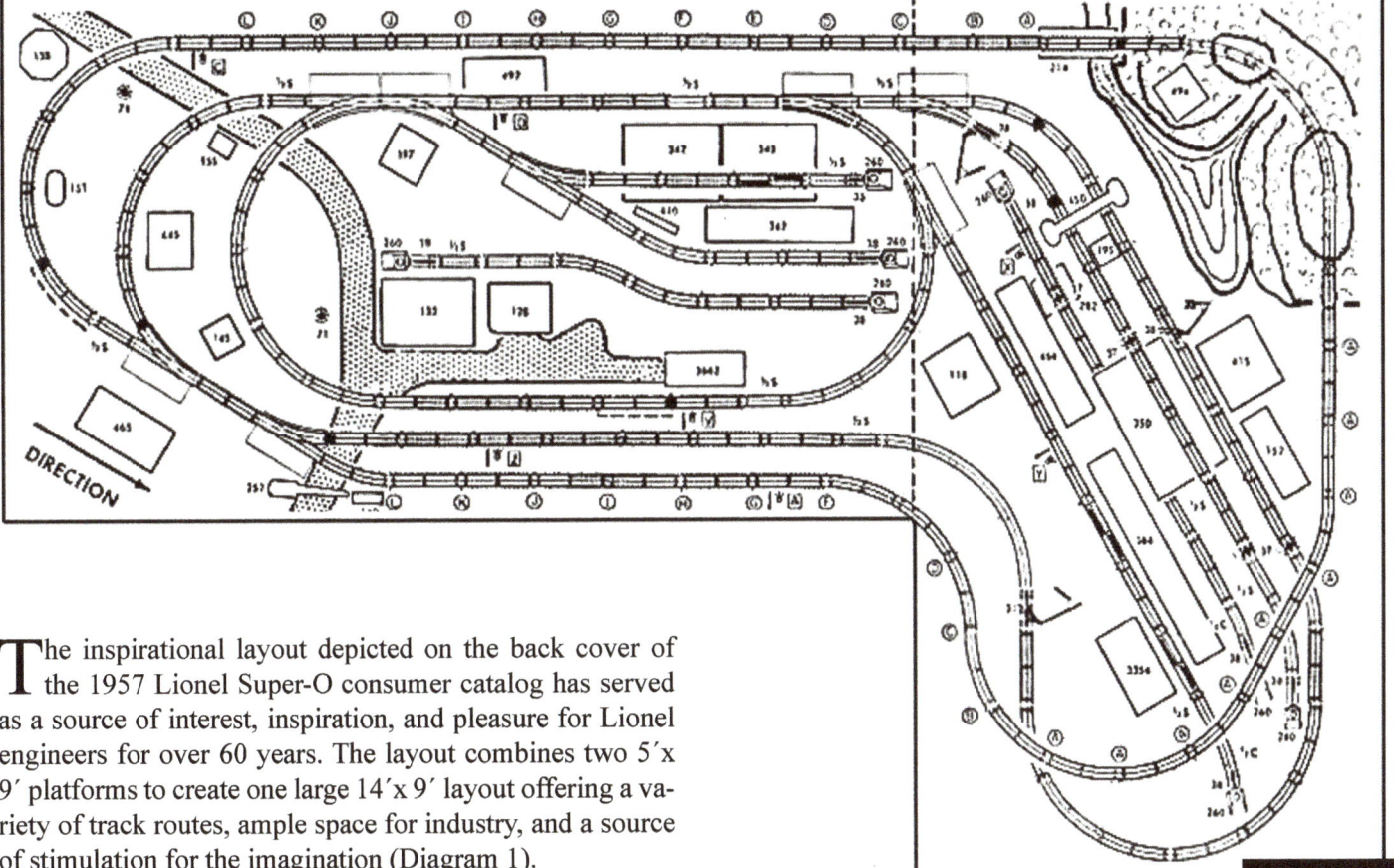

DIAGRAM 1

The inspirational layout depicted on the back cover of the 1957 Lionel Super-O consumer catalog has served as a source of interest, inspiration, and pleasure for Lionel engineers for over 60 years. The layout combines two 5′ x 9′ platforms to create one large 14′ x 9′ layout offering a variety of track routes, ample space for industry, and a source of stimulation for the imagination (Diagram 1).

The updated layout plan I came up with replaces the original plan's Super-O, O36 diameter track with modern Lionel FasTrack sections, which include integrated roadbed at varying diameters from O36 to O96. Atlas O 21st Century track is used on the trestle at the lower right, although FasTrack curves combining O36 and O80 curves can be substituted if desired (Diagram 2). This enhanced track plan features a main line separation to create two independent mains that can connect through O72 crossovers. The inner route is also enhanced by adding a third-route variation consisting of two reverse loops in addition to an inside oval nestled within the inside bent-oval route. A four-track yard made up of 60″ tracks and O60 switches replaces the three-track yard with a back-and-forth trolley run.

The outside main line is a long bent-oval route constructed with a combination of Lionel FasTrack with O48 minimum diameter, and Atlas O used for the elevated trestle over the yard at the lower right a 45″ diameter for a minimum O45 run. Diagram 3 provides a 3-D view that helps to visualize the grades and the elevated trestle.

FasTrack sections of O60, O72, and O96 mix with the O48 diameter in a broad and graceful O96 curve on the upper right providing for excellent train-watching opportunities.

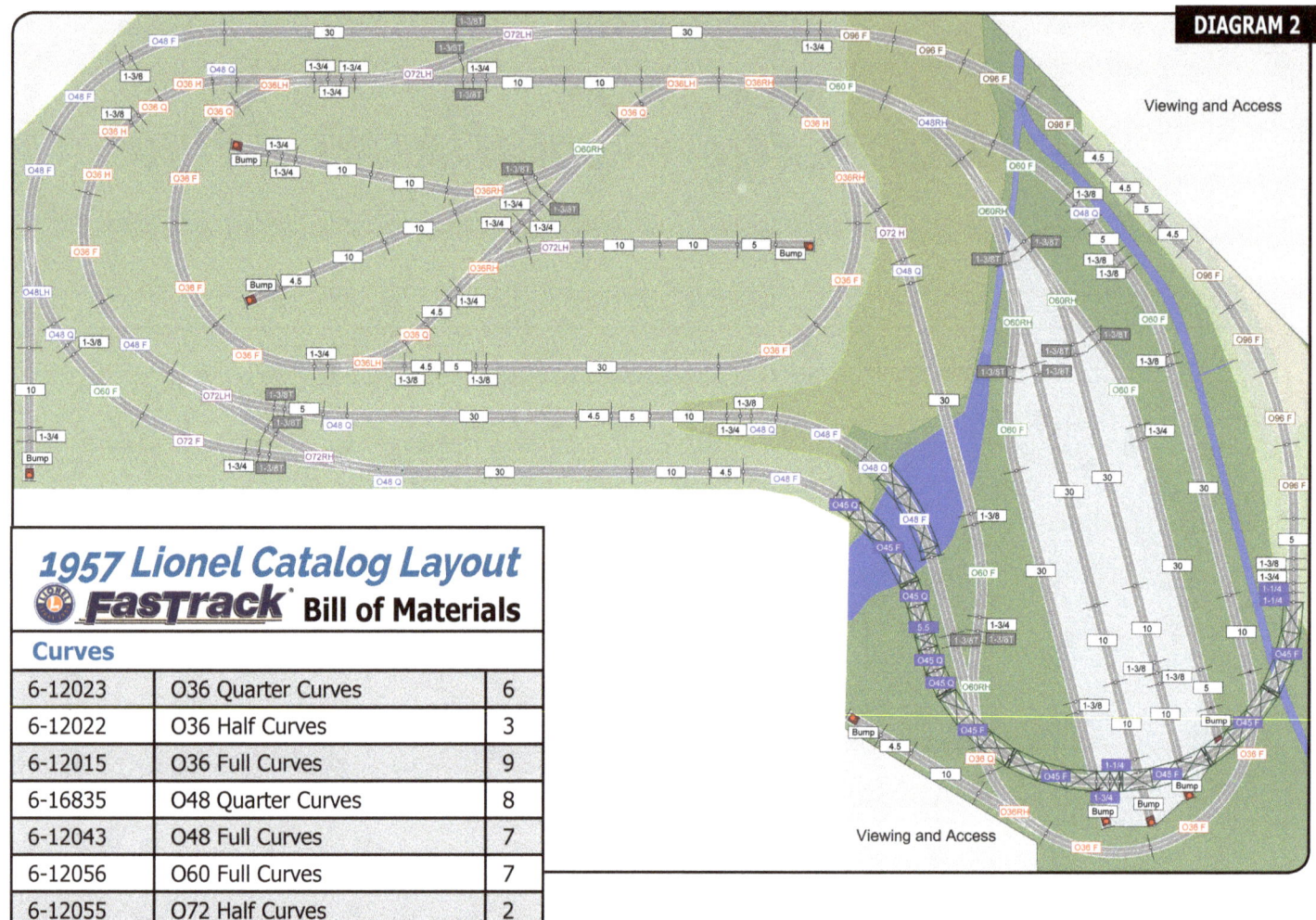

DIAGRAM 2

1957 Lionel Catalog Layout FasTrack Bill of Materials

Curves

6-12023	O36 Quarter Curves	6
6-12022	O36 Half Curves	3
6-12015	O36 Full Curves	9
6-16835	O48 Quarter Curves	8
6-12043	O48 Full Curves	7
6-12056	O60 Full Curves	7
6-12055	O72 Half Curves	2
6-12041	O72 Full Curve	1
6-81250	O96 Full Curves	8

Straights

6-12073	1-3/8" Straights	14
6-12026	1-3/4" Straights	20
6-12025	4-1/2" Straights	9
6-12024	5" Straights	8
6-12014	10" Straights	19
6-12042	30" Straights	11

1957 Lionel Catalog Layout FasTrack Bill of Materials

Switches

6-12046 or 6-81946	O36 Right Remote Only or O36 Right Remote & Command	5
6-12045 or 6-81947	O36 Left Remote Only or O36 Left Remote & Command	3
6-12066 or 6-81948	O48 Right Remote Only or O48 Right Remote & Command	1
6-12065 or 6-81949	O48 Left Remote Only or O48 Left Remote & Command	1
6-12058 or 6-81950	O60 Right Remote Only or O60 Right Remote & Command	5
6-12048 or 6-81953	O72 Left Remote Only or O72 Left Remote & Command	3
6-12049 or 6-81952	O72 Right Remote Only or O72 Right Remote & Command	1

On the left-hand side, a combination of O60 and O72 curves also provides satisfying views as the trains ease through the curves between O48 sections and run through the straight branch with two O72 switches.

The inner main line route is actually three routes in one with lots of variety and action potential. There is an inside oval of O36 FasTrack connecting the town and industries. There also is a connected bent-oval route of FasTrack with a mixture of O48 and O36 curves paralleling the outside route on the left and dropping down on the right-hand side beneath the trestle and around the yard.

DIAGRAM 3

DIAGRAM 4

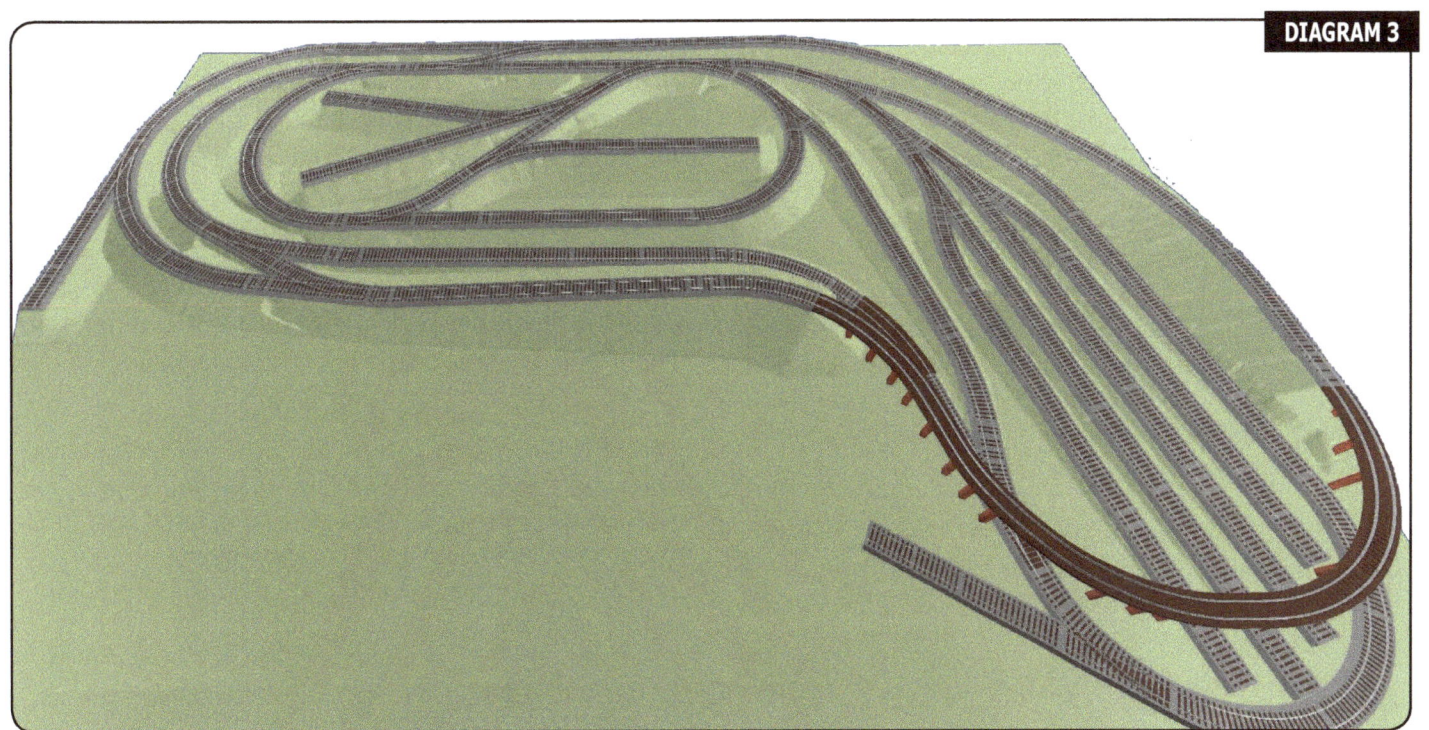

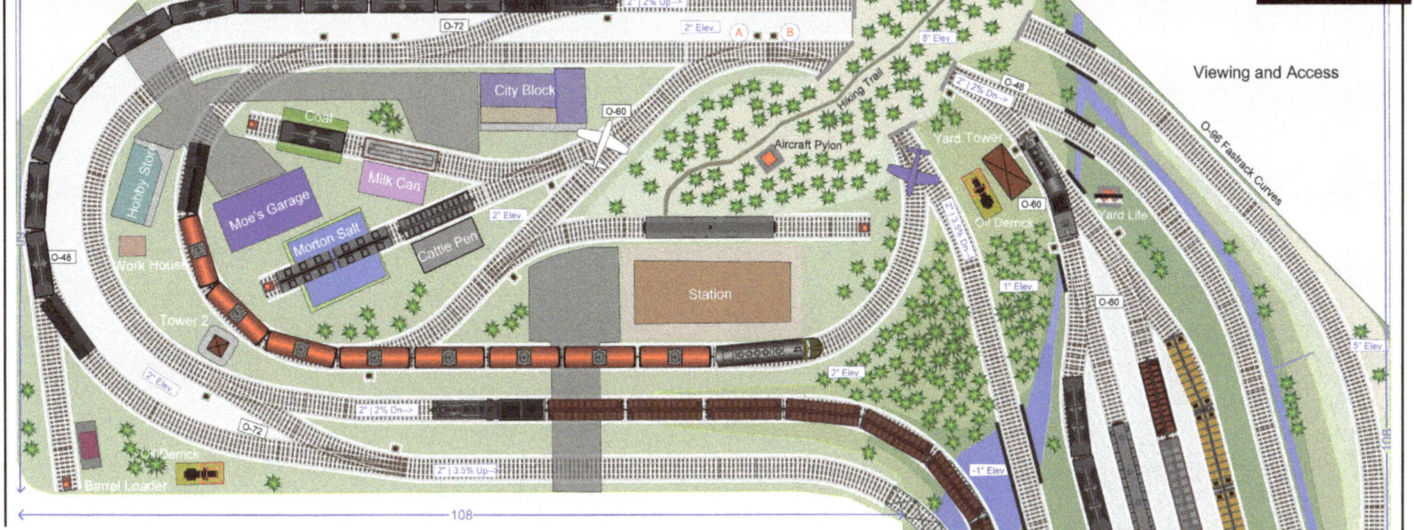

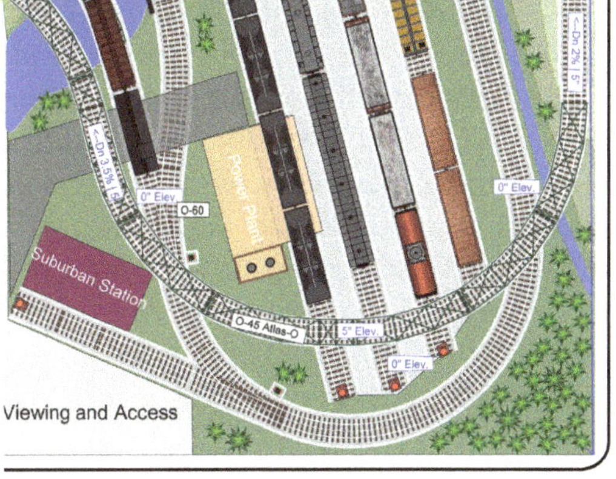

Finally, there is a route comprised of two reverse loops that meet just left of the tunnel in the center, runs though the inner oval on the left, and then around the yard at the right. This enables trains to reverse and alternate their direction of travel.

Switches, as noted, are O36, O48, O60, and O72 and are all easily accessible from the outside edges of the layout. Switches of O36 are unmarked, and other sizes are indicated on the diagram. All switches are on the level except the four descending to the yard at the right, which are on a mild 2 percent grade.

Something Old, Something New

There is ample space on the layout for a number of accessories (Diagram 4). Four traditional Lionel industries are served by the rail lines seen on the left: coal unloader, milk can platform, cattle pen, and barrel loader. A Menards Morton Salt tower is in the center of the left-hand platform. The centerpiece structure is the Menards impressive lighted and detailed station located between the main line and a track that can hold a baggage car, a connecting passenger car, a *doodlebug* self-propelled railcar, a trolley, or other short passenger equipment. A second passenger station is the Lionel Suburban Station, which is located beneath the trestle at the lower right.

Other structures include the Menards Moe's Garage, Hobby Store, and City Block; along with the Lionel Work House with sound, Yard Tower, and operating Oil Derrick with its animated nodding donkey. Also included are a second smaller switch tower, a rotating beacon tower, and a yard light tower.

Railroad operation supports two independent trains on their own main lines, which can swap between the inner and outer routes using the smooth O72 crossovers. The inner route train can alternate between the three possible inner routes. If desired, a third engineer can switch the yard and service the industry tracks in town while two main line trains can share the longer outer main line and use the passing siding formed from the O72 crossovers connecting the two main lines.

Grades throughout the layout are modest, being much reduced from Lionel's original plan with a maximum of 3.5 percent. Most other grades are an even more modest 2 percent, as shown on the layout plan. The trestle at the lower right has a 5″ clearance over the yard. The reduced grades provide for smooth running and unattended operation.

As previously noted, the layout and terrain are formed by two 5′x 9′ platforms, cut as shown for easier access, with the left-hand platform 2″ above the one on the right. This modest platform elevation difference is the key to reducing grades to manageable gradients. The left-hand platform is an intermediate shelf with tracks on grades leading down to the right-hand platform and yard and to the grades up and over the trestle at the lower right. At the junction of the two platforms, terrain will be filled in with a gradual slope starting to the left of the pond and stream to bring the level up to that of the left-side platform. The slope then continues to form the ridge line with tunnels and a hiking trail running along the crest. Another terrain element is the ridge at the far right that supports the smooth O96 curves on the outer loops as it climbs to cross over the yard on the Atlas O trestle.

There are two dense groupings of trees: the woods in the middle of the layout and another at the lower right. Other trees are scattered about as desired.

The plethora of lighted structures, some with animation and sound, combined with the lighted and operating dwarf signals of the FasTrack switches and the lighted bumpers should provide an entertaining light show when operating in the dark.

This updated layout plan should keep one, two, or three engineers engaged for hours or one train watcher viewing two trains running on the two main lines with lots of action and interest from animated industries and structures and lighted buildings. The inspirational Lionel 1957 catalog layout is both updated and enhanced to provide O gauge fun for the next 60 years.

1957 lionel Catalog Layout Highlights
Updated with FasTrack

- Two 5'x 9' tables
- Left at 2" elevation
- Right at 0" elevation
- Two main lines are separated for continuous running.
- Outer Main is O45.
- Inner main is O36 with O48 easements.
- Inside town industry loop is O36.
- Three inside main routes:
    Long bent oval past the yard
    Return loop-to-loop
    Small oval
- Crossovers between main lines are O72 switches.
- Atlas O O45 for the elevated trestle over the yard
- All switches are within 30" reach.
- Switches are O36 except where indicated otherwise.
- Graceful O96 FasTrack Curve at the upper right

Happy Railroading!

Track Combo for the Valley City Northern

FIGURE 1

Driving west from Fargo, North Dakota, across vast plains of wheat and sugar beets, the valley of the Sheyenne River appears without warning. Cut deep and wide as a result of a tremendous outflow of melt water and runoff from glacial Lake Agassi, the valley now cradles the small Sheyenne River winding at its bottom. The Sheyenne flows south through town toward the **Big Bend**, where it then curves to the east and a junction with the Red River (of the North), which flows north through Fargo (forming the border between North Dakota and Minnesota), on to Winnipeg, Manitoba, and then to the far north at Hudson's Bay.

Laid out in 1874 at the then westernmost construction of the Northern Pacific, Valley City was later reached by the Soo Line in 1891, as this subsidiary of the Canadian Pacific drove northwest up the Sheyenne River Valley to an eventual meeting with the CP main lines at Portal, North Dakota.

Not to be outdone, the tiny hamlet of Portal (6,500 people in 2010) was able to boast a third railroad: the electrified Valley City Street and Interurban, which in 1905 began shuttling passengers and freight from the NP through town to North Valley City and the Soo Line connection.

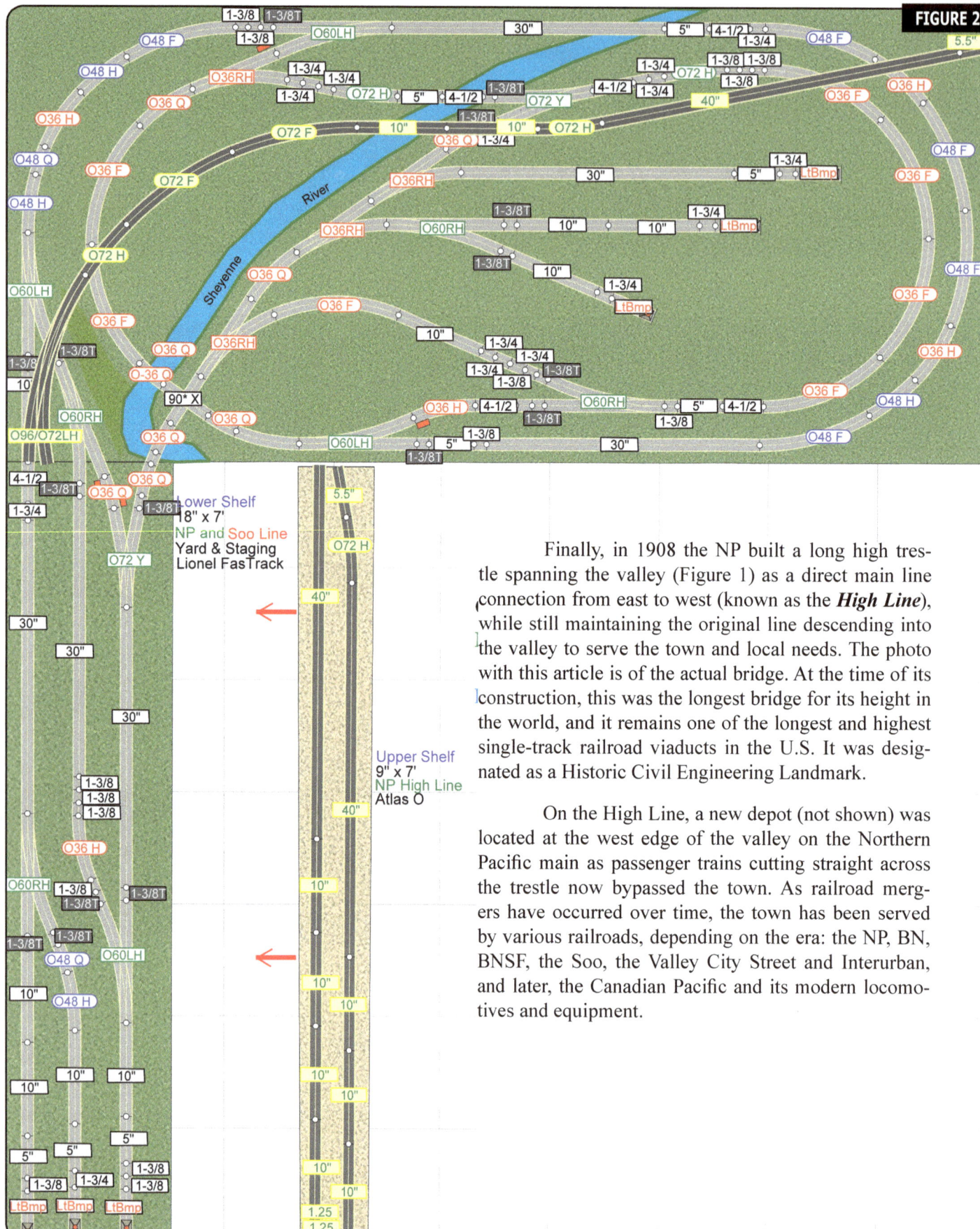

FIGURE 2

Finally, in 1908 the NP built a long high trestle spanning the valley (Figure 1) as a direct main line connection from east to west (known as the **High Line**), while still maintaining the original line descending into the valley to serve the town and local needs. The photo with this article is of the actual bridge. At the time of its construction, this was the longest bridge for its height in the world, and it remains one of the longest and highest single-track railroad viaducts in the U.S. It was designated as a Historic Civil Engineering Landmark.

On the High Line, a new depot (not shown) was located at the west edge of the valley on the Northern Pacific main as passenger trains cutting straight across the trestle now bypassed the town. As railroad mergers have occurred over time, the town has been served by various railroads, depending on the era: the NP, BN, BNSF, the Soo, the Valley City Street and Interurban, and later, the Canadian Pacific and its modern locomotives and equipment.

Valley City Northern RR FasTrack Bill of Materials

FasTrack Curves

6-12023	O-36 Quarter	6
6-12022	O36 Half	8
6-12015	O36 Full	7
6-16835	O48 Quarter	2
6-16834	O48 Half	4
6-12043	O48 Full	5
6-12055	O72 Half	2

FasTrack Straights

6-12073	1-3/8" Straight	17
6-12026	1-3/4" Straight	17
6-12025	4-1/2" Straight	7
6-12024	5" Straight	7
6-12014	10" Straight	9
6-12042	30" Straight	6
6-12035	Lighted Bumper – 5"	6
6-12019	90-degree crossing	1

FasTrack Switches

6-12046 or 6-81946	O36 Right Remote or O36 Right Remote & Command	4
6-12057 or 6-81951	O60 Left Remote or O60 Left Remote & Command	5
6-12058 or 6-81950	O60 Right Remote or O60 Right Remote & Command	3
6-12047 or 6-81954	O72 Wye Remote or O72 Wye Remote & Command	2

Valley City Northern RR Atlas Bill of Materials

Atlas O Curves (High Line)

6062	O72 Half	2
6063	O72 Quarter	3

Atlas O Straights (High Line)

6015	1.25" Straight	2
6053	5.5" Straight	2
6050	10" Straight	9
6058	40" Straight	3

Atlas O Switch (High Line)

6077	Left	1

Track Plan Design

The 4'x 9' Lionel FasTrack/Atlas O layout plan shown in Figure 2 captures this plethora of railroading in a 9'x 11' small-bedroom space, with the NP and the Soo in the valley, connected by the Valley City Street and Interurban, with the spectacular High Line trestle cutting across the valley.

The outer loop is Northern Pacific, while the inner return loop is the Soo Line, sharing trackage rights with the Valley City Street and Interurban. The NP and Soo interchange on a 18"x 7' staging track shelf, which for the NP can be imagined to be the yard at Fargo, ND, where the Valley City locals can originate and return.

The two routes also share main line crossovers and a curved connecting track that completes both routes, allowing both railroads to make multiple circuits around the layout. Trains and locos can be turned on the Soo Line return loop, and the Soo and Interurban can switch industries in town. There are stations for both Valley City and North Valley City, so the Interurban railroad can shuttle freight and passengers between them.

The layout includes the classic Lionel milk car and cattle pen operating accessories, plus the barrel loader, adding some action in town. At the lower-right corner are Lionel's operating oil derrick and oil pump. Even though the real North Dakota oil action is actually further west in the Bakken oil field, the Lionel oil tank supports this theme, along with a scratchbuilt oil transload facility, moving and storing crude between trains and trucks.

The "High Line"

The High Line spans the valley on a tall trestle (at 9" elevation) on Atlas O track, connecting with its own elevated, but narrower, staging track shelf above the main level extension through a O96/O72 curved switch. The High Line does not connect with the main-level railroad, but trains can shuttle back and forth on this O72 line and be positioned on the trestle for visual effect. Cars can be conveniently swapped between the high line staging and main-level staging for additional car storage space. If desired, a widened High Line shelf could support a third small station, which was added by the NP for the High Line.

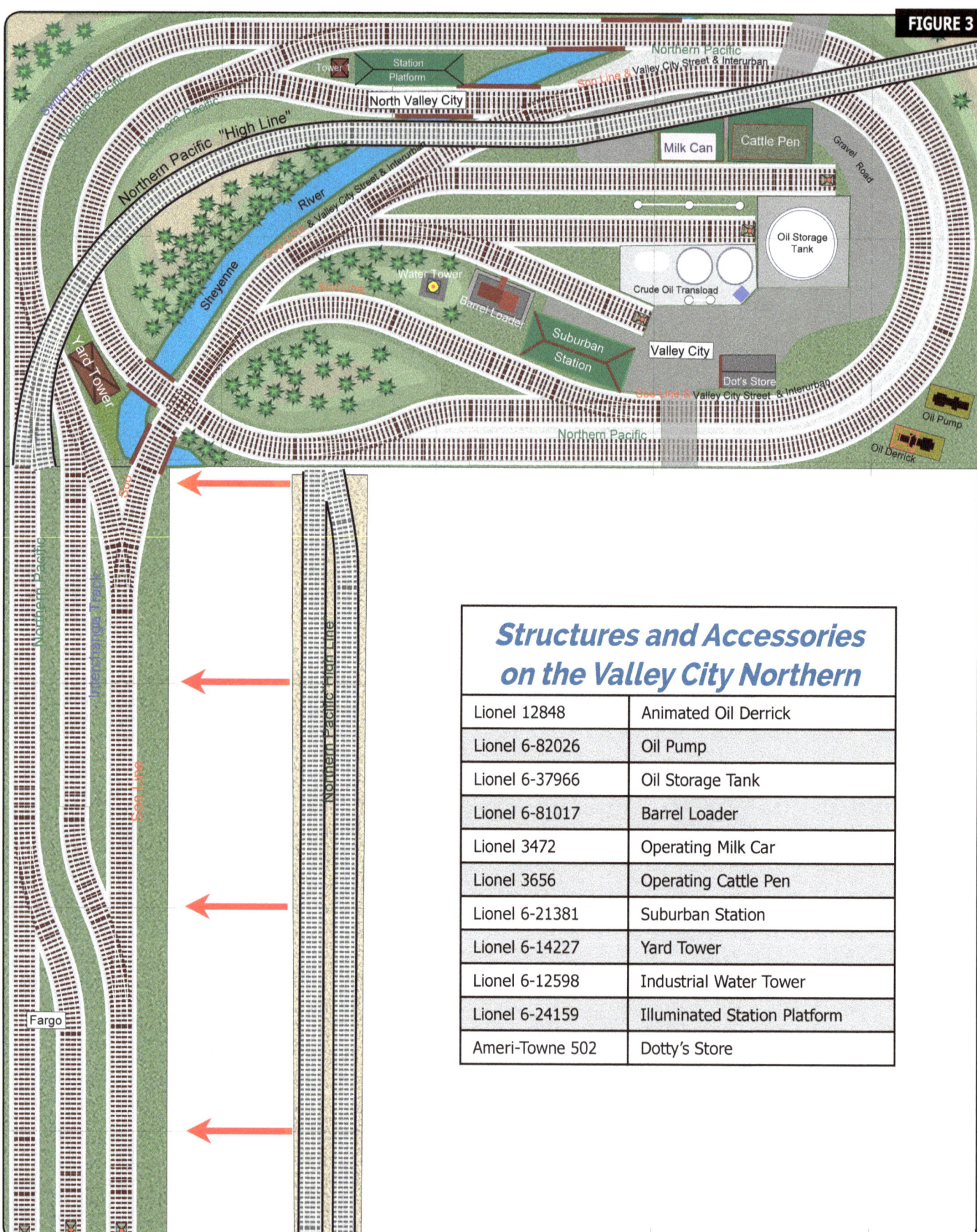

FIGURE 3

Structures and Accessories on the Valley City Northern

Lionel 12848	Animated Oil Derrick
Lionel 6-82026	Oil Pump
Lionel 6-37966	Oil Storage Tank
Lionel 6-81017	Barrel Loader
Lionel 3472	Operating Milk Car
Lionel 3656	Operating Cattle Pen
Lionel 6-21381	Suburban Station
Lionel 6-14227	Yard Tower
Lionel 6-12598	Industrial Water Tower
Lionel 6-24159	Illuminated Station Platform
Ameri-Towne 502	Dotty's Store

Track Minimums and Construction

Minimum FasTrack curve diameter on this 4'x 9' railroad is O36, with some O48 and two O72 half-sections. Switches are O36 and O60, with two O72 wye switches. There are three track sections where the roadbed will need to be trimmed in order to fit switches more closely without using the 1-3/4" half-roadbed fitter sections packaged with the switches, which is easy enough to do with FasTrack plastic roadbed.

The terrain includes steep and tall hillsides cut smooth by the glacial river and covered by grass and sparse trees, with the winding Sheyenne at the valley bottom below grade. If desired, a two-track tunnel in the top left corner could be added for fun, connecting the two high points from the corner to the center-left, with the High Line skirting across the top. The layout foundation can be based on a four-post table with legs on casters to allow the table to roll out for access and construction. Table width is actually 4' and 3/4": a 4'x 9' construction with a 1x4 (about 3/4" width actual dimension) attached level with the top for the additional 3/4" width. The two-level staging extension can also be made detachable and movable.

Operating and Expansion

This track plan (Figure 3) can keep two engineers busy, taking turns making-up trains in the staging yard, running the loops, switching the town with interchange between the two roads, then returning around the layout back to the staging yard. Plus, you can also run the Interurban serving North Valley City and Valley City, running trolleys, RDCs, or very short freight and passenger trains.

The layout can be easily stretched to make use of a larger space, by expanding to the right with additional straight sections to 4'x 10', 4'x 11', 4'x 12', or larger. Connection with a layout expansion or connecting railroad can be made at the upper right, with a drop-in O48 switch on the outside NP main line, cutting beneath the NP High Line through a tunnel. An optional connection can also be made with another drop-in O48 switch at the lower-right NP main line, dislocating the oil pumps.

The Valley City Northern track plan features all these design elements:

- Two-train operation
- Continuous loop running
- Return loops
- A passing siding
- Switching lead for the staging yard
- Two wye switches,
- Wye track arrangement for completing the return loop
- Staging track storage
- The High Line for display and car storage.

Happy Railroading!

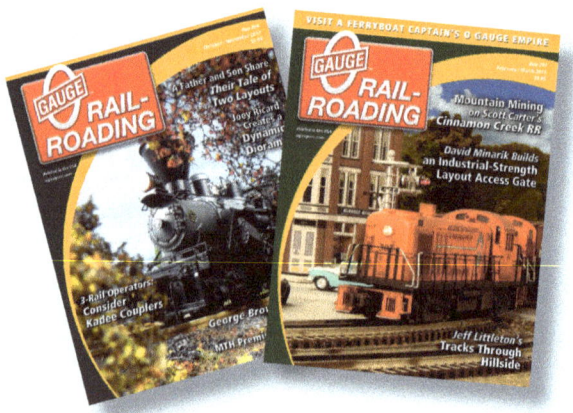

The Triple-R Railroad

The Triple-R Railroad is an updated version of a classic layout plan for three times around operation with level crossings using Lionel's FasTrack sectional track. It uses O48 minimum diameter curves and is designed to fit in a 7'x 12' space.

The layout setting could be eastern mountains, western high country, southern valleys, or mid-country rolling countryside. The long thrice-around spiral run goes through O60 switches with plenty of length for two trains to follow each other along this route. The layout's minimum diameter O48 curves with O60 switches will allow locomotives and rolling stock designated for O42 and smaller curvatures to run gracefully everywhere on the layout.

Additions updating the basic thrice-around plan include a connecting route at the upper-right, making an outside perimeter route of O60 minimum diameter through O72 switches. This new perimeter loop route will allow O54 equipment to run on the layout. By adding an O72 crossover in the center-top, a middle-track loop of O48 minimum diameter through O72 switches is created. Two trains can run unattended through the two loop routes when not running the thrice-around spiral route.

With the thrice-around spiral route, plus the two loop routes, the layout offers multiple train running options for two trains. Three or more trains can even work the layout: a short third train could be parked in the tunnel at the upper-right while two trains run the spiral thrice-around.

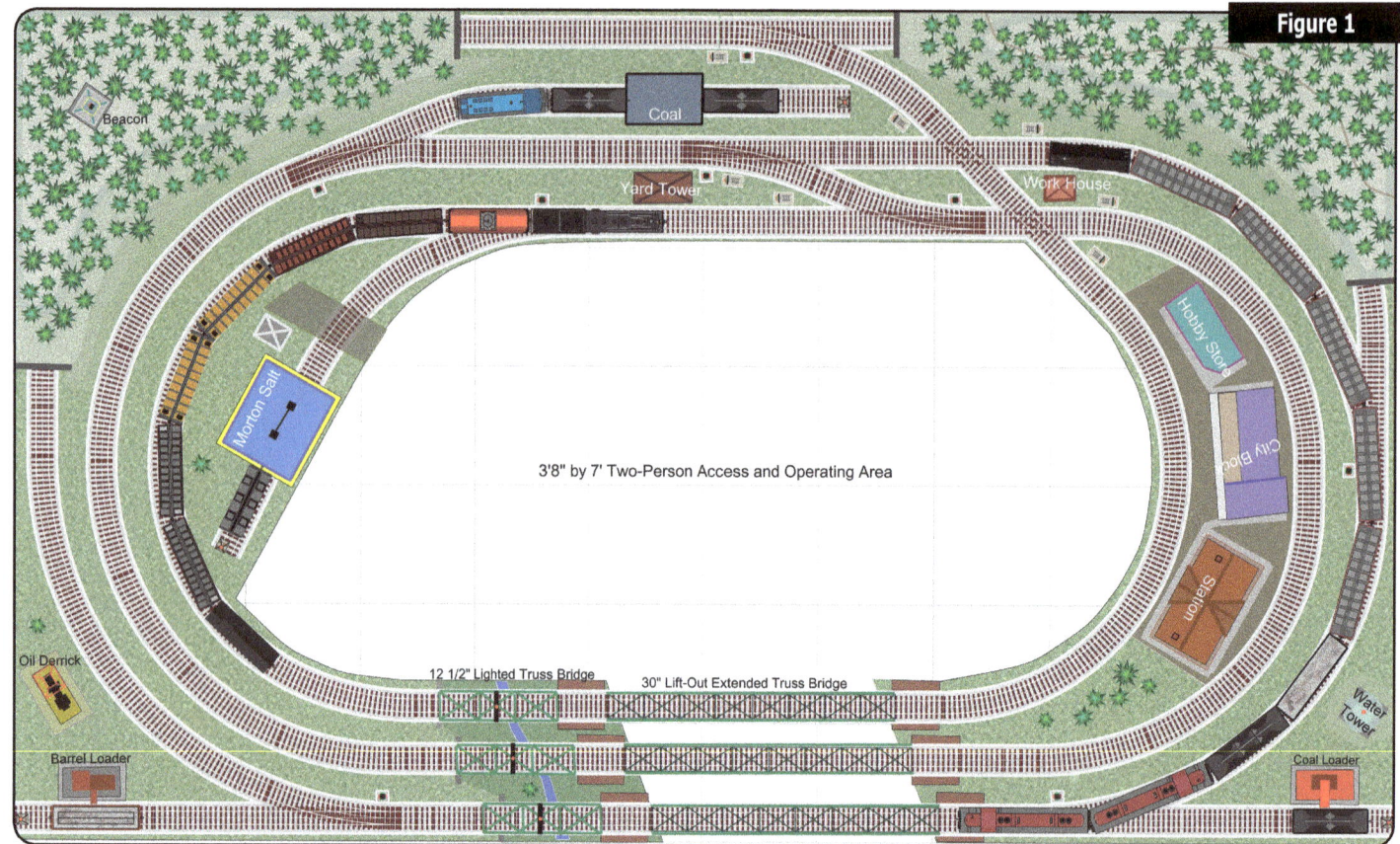

Figure 1

Figure 1 above shows a switcher and three cars waiting on the coaling track at the top center. There is a comfortable two-person operating area in the center, accessed conveniently through three of Lionel's Extended-Truss Lift-Out Bridges. No need for duck-unders, crawling, or climbing to reach this center operating and access area, which provides easy reach to the entire layout and all switches.

Expansion options and possible connection to a staging yard can be achieved leading off from either or both of the O72 switches at the bottom of the O60 perimeter route.

Bridges

This plan includes six impressive bridges: three Lionel Extended-Truss Lift-Out Bridges (Photo 1 above), and three Lionel Lighted Truss Bridges (Photo 2). This is a well-engineered structure with multi-height supporting piers. These bridges include a 30" length of FasTrack on the bridge itself and two 5" sections of FasTrack on the two piers. The height of the piers is adjustable, being built up of multiple sections that snap together.

The other three bridges are Lionel's Truss Bridge with flashing warning light at the top. FasTrack lengths run through the center of these truss bridges.

Scenic and Structure Concepts

Attractive scenic elements include the three striking Lionel Extended-Truss Lift-Out bridges with three lighted truss bridges on the approach from the left with blinking red lights on top of each bridge. The center top trackwork is an interesting arrangement that will draw attention as trains cruise through the double-diamonds and the O72 crossover.

There are two mountains and tunnels for trains to travel through on the outside perimeter. There is also a town center with station and lighted and detailed structures on the right, and on the left a track serves Menard's eye-catching Morton Salt tower with its brilliant blue and yellow colors. The two lower corner tracks each create even more interesting scenes with operating accessories.

In addition to the lighted and detailed structures, there are six operating Lionel accessories shown: Lionel's Barrel Loader, Coal Loader, Rotating Beacon, Coaling Loading Station, Oil Derrick, and Work House with Sound. Other structures include Lionel's Yard Tower, a water tower, Menard's Morton Salt, City Block, Hobby Store, and a station.

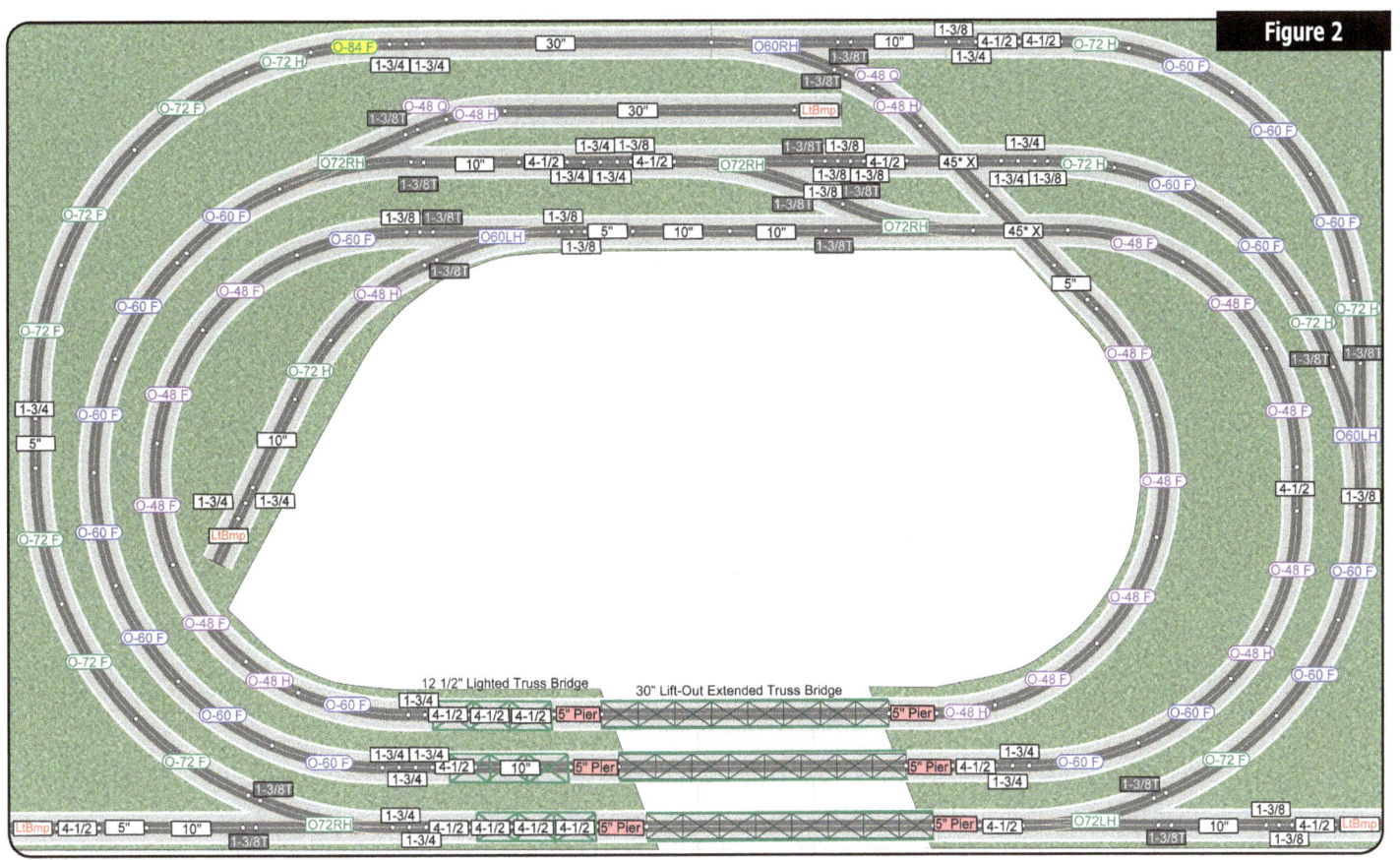

Figure 2

Triple-R Railroad FasTrack Bill of Materials		
Straights		
6-12042	Straight 30"	2
6-12014	Straight 10"	8
6-12024	Straight 5"	8
6-12025	Straight 4-1/2"	17
6-12026	Straight 1-3/4"	19
6-12073	Straight 1-3/8"	31
6-12035	Lighted Bumper - 5"	4
Curves		
6-12041	O72 Full	7
6-12055	O72 Half	6
6-12043	O48 Full	13
6-16834	O48 Half	5
6-16835	O48 Quarter	2
6-12056	O60 Full	18
6-12061	O84 Full	1
6-12051	Crossing 10", 45 degree	2

Switches		
6-12048 or 6-81953	O72 Left Remote or O72 Left Remote & Command	1
6-12049 or 6-81952	O72 Right Remote or O72 Right Remote & Command	4
6-12057 or 6-81951	O60 Left Remote or O60 Left Remote & Command	2
6-12058 or 6-81950	O60 Right Remote or O60 Right Remote & Command	1
Bridges		
6-82110	Lionel Extended-Truss Lift-Out Bridge (30" with two 5" piers)	3
6-12772	Lionel Truss Bridge	3

Construction and Wiring

Lionel FasTrack components needed for the layout are listed at left and above and are shown in Fig. 2. Of course, other types or brands of track might be used, perhaps with some modifications or adjustments depending on what is selected.

The Triple-R Railroad

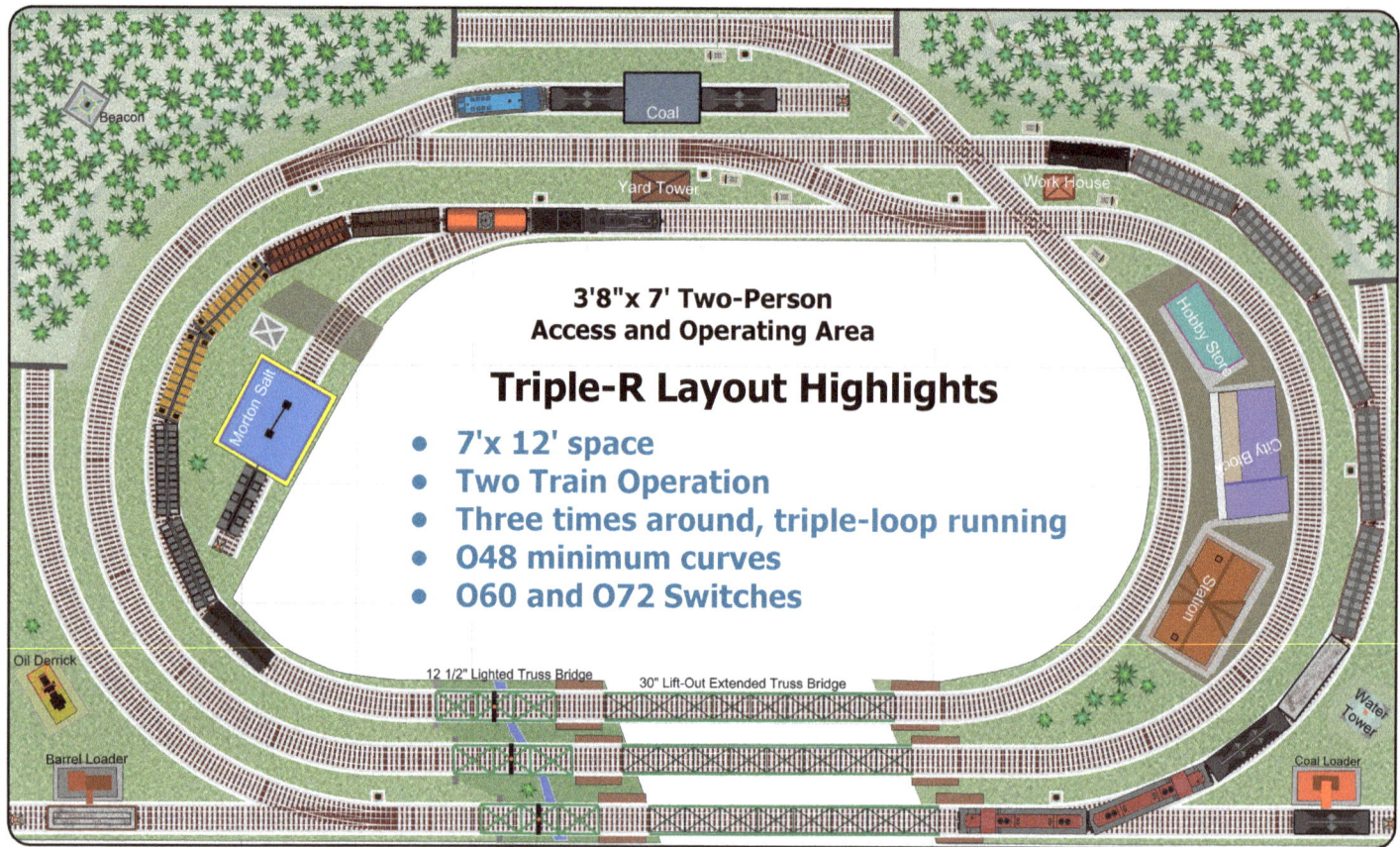

A variety of construction concepts could be employed to build this layout: a traditional plywood surface or 2" foam sheet surface can comprise the layout surface, supported by 2" square or 2x4s, without the need to be strong enough to support your weight during construction since the entire layout is within easy reach from the center operating area.

The layout can be wired conventionally for block control, or wired for command control using Lionel TMCC/Legacy/LionChief, or DCS from MTH Electric Trains. Since all switches are within easy reach, switches can be manual, remote, or command controlled.

The major expense items to build this plan are the three Lionel Lift-Out Extended Truss bridges and the seven FasTrack switches: five O72 and two O60.

A Flexible and Modern Layout Plan

This update to the classic thrice-around spiral track plan adds multiple train-running options for two or three trains and two engineers, designed to fit in a comfortable 7'x 12' layout space with operating and access area. The layout is updated with Lionel's modern FasTrack 3-rail sectional track with integrated roadbed and O48 minimum diameter curves with O60 and O72 switches, and includes multiple attractive scenic features, with the added feature of being able to operate larger or longer equipment designated for O54 minimum curves on the O60 perimeter route.

Happy Railroading!

John Allen's Timesaver in O Gauge

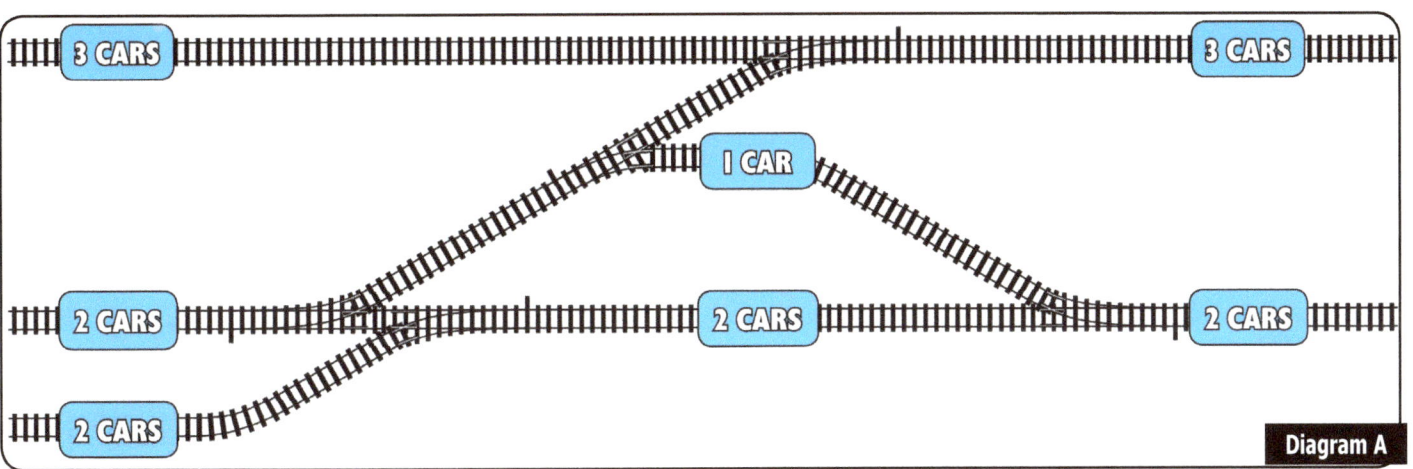

Diagram A

John Allen's (1913-1973) Timesaver layout, as depicted above in Diagram A, has long been popular with model railroaders in all scales. As conceived and designed by Allen, the Timesaver is a model railroad switching puzzle consisting of a specific yard-type track layout with five switches (three left hand, two right hand), five tracks, and a runaround track at the center. Several freight cars are placed on the track, and the challenge is to move all of them to clearly marked destination positions. Operational considerations include a set of initial conditions, a defined goal, and rules which must be followed while performing the switching operations. Timesaver packs a whole lot of operational challenge and fun in a compact space.

This is a 3-rail O gauge version of the Timesaver switching puzzle assembled here with Lionel FasTrack track and switches and using FasTrack's 5" remote uncoupler sections (Diagram B). Shown are more uncouplers than are generally used, in recognition of the simple fact that our O gauge claw-type couplers are often not as flexible as Kadee-style couplers. Nevertheless, this does not change the game parameters. All of the car-length sections are sized for 40' scale cars (typically boxcars, but could be other types) and a diesel switcher. The entire switching layout fits in a 2'x 9'3" space.

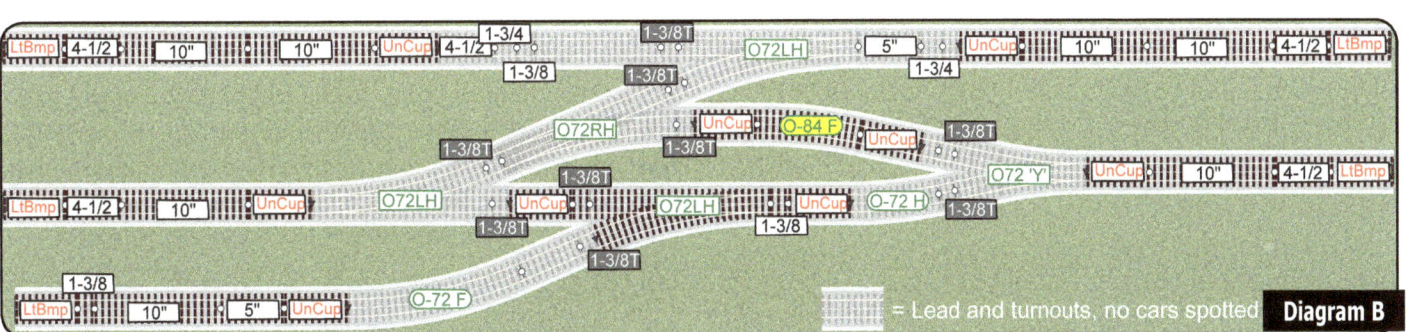

Diagram B

John Allen's Timesaver in O Gauge — Page 49

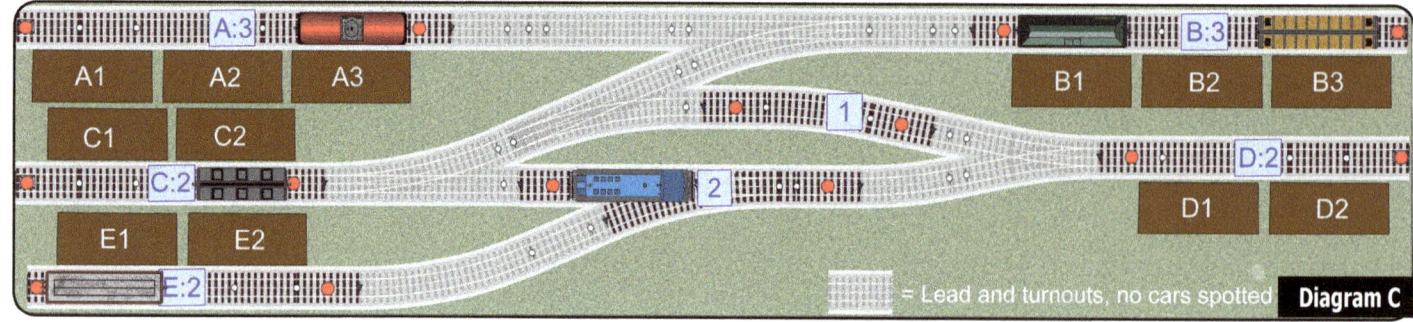

Diagram C

The idea of this switching game is to begin with cars initially spotted at various industries, and the engineer must then move the cars to, and spot them at, select other destinations. There are several ways to play the game. The engine crew can either work against the clock to accomplish the assigned tasks in the shortest time possible; attempt to complete the switching operations with the minimum number of moves; or compete the game in competition with another engineer. There are 15 spots on the layout to accommodate cars, and the game generally starts with an engine (preferably a small switcher) and five cars.

The red dots seen on Diagram C indicate the center of the FasTrack 5" uncoupling tracks and the lighted FasTrack bumpers. Cars can only be spotted between the red dots of the uncouplers and lighted bumpers. Shown are leads to extend the tracks and make switching a bit more prototypical—cars cannot be spotted or stored on these tracks.

Track, Construction, and Wiring

Switches are O72, along with one O72 wye switch. There are three broad curved sections: one full size O72, one half-O72, and one half-size O84, so couplers will tend to be centered over the track for coupling and uncoupling. Using TMCC/Legacy for operating, FasTrack command control switches can be controlled remotely. The nine remote uncouplers can also be operated using one of the other TMCC/Legacy components (Operating Track Controller or ASC2 device), thus enabling the entire game to be operated from the TMCC/Legacy remote. The layout can also be built with manual switches and push-button uncouplers.

This O gauge FasTrack Timesaver plan exceeds the eight-foot length of a single 4x8 sheet of plywood or 2" thick foam and might instead be constructed with a light-weight 1"x 3" frame for supporting the extended layout surface.

TimeSaver Track Items
FasTrack Bill of Materials

	Straights	
6-12014	Straight 10"	8
6-12024	Straight 5"	4
6-12025	Straight 4-1/2"	5
6-12026	Straight 1-3/4"	2
6-12073	Straight 1-3/8"	5
6-12020	Uncoupling track 5"	9
6-12035	Lighted Bumper 5"	5
	Curves	
6-12041	O72 Full	1
6-12055	O72 Half	1
6-12061	O84 Half	1
	Switches	
6-12048	O72 Left	3
6-12049	O72 Right	1
6-12047	O72 Wye	1

Structures and Operations

Timesavers can be constructed with or without structures and scenery. Footprints for industries are shown if you want to populate the Timesaver with appropriate structures and industries for spotting cars. You can also set up pairs or triplets of compatible industries so cars can logically move from a source to a destination where their loads could originate, or they might be spotted at industries that typically would make use of their contents. Boxcars can, of course, hold a wide variety of goods, and freight warehouses can store an equally diverse variety of products.

There is a wealth of Timesaver layout information available on the internet. Do a Google search using the key words "Timesaver layout" to see John Allen's original Timesaver layout.

Happy Railroading!

Action on the Peach Grove Line

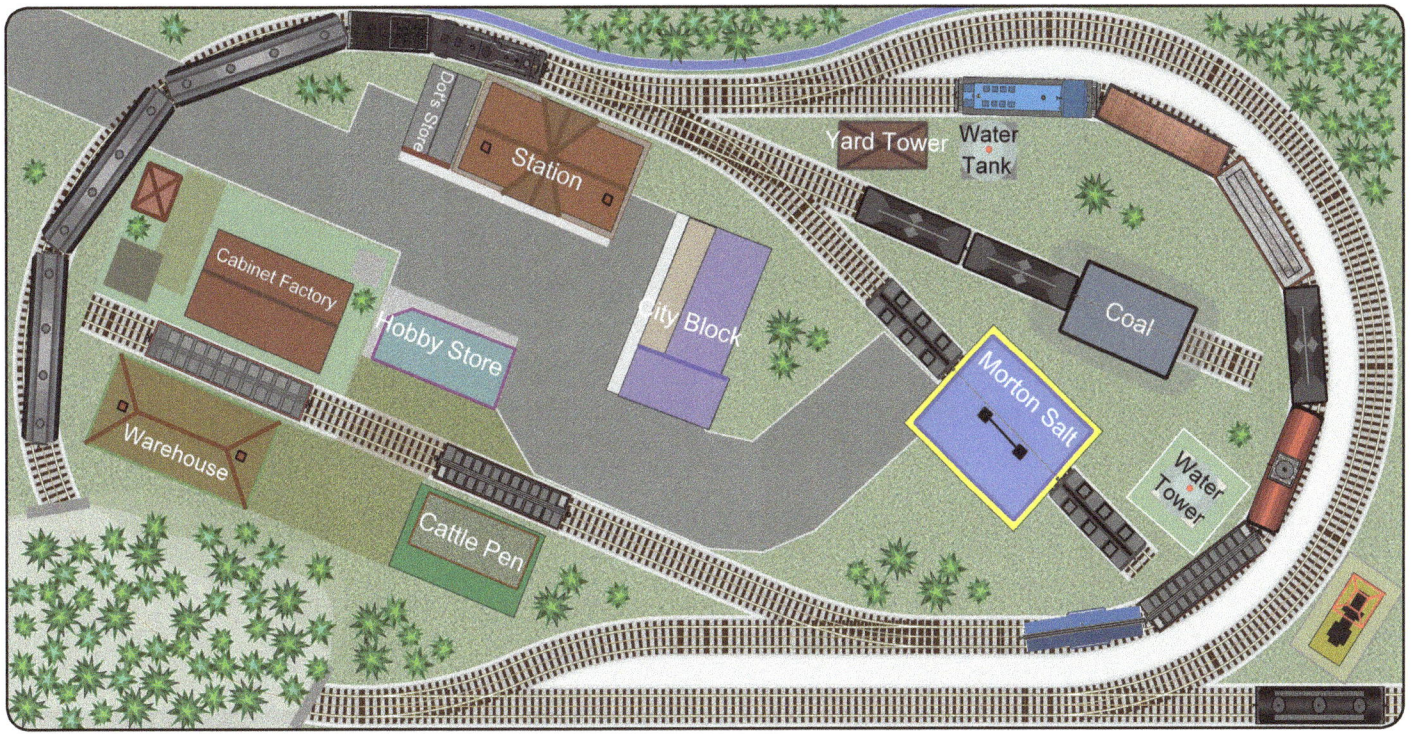

O gauge railroaders are fortunate to have a number of excellent track systems to choose from. This layout design uses the Atlas O 21st Century track system with its solid and realistic rails and ties with a blackened center rail. The 4'x 8' track plan uses sectional track of O36, O45, and some wider diameters; accommodates O42, O36, and smaller equipment; and makes for an excellent first layout or temporary/movable layout.

The Track Plan

The track plan is a simple oval with passing-track, three tracks, and an interesting indent at the top formed with two O63 curves and two O54 switches. The layout's minimum curve diameter is O36, which is used to form the inside passing track, with a broader O45 for the perimeter main line loop. This track plan will accommodate O36 equipment everywhere on the layout and O42-specified locomotives and rolling stock on the outside main line and on the tracks near the station.

The switch standard is generous at O54, allowing O42 locomotives to be parked on the tracks near the station and to service those tracks. The long 52" track serving the cattle pen and cabinet factory is accessed from the O36 passing track, which excludes most O42 or longer wheelbase equipment from accessing this track. There are easements of O54 and O63 to the switches, which provide free-flowing and reliable operation and also help to make the trains look good when they are running on the layout. The optional O45 switch at the lower-right is an exception to the O54 standard and can be used for future expansion, an extension to a yard, or a connection to another railroad or main line.

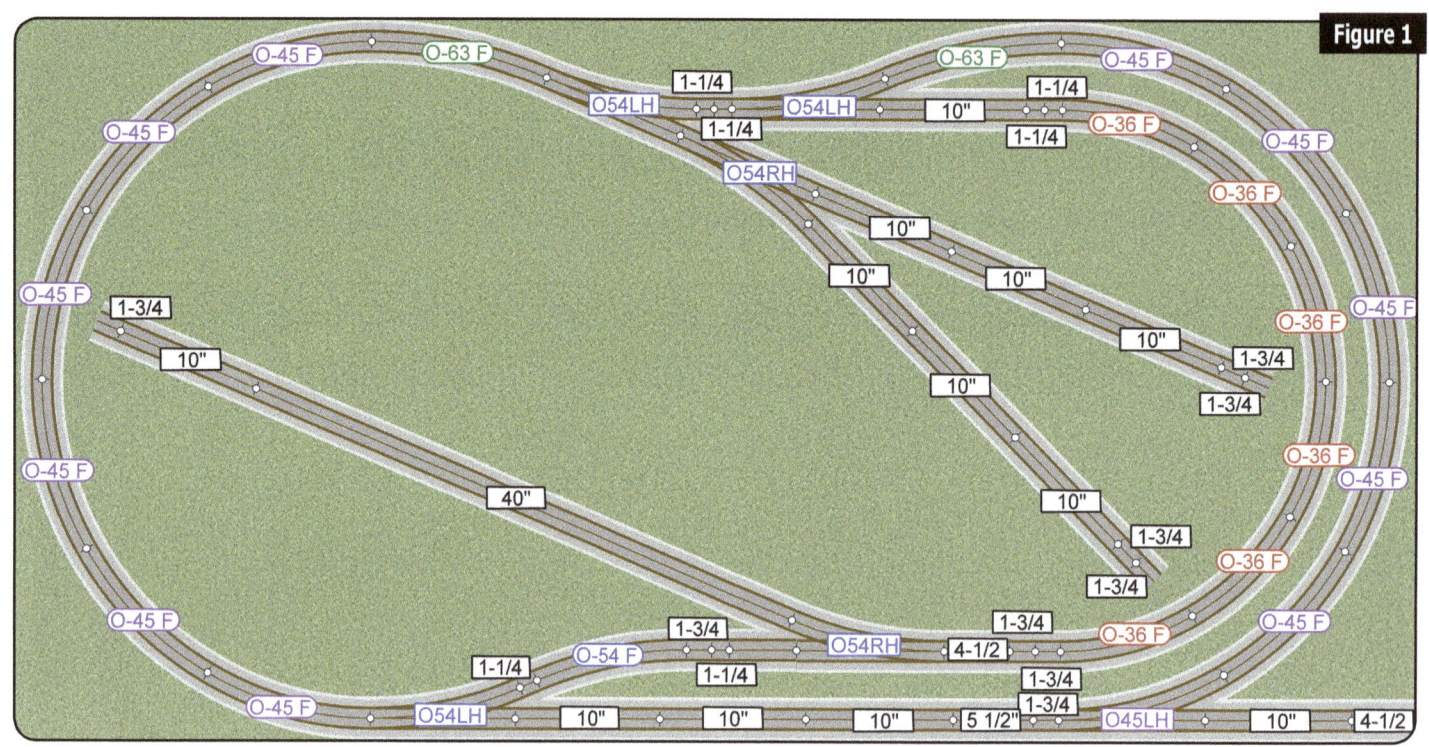

Figure 1

Peach Grove Line
Bill of Materials

Straights		
6015	Straight 1-1/4"	6
6052	Straight 1-3/4"	9
6051	Straight 4-1/2"	3
6053	Straight 5-1/2"	1
6050	Straight 10"	12
6058	Straight 40"	1
Curves		
6066	O36 angle 30°	6
6045	O45 angle 30°	11
6060	O54 angle 22.5°	1
6064	O63 angle 22.5°	2
6085	O45 Left	1
6070	O54 Left	3
6071	O54 Right	2

Operation

This simple layout offers continuous running around the perimeter route and switching operations on three tracks. Two trains can operate on the layout, taking turns switching the tracks and running the loop. With command control (TMCC/Legacy, DCS, or LionChief and LionChief+) two engineers can work the layout. Small traditional equipment or LionChief and LionChief+ engines will be ideal fits on this layout.

Construction and Wiring

Any conventional construction technique will work for this 4'x 8' plan, including using a 2"-thick foam sheet for the layout base, preferably underlaid with a sheet of plywood to provide a more rigid base that is less susceptible to damage.

The O45 curves are the maximum diameter that will fit on a 4'x 8', with the ballasted roadbed running almost the entire width of the layout surface. Ties are set back about 3/8" from the edge. If you are concerned about running trains that close to the edge of the layout, you can surround the layout with a 1"x 4" framework, using 1x2 or 2x2 runners beneath the layout base and providing support. In order to avoid any clearance issues with locomotives or rolling stock, the outside framework should rise no more than 3/8" above the layout base.

This small layout will be light and manageable enough to slide under a bed or perhaps stand in the back of a large closet when not in use. Construction with the 2" thick foam sheets will result in a light and surprisingly strong layout that can be easily moved and stored when not in use.

The layout can be wired for conventional operation with three blocks: two for the perimeter main line and one for the passing track. The three tracks can be isolated with power to the center rail using On/Off SPST switches. Command control wiring is even easier, with two power drops at the center of each main line curve; one drop for the inside passing track, and a drop for each track.

Figure 2

Ballasting

Atlas O 3-rail track does not come with integrated roadbed, such as that already fitted on Lionel's FasTrack or MTH RealTrax components; and some hobbyists regard ballasting as a tedious and time-consuming process. Ballasting can indeed involve a bit of time and effort if you want it to look really good (as seen on the prototype), but a temporary work-around is to use O gauge cork roadbed and simply spray paint it lightly using a Rustoleum textured spray can color prior to installation on the layout (see the photo above). A light spray preserves the texture of the cork roadbed, with additional variations in color coming from the textured spray paint. The track can be ballasted later, if so desired and when time permits, but in the meantime this technique yields a passable result with the extra-tall ties of Atlas O track.

Structures

The town center features:

- An MTH station
- Menard's City Block
- Hobby Store
- Cabinet Factory
- Ameri-Towne No. 502 Dotty's Store

Operating accessories include:

- Lionel Cattle Pen
- Lionel Coaling Station
- Lionel Oil Derrick with **nodding donkey** pump
- Lionel Yard Tower
- Menard's eye-catching Morton Salt Tower
- Warehouse
- Water tower
- Line-side water tank.

A 4'x 8' First Layout or Temporary Layout

The Peach Grove Branch Line makes for a fine first layout, with its wide-diameter curves and broad switches that will accommodate operating two trains using either conventional or command control. A great deal of fun can be had building and operating this modest railroad using the outstanding Atlas O 21st Century track system. For those interested, I used AnyRail (www.anyrail.com) and TrainPlayer (www.trainplayer.com) software to produce the track plan and layout images seen here.

Happy Railroading!

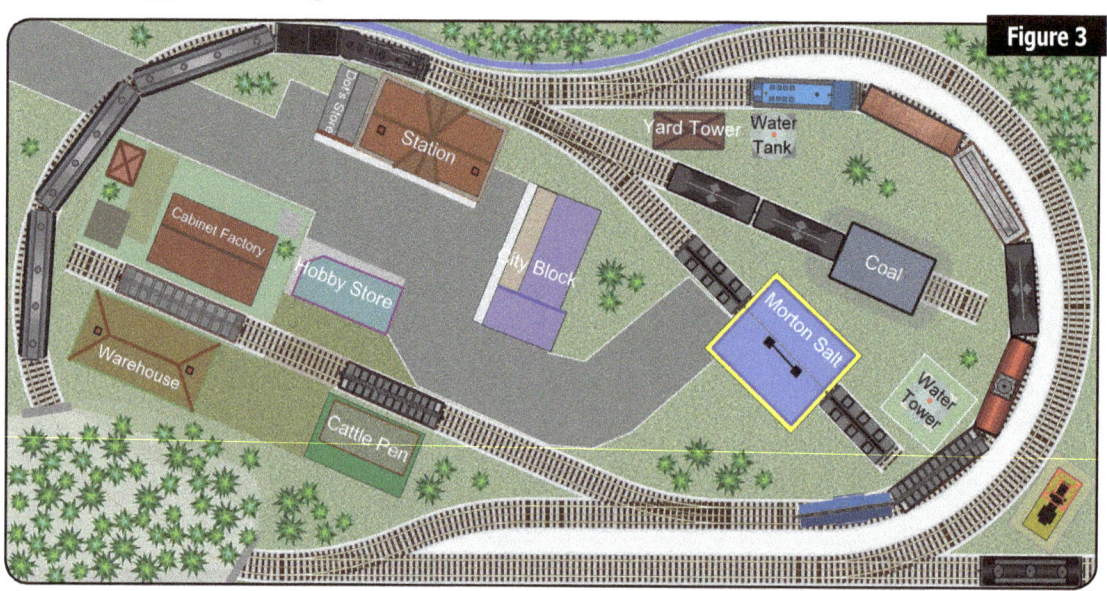
Figure 3

Pumping Iron on the DM&IR

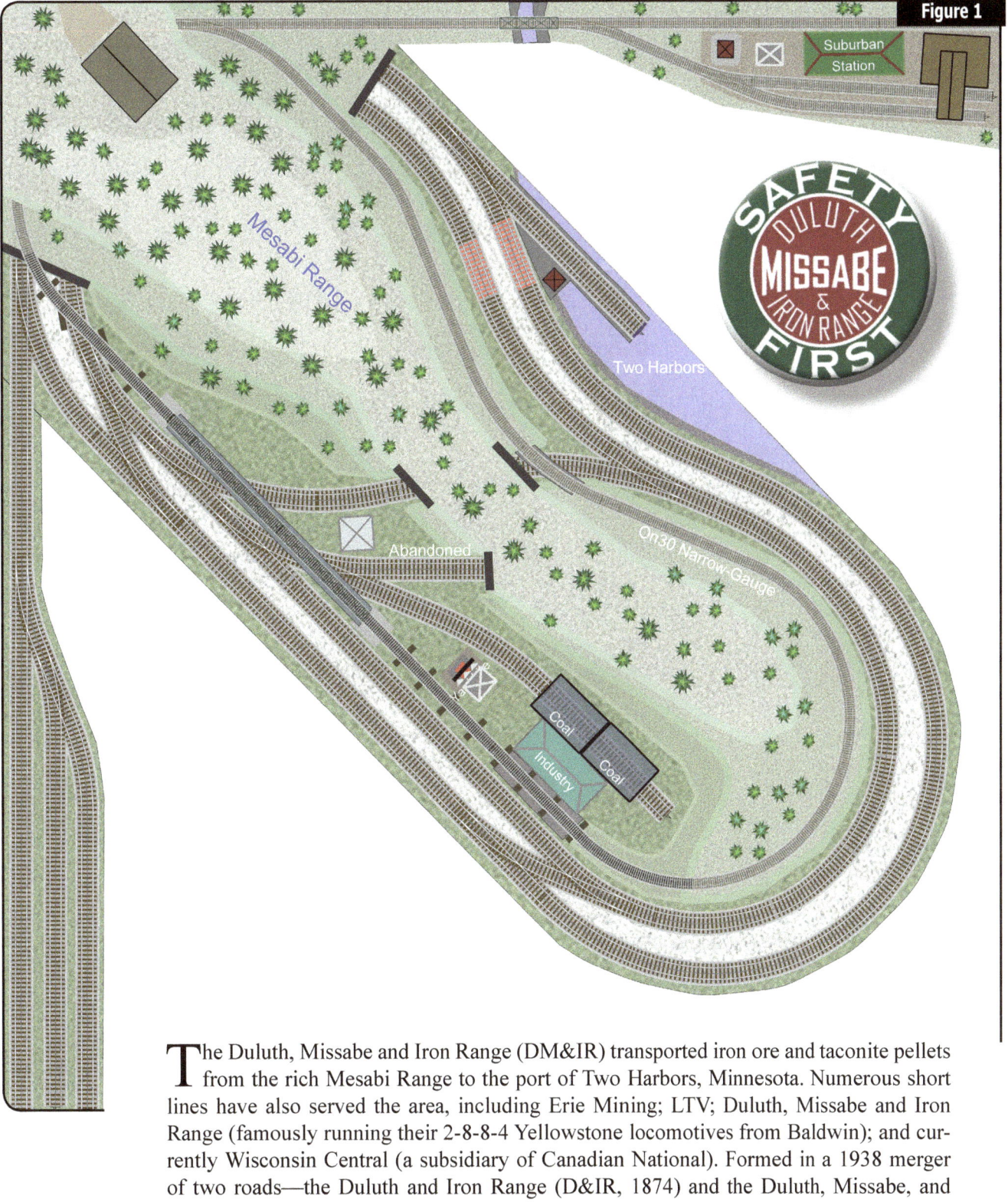

Figure 1

The Duluth, Missabe and Iron Range (DM&IR) transported iron ore and taconite pellets from the rich Mesabi Range to the port of Two Harbors, Minnesota. Numerous short lines have also served the area, including Erie Mining; LTV; Duluth, Missabe and Iron Range (famously running their 2-8-8-4 Yellowstone locomotives from Baldwin); and currently Wisconsin Central (a subsidiary of Canadian National). Formed in a 1938 merger of two roads—the Duluth and Iron Range (D&IR, 1874) and the Duluth, Missabe, and Northern (DM&N, 1891)—the DM&IR was merged into the Wisconsin Central in 2011.

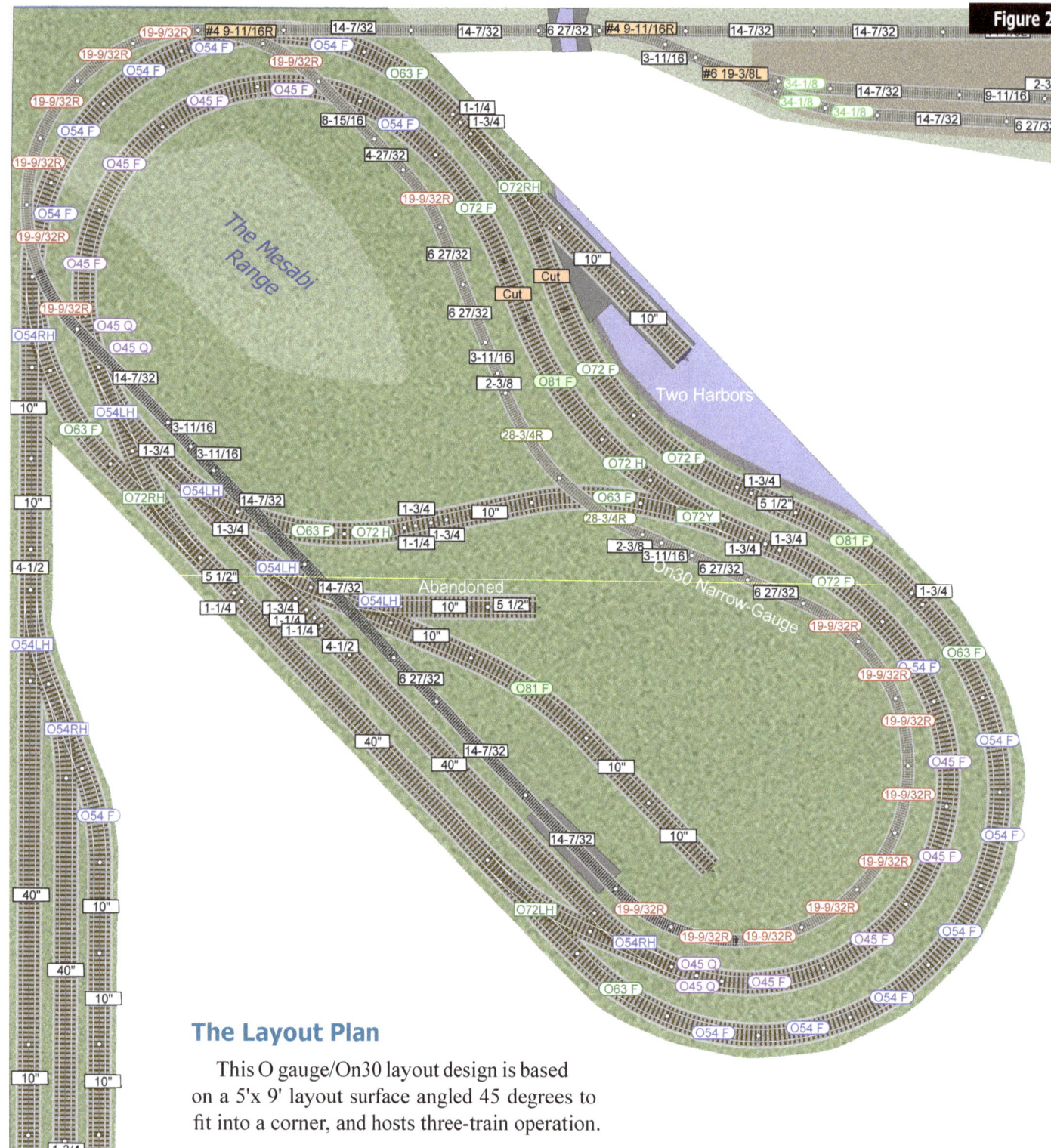

Figure 2

The Layout Plan

This O gauge/On30 layout design is based on a 5'x 9' layout surface angled 45 degrees to fit into a corner, and hosts three-train operation.

The track plan features two smoothly aligned O gauge main lines made up of Atlas O track, and a narrow gauge route using On30 narrow gauge track or HO track. This plan is designed using Kato Unitrack (Figure 1). The corner area allows the double-track main line loops to extend about 18" into the corner for a longer main line. The outer main line is O54 minimum diameter, with O54 minimum switches and O63 easements. The inside main line is O45 minimum diameter, with O54 minimum switches and O54 easements. The crossovers between loops are O54-O72 switch pairs for a smooth crossover without internal S curves.

DM&IR Railroad
Bill of Materials (Atlas)

Straights

6015	Straight 1-1/4"	5
6052	Straight 1-3/4"	12
6051	Straight 4-1/2"	4
6053	Straight 5-1/2"	3
6050	Straight 10"	13
6058	Straight 40"	4
6056	Flex 40"	1

Curves

6045	O45 Full Curve	8
6046	O45 Quarter	4
6060	O54 Full	14
6064	O63 Full	6
6062	O72 Full	4
6063	O72 Half	2
6011	O81 Full	3

Switches

6070	O54 Left	6
6071	O54 Right	2
6072	O72 Left	1
6073	O72 Right	2
6074	O72 Wye	1

Kato Unitrack HO Track Bill of Materials

Kato Unitrack HO Straights

2-105	Straight 2-3/8"	3
2-111	Straight 3-11/16"	5
2-130	Straight 6-27/32"	7
2-140	Straight 4-27/32"	1
2-150	Straight 9-11/16"	1
2-160	Straight 8-15/16"	1
2-180	Straight 14 17/32"	12

Kato Unitrack HO Curves

2-240	Curve radius 28-3/4", angle 22.5°	2
2-270	Curve radius 19-9/32", angle 22.5°	17
2-290	Curve radius 34-1/8", angle 10°	3

Kato Unitrack HO Switches

2-841	Right 9-11/16" (manual)	2
2-860	Left 10 (remote)	1

There are two parallel short sections of straight track, trimmed to fit, near the bay and port. These can be cut from a single section of Flex-Track or 10" straight sections.

There is one reversing connection on the inside O gauge main, with O63 minimum curvature. One side of the double-track main is a long straight run, and the other side is indented around the bay and port with a shipping pier with O72 and O81 curves.

This corner layout fits into a 11'x 10' space as shown, with two extensions along the walls, though a 11'x 11' space would offer more room for engineers. The O gauge extension leads to a three-car yard, with an optional connection to another railroad or interchange.

The On30 narrow gauge line is an indented loop, with an extension along the wall to the mine area. The mine area also includes a track that can be used as a run-through track to another main line, with a small station adjacent. The track component diagram (Fig. 2) shows the narrow gauge line as constructed with Kato HO Unitrack at 19-1/4" radius, which features thin rails and tie spacing similar to typical narrow gauge lines. The integrated roadbed and special Unijoiners keep the HO track sections tightly together with solid electrical connections. The narrow gauge line could, as an alternative, be constructed and ballasted with Peco On30 switches and flextrack, or even converted to use O36 diameter O gauge track.

As shown, the layout is imagined to represent upper northeast Minnesota, an area rich with Mesabi Range iron ore, now shipped as taconite pellets. The actual DM&IR did not operate a narrow gauge railroad as shown in this layout plan. Alternatively, the layout could be geographically relocated to represent a scene in Colorado, with the port and shipping pier then converted to a smelter operation.

Operation

Trains operating on the layout move ore from the narrow gauge mines to an elevated ore car dump, where the ore is crushed and sorted, and then conveyed up to one of two ore-dumping bins. The bins in this case are Lionel's operating coal-loading accessories spanning Atlas O track, repurposed to handle ore. Loaded ore cars are then moved around the inner and then outer O gauge main lines to the dock for loading into the holds of ships.

For continuous running and train watching, three trains can be operated: two on the O gauge main line loops, and one on the narrow gauge mountain line. The inside main line loop features a connecting and reversing track so trains can reverse direction with a head-in move in one direction and a backing move in the other.

Construction and Access

The use of the extension into the corner allows the O gauge main lines to extend into the corner area 18" beyond that of the 5'x 9' layout base, as if a 5'x 10'6" layout base in overall length. The bottom-right end of the 5'x 9' layout benchwork is curved for easier movement around the layout from one side the other. The layout has excellent reach access around three sides of the layout: the two along-the-wall extensions narrow as they connect to the main layout surface to ease access in toward the corner. To allow access to the track inside the long tunnels in the upper-left corner, the ridge/mountain can be hollowed-out so a person can pop his or her head up inside the mountain to access the main lines in the tunnel (Fig. 3).

There are three aspects that guide your choice of construction technique:

- The curved layout base around the outer main line at the lower right
- The need for access inside the long tunnels in the upper left corner
- The depressed water areas for the river and the port/bay

Keep these in mind when choosing how you will build your layout because they may affect the framework construction method you decide to use.

The layout can be permanently built in place and attached to the walls if desired. Or the layout can be built as three separate modules, including a main layout with two extensions so the layout can be transported in the event of a move, or even to a different location in the same house. To build the elevated terrain above the layout base, any traditional technique can be used, but perhaps using 2"-thick foam insulating sheets would be most convenient. The elevated narrow gauge line is level at 6" above the base (there are no grades on the layout), suggesting layering and shaping three layers of 2" foam sheets to build the mountain ridge. The foam sheets are light and easy to work with, with minimal foam residue when trimming. If a hot foam cutter is used, no dust is created in the cutting/forming process.

The mountain ridge that divides the main layout into two scenes extends 14" above the base at its peak. Hollowing out this ridge for corner access to the hidden main lines allows 9" or so of **head space** beneath the layout. Positioning a low, rolling office chair beneath the layout makes for easy access, scooting in and out in comfort.

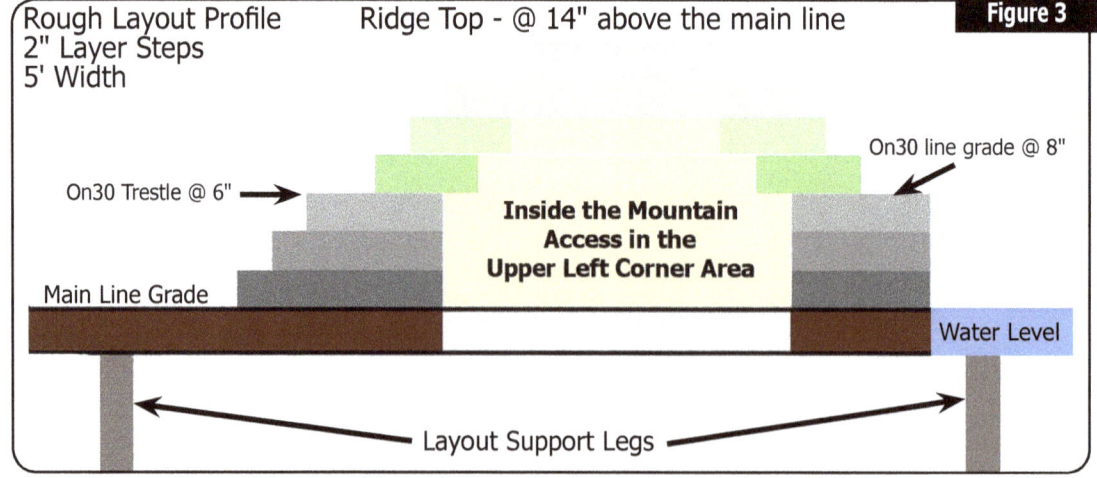

Scenery

This layout emphasizes beautiful scenery with flowing track work, bridges, trestles, tunnels, mountains, and water features, but with a minimum of structures. The scenery as shown is lightly wooded, but more trees should be added for a Minnesota mining operation. Even a western location will have some thickets of denser trees.

There is one short river section at the top, crossed by a bridge, which can be about 2" deep below the track level and the main layout surface. The port/bay area is also depressed 2" below the main line grade. If the main layout surface is built on 2"-thick foam sheets, it will be relatively easy to build and shape the depressed areas below the main line grade, but other techniques can also be used to construct the areas below the main line grade.

The narrow gauge line runs on the left side over an elevated trestle with a bridge and piers to span the O gauge main lines below. This bridge is about 32" long at 6" high, with a clear span beneath. At the lower left, the narrow gauge allows bottom-dump ore cars to drop their contents below, to be subsequently processed by the crusher and ore sorter beneath and then lifted by conveyors to the ore holding bins (the Lionel coal-loading accessories repurposed to handle ore).

There is an abandoned O gauge iron ore mine in the lower left area adjacent to the ore crushing-and-sorting facility that can be maintained in active use for switching purposes, or made to look dilapidated and fading for a fun scenic effect.

Structures and Wiring

At the narrow gauge mining area in the upper right, there is a small station/freight/office building. Also in that location is a small switch tower, Lionel's Work House with Sound, and a small mine structure. There is one MTH house on the Mesabi range mountain.

At the lower left at the ore-crushing-and-sorting area, there are the two Lionel coal-loading accessories, and an ore crushing-and-sorting structure based on the Lionel Suburban Station in size—a candidate for possible kitbashing. Also, there is another Lionel Work House with Sound, and a Lionel Yard Light tower. Further along is an MTH switch tower.

For command control, the layout wiring for the O gauge lines is simple, with a separate control or power pack for the narrow gauge. For conventional wiring, each of the two O gauge loops should be divided into two blocks. The two along-the-wall extensions should each be a separate block, with the tracks connected to power through an on-off switch. The connecting track that builds a reverse loop through the center should be a separate block.

Conclusion

The Duluth, Missabi and Iron Range O gauge layout is based on a 5'x 9' platform, smooth track work, and mountain scenery that allows O54 equipment to run on the outside loop and O42 or tighter curve trains on the inside loop and everywhere else, with the longer runs of a 5'x 10'6" layout using the corner area. If built with the On30 section as illustrated, you can enjoy a somewhat different experience and pace using Bachmann or other makes of On30 trains and rolling stock. Operating either as a three-train continuous-running operation for pleasure, or in a more prototypical manner moving ore from mine to port, the DM&IR will provide years of fun and O gauge excitement.

Happy Railroading!

A 3-Rail Gorre & Daphetid
An O Gauge Version of John Allen's Iconic G&D Layout

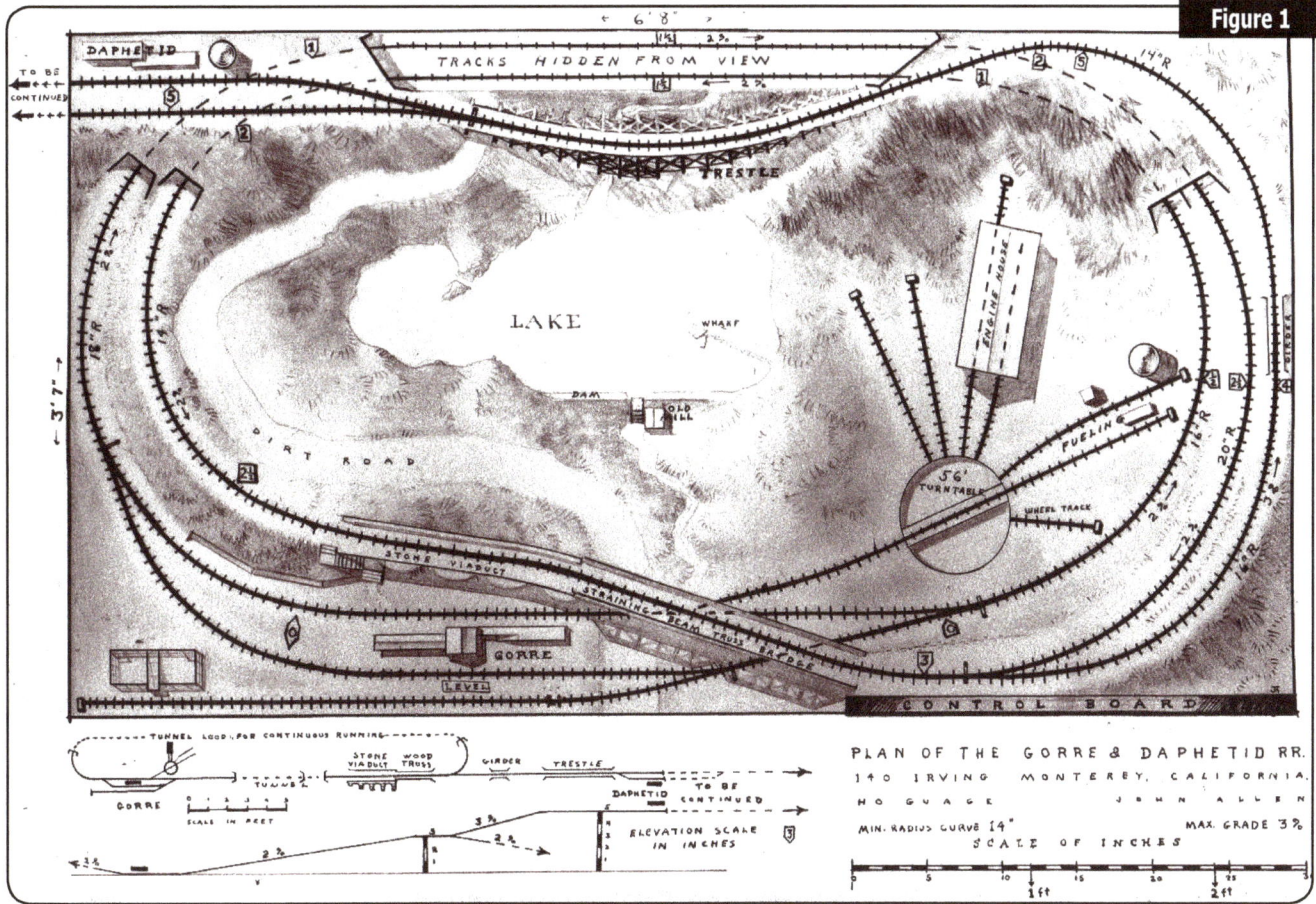

Figure 1

John Allen's classic Gorre & Daphetid (pronounced Gory & Defeated) HO model railroad design has inspired, entertained, and instructed model railroading enthusiasts since its 1946 inception. John's layout illustration of the G&D, seen here in Fig. 1, is artfully composed and detailed in a blueprint style with formal notations and notes, and it was intended to fit a 3'7"x 6'8" space. Inspection of the plan reveals its basis as an up-and-over twice-around main line, with a branch line diverging at the highest point and climbing even further to cross over the main lines to reach Daphetid. Near the pond, the town of Gorre features a small turntable, a passing track, and a single siding. The minimum curve radius is very tight for HO at 14". As a professional photographer, John created a layout plan that emphasized scenery and viewing angles, with somewhat basic operating possibilities.

A G&D for the O Gauge Hobbyist

This O gauge interpretation of the G&D is just short of double the size of John's *Half-O* plan, coming in at 7'6"x 12'. As an O gauge plan, a number of features have been added or revised from the original HO plan to meet O gauge enthusiast expectations. Three new tracks have been added, along with an interchange track to a connecting railroad, hidden staging tracks, more structures, and some operating accessories.

The elevated town of Daphetid has been given a coal mine that originates loads to be used in the power plant and distributed through the interchange track to other connections.

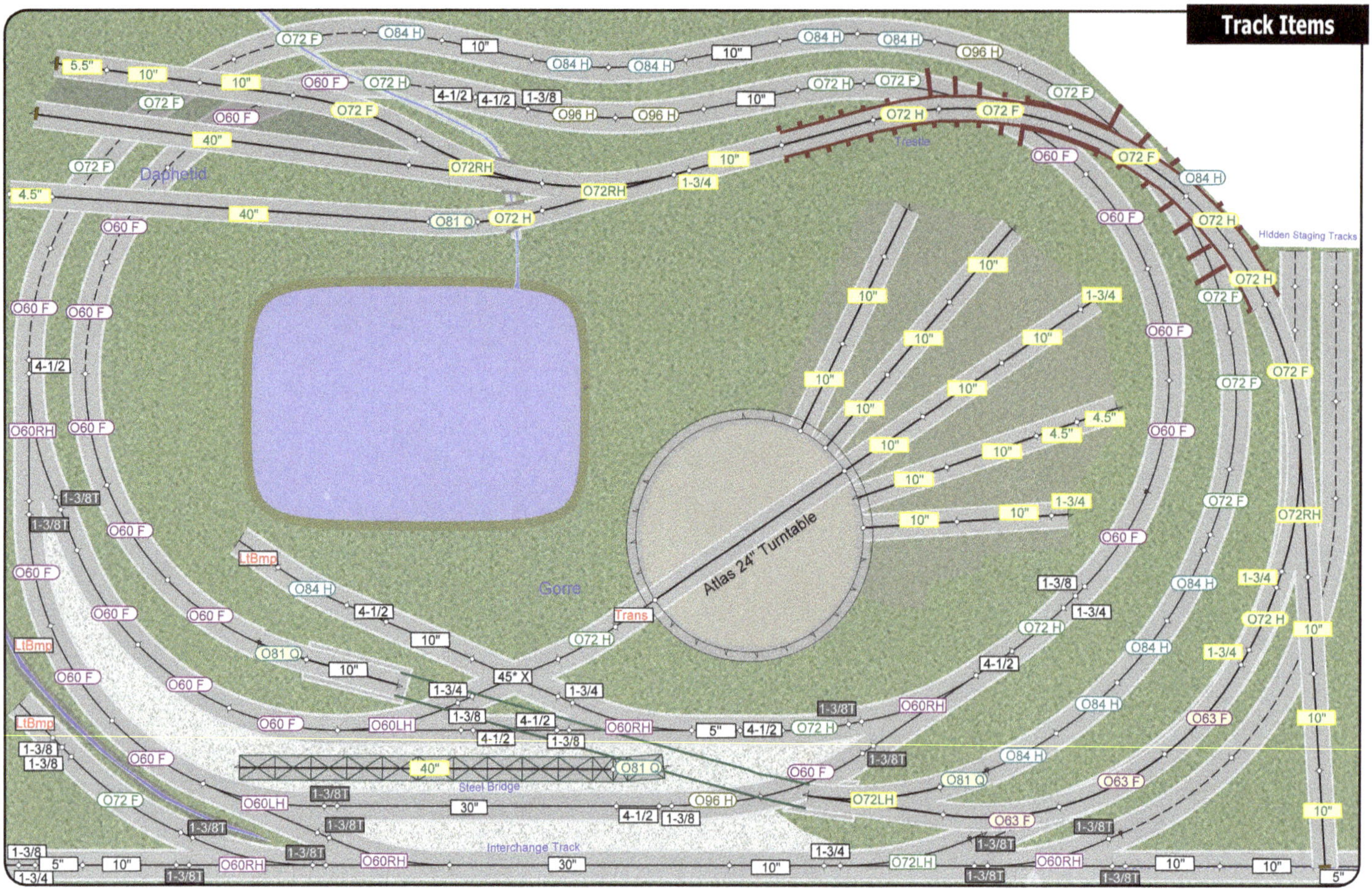

Two additional tracks have been added: the coal-burning power plant track at the lower right, and the warehouse track in Gorre, left of the turntable and below the pond. At Daphetid, a separate track serving the station is located below the two tracks of the mine facility, which can continue to the left, if desired, to reach points beyond.

At Gorre, an interchange track and connecting railroad has been added, creating more operating possibilities as well as both a source and destination for rail traffic.

At the lower right, new tracks have been added for hidden staging tracks coming off of the interchange/connecting track. These can be used for staging of trains and holding cars during operating sessions. Since there is no yard in John Allen's plan, these staging tracks provide part of that functionality.

The 24" Atlas O turntable in the O gauge plan takes up quite a bit of space and dominates the right side of the layout interior. Its larger size allows turning a greater variety of locomotives than John's 56' scale turntable (14").

Two different track systems are in use in this plan: Lionel's FasTrack and Atlas O's 21st Century 3-rail track. Both are excellent systems, and either could be used to create the entire layout alternatively. FasTrack for the main lines is used by many modelers today and is easily available and highly reliable with outstanding switches, while the Atlas track without the integrated roadbed makes for good trestles and bridges. Also, Atlas offers a reasonable turntable with its track system. The two different track systems and the transition from one to the other helps to create a sense of a railroad going from here to there with the

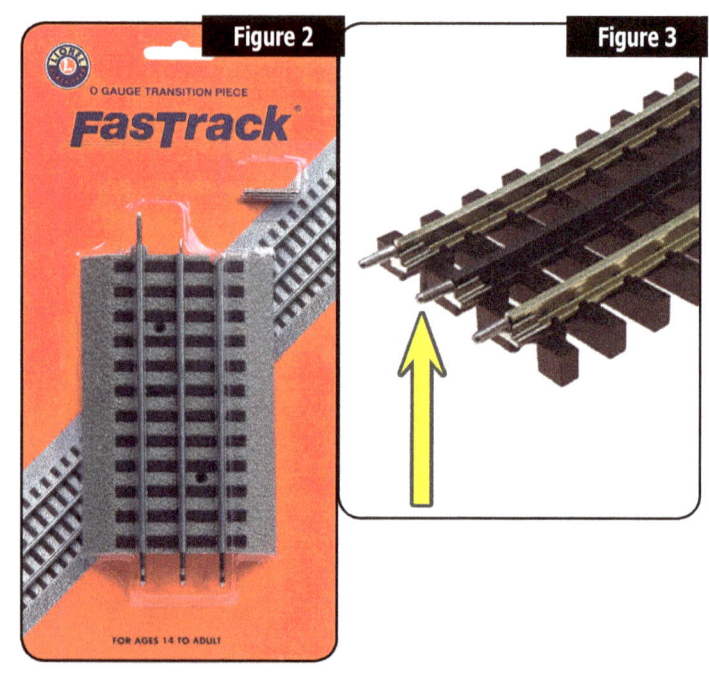

Figure 2

Figure 3

change in track—it emphasizes the departure from the main line loops to the elevated branch line climbing to Daphetid. Lionel makes a transition track to traditional tubular O scale track (Fig. 2), and Atlas makes conversion rail joiners to mate its track to tubular (Fig. 3).

The O gauge track plan improves on the tight 14" radius of the HO plan, with 60" minimum diameter for the FasTrack main lines with O60 switches, and O63 minimum diameter for the branch line to Daphetid with Atlas track and O72 switches. Thus, O54 scale equipment can run anywhere on the layout, perhaps limited by the length of the 24" turntable for locomotives. Grades are 3% throughout, the same maximum grade as John's HO plan.

Operating Plans

The layout track plan is a simple loop with a branch-line extension, plus an interchange track and hidden staging tracks, but a number of fun operations can be devised.

You can, for example, take loaded coal hoppers from the mine and run them over to the power plant. The location of the locomotive at the wrong end of the train at one location or the other suggests the train would run down to Gorre and use the siding to run around the train in order to access the tracks. The power plant has only one track, so an additional move taking the empties from the plant back to the mine should proceed the train toting coal to the plant.

Coal can move from the mine over the loops to the interchange track. Then the cars can be run into the hidden staging to continue beyond the layout. There is a short section of the interchange track in a tunnel at the lower right that can house a locomotive to make car shuffling easier. Empties can then come from off-layout to the interchange track, and then be picked up for a train returning them to Daphetid.

A short passenger consist can hide in a hidden staging track, to be run out occasionally to the station at Gorre, then cycled around and up to Daphetid, and then returned back to staging. An engine run-around at the Gorre passing track may be needed in order to push the passenger consist up to Daphetid, and then be able to return to Gorre with the locomotive leading the train.

Gorre & Daphetid Railroad FasTrack Bill of Materials

FasTrack Straights

6-12073	Straight 1-3/8"	9
6-12026	Straight 1-3/4"	7
6-12025	Straight 4-1/2"	10
6-12024	Straight 5"	5
6-12014	Straight 10"	12
6-12042	Straight 30"	2
6-12040	Straight transition 5"	1
6-12059	Buffer/Bumper 3-5/8"	2
6-12035	Buffer/Bumper (Lighted) 5"	2
6-12051	Crossing 10"/45°	

FasTrack Curves

6-12056	O60 Curve, angle 22.5°	20
6-12055	O72 Curve, angle 11.25°	8
6-12041	O72 Curve, angle 22.5°	14
6-12061	O84 Curve, angle 11.25°	11
6-81250	O96 Curve, angle 11.25°	4

FasTrack Switches

6-12057 or 6-81951	O60 Left Remote or O60 Left Remote & Command	4
6-12058 or 6-81950	O60 Right Remote or O60 Right Remote & Command	4
6-12048 or 6-81953	O72 Left Remote or O72 Left Remote & Command	1

Gorre & Daphetid Railroad Atlas Bill of Materials

Atlas O Straights

6015	Straight 1 1/4"	1
6050	Straight 10"	20
6051	Straight 4 ½"	3
6052	Straight 1 3/4"	5
6053	Straight 5 1/2"	2
6058	Straight 40"	3

Atlas O Curves

6064	O63 Curve, angle 22.5°	3
6062	O72 Curve, angle 22.5°	4
6063	O72 Curve, angle 11.25°	3
6012	O81 Curve, angle 7.5°	4

Atlas O Switches

6072	O72 Left	1
6073	O72 Right	3

Atlas O Accessory

6910	Turntable diameter 24"	1

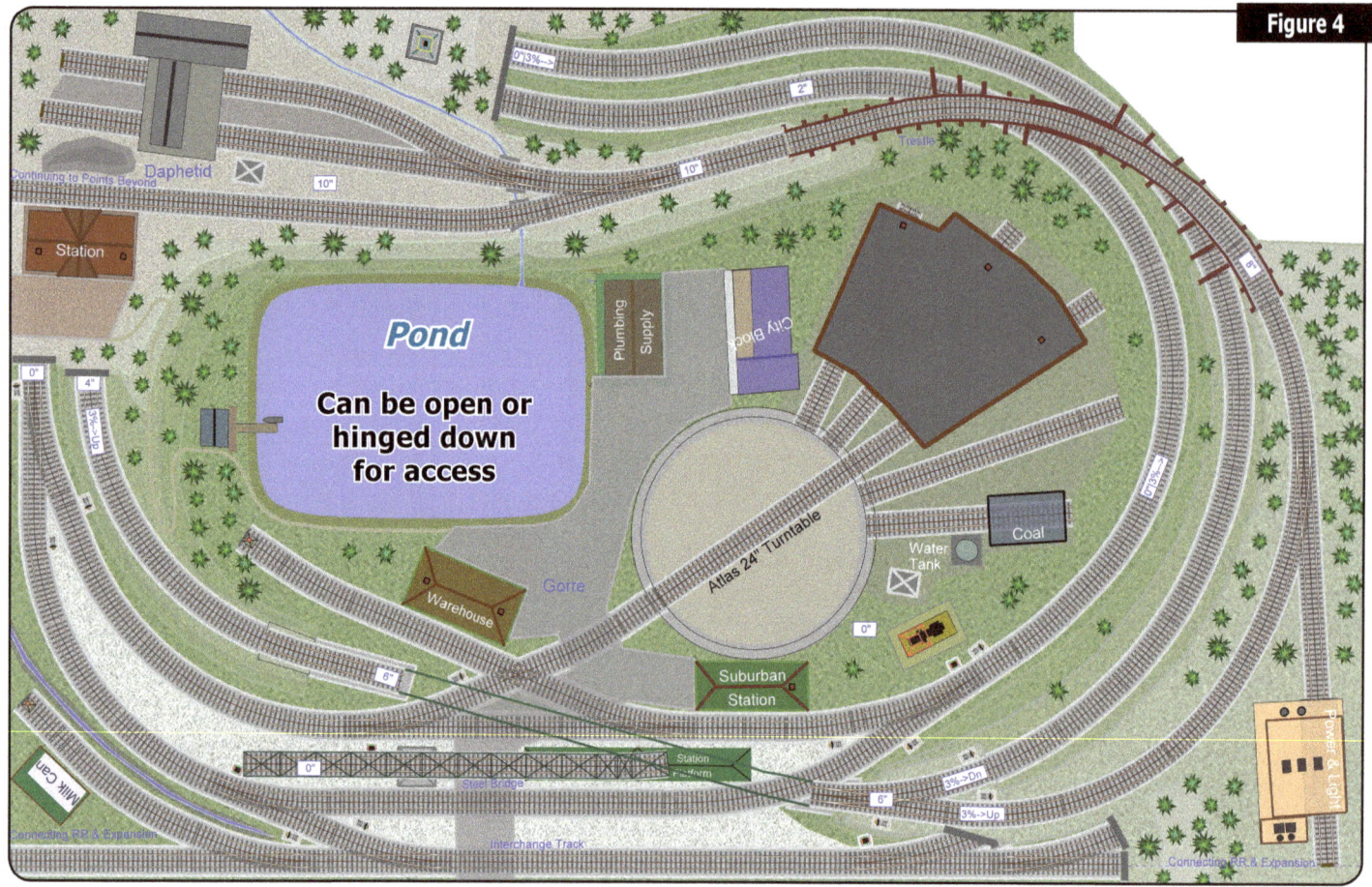

Figure 4

Clearances, Grades, and Scenery

Daphetid is level at 10" in height, sufficient to clear the ascending and descending FasTrack main lines below plunging through parallel tunnels. Elevation drops steeply to the pond at Gorre, but the high ground has fingers that stretch out along the track alignments. The tunnel portals to the right, under Daphetid, are partially obscured from the front of the layout, blocked by the branch line, which curves from Daphetid to the right and passes over the main lines on a trestle. Daphetid itself has the coal mine, a station, and a small ridge with the rotating beacon tower.

At Gorre, the main line crosses over itself on a steel bridge, with interesting track work beneath with the crossing, switches, and the lead to the turntable. The main line is level through Gorre, but heading to the right, out of town, begins climbing at 3% to reach the steel bridge. This main line loop enters the tunnel at about 2" in elevation and exits the tunnel at about 4" in elevation, then continues to climb to the elevated steel bridge at 6" in height. Daphetid, at 10" in height, has sufficient clearance for this FasTrack main exiting the tunnel beneath it at 4". One could make the branch line grade steeper and more challenging at 4%, making Daphetid 12" or more in height with more clearance beneath. Tracks, the passing track, and staging tracks tend to limit train length to short trains that can easily handle 4% grades.

The main line leaving Gorre to the left, curves to the tunnel and begins its ascent at 3%, exiting the tunnel at about 2", then continues to climb to the steel bridge at 6".

At the right side of the layout there is another elevated section of terrain, which gradually steps down toward Gorre from 6" to 0" while supporting the two FasTrack loops. This elevated area hosts one track serving the coal-fired power plant. As this terrain and the branch line continue toward the top of the plan and access area, it ascents to 8" at the trestle over the mains and to Daphetid.

There is a town center for Gorre, between the turntable and the pond. The pond has a fishing shack with a dock and rowboat. A stream cascades down a waterfall from Daphetid to fill the pond.

Construction and Access

Construction can create a level layout base of 12' on 2x4 runners on solid posts, with 1/2" plywood creating a solid surface and a clear space beneath. Alternatively, instead of a plywood base, a layer of 2" thick foam sheet is strong enough to support the layout on 16" centers, but would not sustain a person crawling over the layout during construction. Elevated terrain can be created on top of this base, with cut-outs for the pond and around the tunnel tracks under Daphetid. Any terrain technique can be used, but the use of 2" thick foam sheets might be convenient, and layout elevations at 2" intervals are marked on the layout plan.

A midsize layout plan of this type has issues with reach and access during construction, and with accessing the occasional derailment. The pond in the center is an access hole of about 2' by 3' and can be made to lift out, drop down, or simply remain open with the shoreline detailed to represent a lake filled with water. At the upper-right corner is another access and viewing area.

Access inside the hidden staging tracks under the power plant and terrain is from the front of the layout, and also from the access area in the upper right. Access to the track in the tunnels under Daphetid is inconvenient, but doable, with the area under Daphetid open to allow you to reach the tracks from beneath the layout. A layout surface a bit higher at up to 44" will help getting under and moving around, perhaps seated on a low rolling office chair, so that you can comfortably reach the pond access area, and from there access the track in the tunnels under Daphetid.

Once the layout base has been created, the surface can be prepared. A layer of 2" foam sheet could be laid down, which can be carved for areas below grade (the pond shore and streams). A grass mat with a sound-deadening vinyl base might be layered on top of the level areas around Gorre. Then the track can be laid down temporarily, with Woodland Scenics flexible foam inclines following the track alignments to create consistent and smooth grades without needing a lot of calculation and measuring to get it right. Scenery slopes can then be created inside the tracks and inclines. The Woodland Scenics inclines are wide enough for Atlas track to ride on top, but FasTrack is a bit wider than the inclines. It might be easiest to use two incline sets laid side-by-side for the FasTrack alignments and then trim them to match the slopes and scenery. Lay the inside curve incline first, and then gently stretch the outside incline to match. Alternatively, either a wider top can be laid on top of the foam inclines to support the track, or the FasTrack track can be filled with expanding spray foam and trimmed to make a level base to span the inclines, which would also serve to deaden track noise.

Structures

A variety of structures decorate the layout—more than displayed on the original HO G&D plan. Six operating Lionel accessories are included: the milk can unloader, a coal loader near the engine house, a rotating beacon at Daphetid, an oil derrick with nodding-donkey pump near the engine service track, and two of Lionel's sound-equipped work houses. At Daphetid, the coal mine is scratchbuilt, or perhaps modified from an S-scale structure, and the station is a Walthers kit. The coal-fired power plant at the right is by Menards. At Gorre, the City Block and Plumbing Supply are also Menards products. There is a water tank for steam locomotives, and the engine house is scratchbuilt. An MTH switch tower is positioned between the passing tracks. There are two station platforms under the steel bridge, and the Gorre station is a Lionel Suburban Station.

Control

Command control simplifies layout wiring and locomotive operation. For conventional control of two trains with two transformers, the main loops have each been divided into two blocks, breaking at the switch to Daphetid (just past the top of the grade and steel bridge). The plan shows block signals at this location protecting each block. The branch line is, of course, a separate block, as is each passing track and the interchange track. Each track should have an on/off switch, including the turntable tracks. Two power connections for each of the four main line blocks will provide ample power, and the other blocks will need only one power connection each.

Conclusion

The O gauge Gorre & Daphetid allows scale-size equipment capable of handling O54 minimum curves anywhere on the layout and provides a number of satisfying operations. The basic design combined with interesting scenery will make this an entertaining layout that is true to John Allen's original concept, design, and intent for the layout, but now in O gauge.

Happy Railroading!

Exclusively from OGR Publishing!

Building a Layout
by Jim Barrett

Order Today!

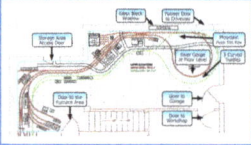     

The *Complete* Chronicles of 45 *OGR* Backshop Articles
Detailing the Building of Jim Barrett's Personal Layout

250+ Full Color Pages, with over 650 Photos
of Tips You Can Implement on Your Layout

Visit www.ogaugerr.com/jim/ to Order Your Copy!

OGR Publishing, Inc.
1310 Eastside Centre Court, Ste. 6
Mountain Home, AR 72653

"All major credit cards accepted"

www.ogaugerr.com

Model the Nickel Plate Road
A Double Main Line FasTrack Layout in a Small Space

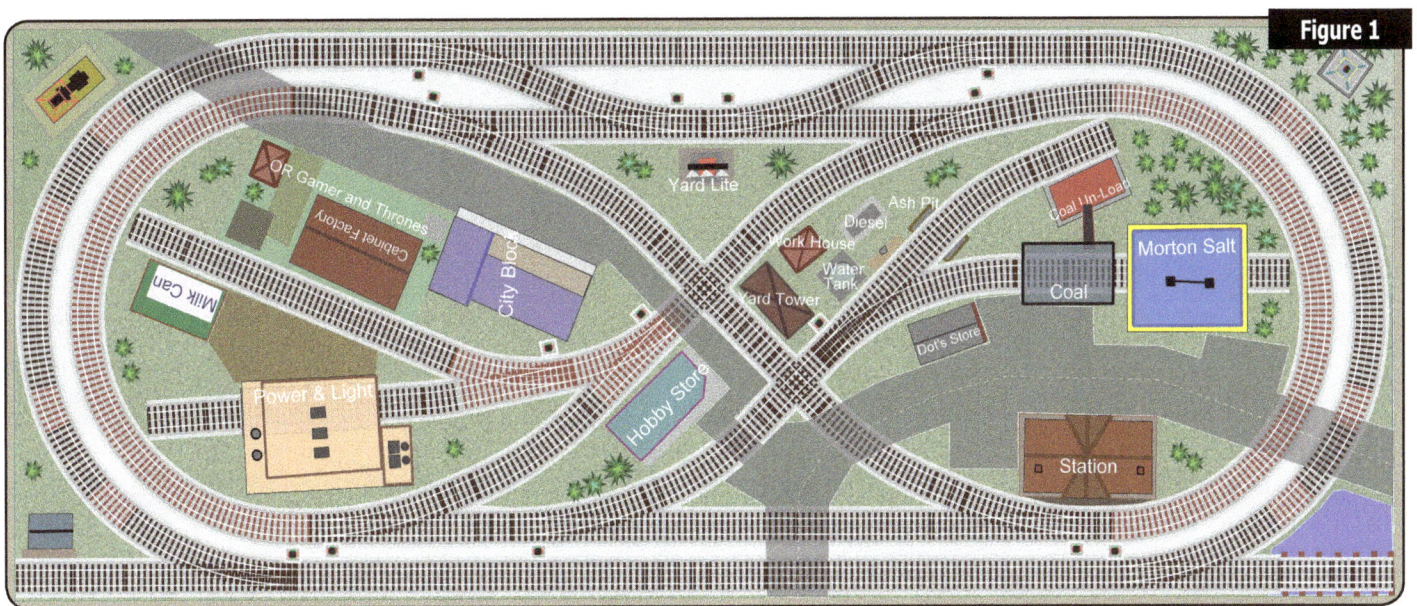

Figure 1

This Nickel Plate Road layout is a double-track FasTrack road in a compact 4x10 feet. Creating two parallel routes in a mere 4' width without resorting to O31 diameter curves is certainly a bit of a challenge. The solution here is what is known as compound curves, where two (or more) diameters are combined to create an intermediate diameter curve. Here, FasTrack O48 curves are combined with short O36 sections to create a half-circle of O44.5, which encloses the interior O36 circle with a figure 8. The 180° turn-around curves at both ends are mostly O48, but with four quarter-sections of O36 (each 12.5°) interspersed. The curves start with O48 easements leading to a quarter-O36, then 15° of O48, followed by another quarter-O36 to create a very smooth curve nicely paralleling the interior O36 curves.

A Bit about the Nickel Plate Road

The New York, Chicago & St. Louis Railroad (aka the Nickel Plate Road, abbreviated NKP) was a Midwest road linking Buffalo with Chicago, St. Louis, and Peoria. The main line ran through Cleveland, Ohio. The NYC&StL gained its famous Nickel Plate Road nickname from a Norwalk, Ohio, newspaper columnist who complemented its high standard of construction by referring to it as a "double-tracked, nickel-plated railroad." The Nickel Plate's 2,200-mile network operated in the hotly competitive Midwestern rail transportation market. During the railroad merger years, the Nickel Plate Road was merged with the Norfolk & Western, and it now operates as part of the current Norfolk Southern system.

The Nickel Plate was known for its high-speed freight trains running behind its famous Berkshire locomotives. Lionel has produced a fine LionChief Plus 2.0 Berkshire, No. 765 (product number 1932030). The LC+2.0 steam locomotive features upgraded sound with four chuffs per revolution and with smoke emissions timed with the exhaust chuffs. The upgraded LC+2.0 command control system integrates TMCC with LionChief Plus features, including Bluetooth to allow operation with a handheld device or smart phone, or controlled through a TMCC controller (or Legacy controller in TMCC mode) and Lionel's Universal Remote. This excellent locomotive runs on O36 curves, so will run anywhere on this layout, inside or outside main lines.

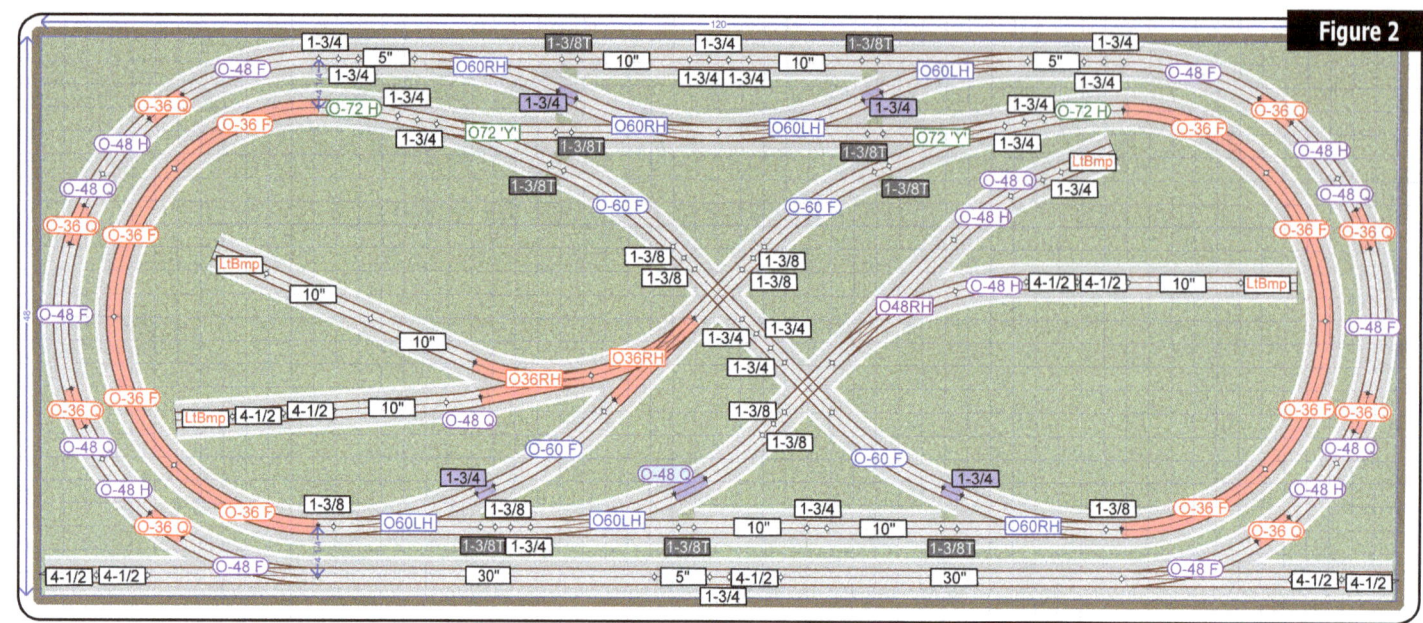

Figure 2

NKP Railroad FasTrack Bill of Materials

Lionel FasTrack Components

6-12042	Straight 30"	2
6-12014	Straight 10"	8
6-12024	Straight 5"	5
6-12025	Straight 4-1/2"	6
6-12026	Straight 1-3/4"	15
6-12073	Straight 1-3/8"	17
6-12035	Lighted Bumper	5
46-12019	90° Crossing 6"	2

Curves

6-12023	O36 Curve, angle 11.25°	8
6-12015	O36 Curve, angle 45°	8
6-16835	O48 Curve, angle 7.5°	7
6-16834	O48 Curve, angle 15°	7
6-12043	O48 Curve, angle 30°	4
6-12056	O60 Curve, angle 22.5°	4
6-12055	O72 Curve, angle 11.25°	2

Switches

6-12046 or 6-81946	O36 Right Remote or O36 Right Remote & Command	2
6-12065 or 6-81949	O48 Left Remote or O48 Left Remote & Command	1
6-12066 or 6-81948	O48 Right Remote or O48 Right Remote & Command	2
6-12057 or 66-81951	O60 Left Remote or O60 Left Remote & Command	4
6-12058 or 6-81950	O60 Right Remote or O60 Right Remote & Command	3
6-12047 or 6-81954	O72 Wye Remote or O72 Remote & Command	2

Nickel Silver Track for the Trestle

6051	Straight 4 ½"	1
6052	Straight 1 ¾"	3

Model The Nickel Plate Road

Layout Design

The Nickel Plate Road features double-track main lines. There is also a high-speed O60 double crossover so trains can transition between the inner and outer main lines. The inside main line also features two reverse loops, creating a figure-8 interior route and allowing trains to reverse direction.

The layout is for trains running on conventional, LionChief+/2.0, and/or MTH capable of running O36 (or the O44.5 compound described earlier). But the layout also has some fun switching opportunities, and could even be run like John Allen's renowned Timesaver switching puzzle. The O36 track sections and switches depicted in the diagrams are highlighted in a rusty-red color.

There are two O36 industry switches, and all other switches are O48 or wider diameter. Main line switches are generous—O60 and O72 wye—with two O48 switches at the bottom corners to create an optional connecting railroad and a short interchange track.

The minimum main line center-rail-to-center-rail separation is 4-1/4", which has been constructed and tested and will run the SCALE LionChief Plus SD60M and Menard's double-stack cars on the outside main line, with the LC+ Berkshire and compressed RailKing MTH SD70 on the inside main line without conflict (though close!).

The inside figure-8 curves (also forming the reverse loops) are O60 and O72 switches, with O60 curves. These curves are gentle, as trains roll through with less chance of locos and cars bumping off the rails over the two crossings at speed, because there is only moderate force from the drag of a long train reversing direction thanks to these wide curves and switches (wide relative to O36 and smaller equipment anyway).

Layout Construction

I have begun construction with the double-track main lines; and I have been running trains with the above-mentioned locomotives, and also with Menards double-stack container cars (a set of five). The double-track main line looks particularly good to my eyes, and I have oriented the long straight section at the front for train viewing. This puts the switches for the crossovers at the top of the layout, usually a less than ideal practice due to the risk of derailments outside of convenient reach, but in my construction the layout table rolls out for access. And FasTrack switches are really superb and reliable. I plan to operate my switches through TMCC command control.

If constructed with 2" foam sheets, as I have done, this creates a lightweight and movable layout, or even a temporary layout. The 3/4" width of the alternative construction outside framework provides additional overhang clearance as locomotives and equipment operate on the layout.

The layout could also be constructed with a 4x10 layout surface within an outside frame of 1x4s. The outside framework could also extend higher than the table surface, if desired. FasTrack roadbed, plus rail height, adds up to about 1/2" above the layout surface, so the framework could extend that high above the layout surface with zero chance of interference with moving equipment.

There are three small FasTrack sections that need to have the roadbed trimmed to match up to O60 switches: one O48 quarter-curved section, and two 1-3/4" straight sections. The plastic roadbed is easy to cut with a variety of hand tools or a Dremel to make a close fit with the O60 switches.

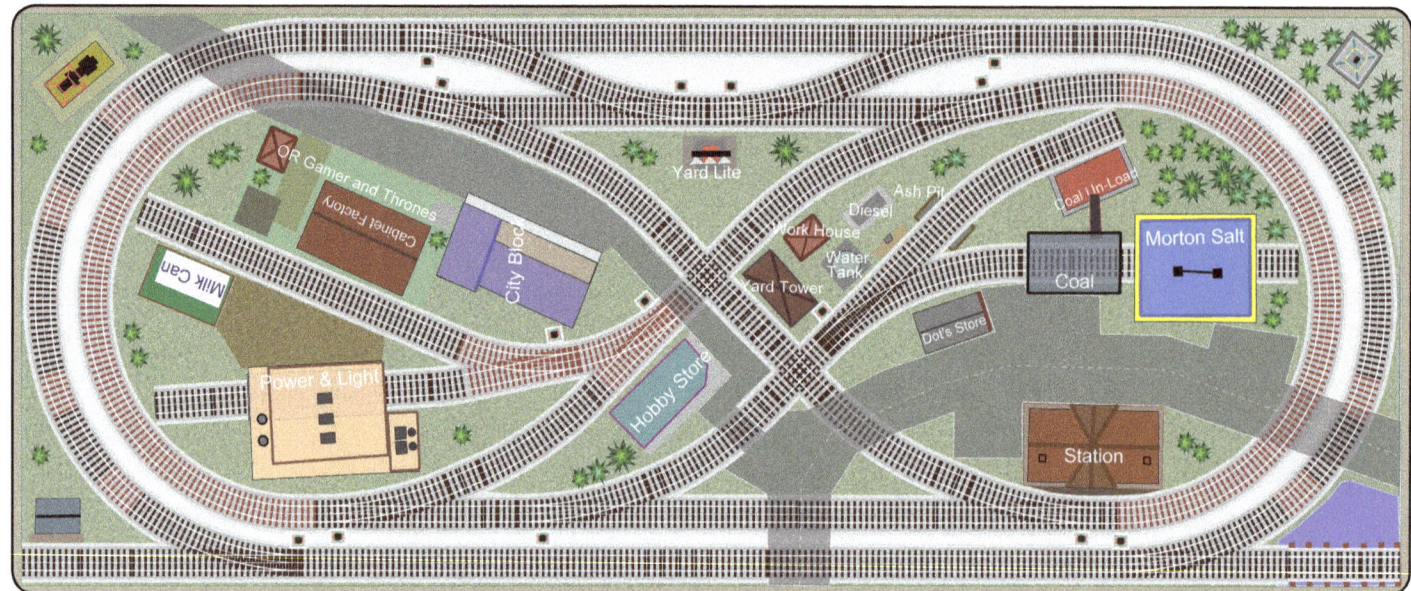

Structures

The layout includes OGR's Dotty's Store (Ameri-Towne No. 502), and a water tank and coal loader for steam locomotive servicing. Also, the new Menards Gamer and Thrones structure is the same size as the Cabinet Factory, so is an option there. There also is some traditional Lionel layout action with operating accessories including the Bubbling Oil Derrick with nodding donkey, Milk Can Unloader, Yard Light, Work House w/Sound, Rotating Beacon, Coal Loader, and Coal Unloader.

The engine-servicing facilities are highlighted: an operating conveyor could be installed to lift coal from the unloader bin up into the coal-loading bin with coal for steam locomotive tenders. A diesel standpipe and holding tank are shown, along with an ash pit to make a small locomotive servicing facility.

Scenery

The scenery is fairly easy on this mostly flat 4x10, with one modest hill with the rotating beacon in the upper-right corner, and a depressed pond area in the lower-right, with a trestle carrying the rail line. This trestle can be homemade with dowels or scale timber, fitted with a short section of Atlas (or other) non-roadbed track, which will look good on a trestle. Then lots of trees and vegetation can be added over a grass-mat base. Woodland Scenics grass mats are on a vinyl mat, which cuts down on FasTrack noise since there is no direct contact between the roadbed/track and the layout surface. In my experience, the 2" foam tends to reduce noise as well.

The Nickel Plate in 4x10

High-speed freight service returns, headed by the magnificent Nickel Plate Road Berkshire locomotives! This innovative double-track main line layout truly lives up to the road's nickname "as a double-track, nickel-plated railroad" with closely-parallel main lines of shiny Lionel FasTrack.

Happy Railroading!

Lionel's 56" x 86" Train Table
A First Layout in a Small Space

Lionel 56" x 86" Table Part No. 1904010

Photo 1

Lionel offers an attractive train table (Photo 1) that is sized to fit many spaces in a typical household, and it is a good size for a first layout. This might make a perfect gift layout for the kids or grandkids, or a nice layout for those with limited space for trains, such as in an apartment and condo, or even as a second layout in a spare bedroom while the main layout is in the basement or attic.

Track Plan

Lionel's table, at 58" wide (56-1/2" between the sides), will accommodate an oval of O48 FasTrack with another O36 loop nestled inside, leaving a generous amount of space and clearance between the track sections and the table sides.

In this plan, the outer O48 oval includes O60 easement track sections leading into each half-circle, and this track loop will run O42 and smaller locomotives and equipment. One good possibility is the Lionel No. 2022010 Granite Run Quarry Set shown here, but that is just a suggestion.

The inside oval is O36, also with O60 easements leading into each half-circle, matching with the O60 switches providing the crossover to the outside loop. These crossovers are formed with two O60 switches arranged so there is no *S* curve, or reverse curve, for smooth and fast running. The minimum center rail spacing is 4-3/4" at its narrowest on the curves, which is just fine for traditional and LionChief locomotives and rolling stock.

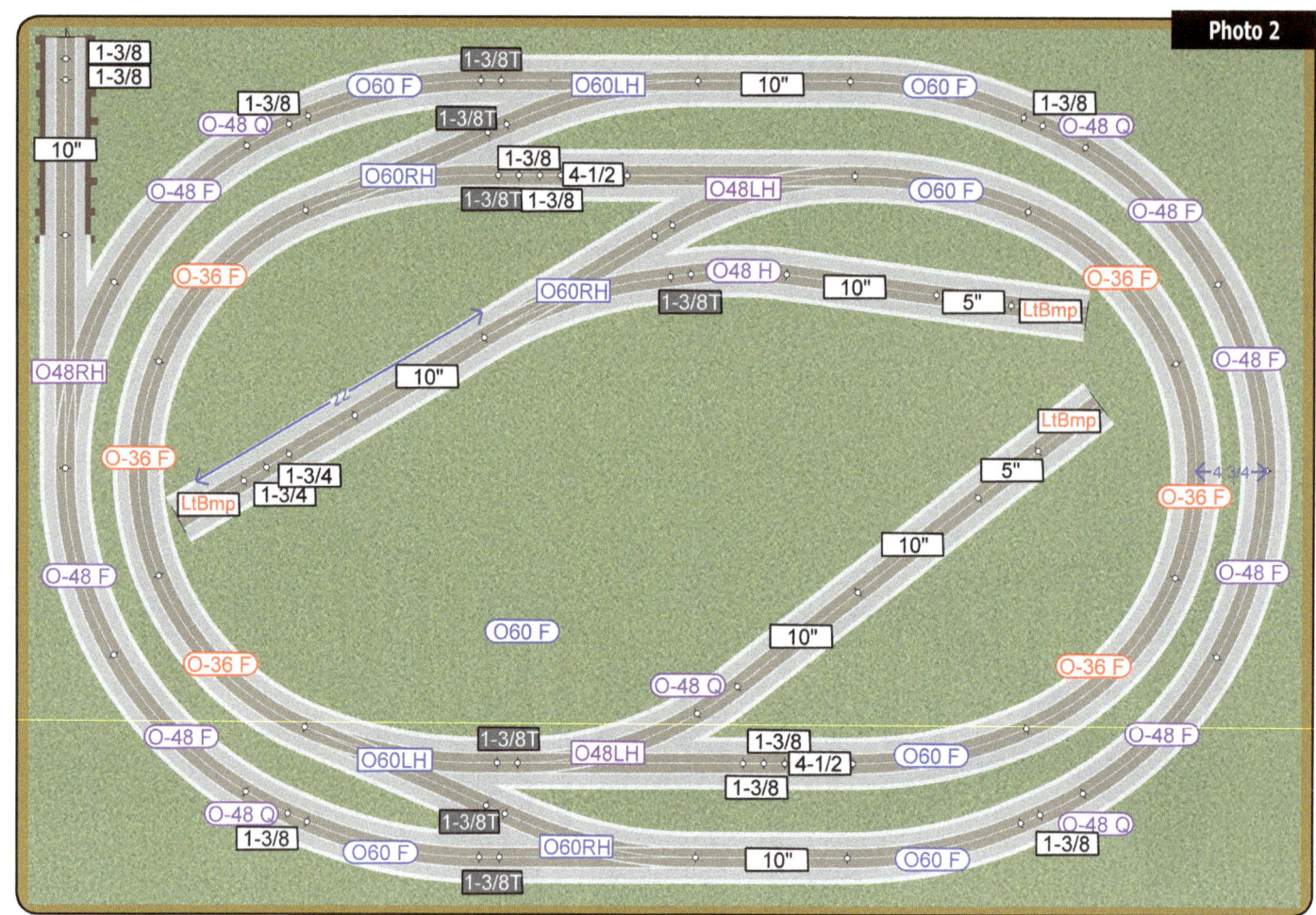

Lionel Train Table FasTrack Bill of Materials

Straights		
6-12014	Straight 10"	7
6-12024	Straight 5"	3
6-12025	Straight 4-1/2"	2
6-12026	Straight 1-3/4"	2
6-12073	Straight 1-3/8"	10
6-12035	Lighted Bumper 5"	3
Curves		
6-12015	O36 Curve, angle 45°	6
6-12043	O48 Curve, angle 30°	7
6-16834	O48 Curve, angle 15°	1
6-16835	O48 Curve, angle 7.5°	5
6-12056	O60 Curve, angle 22.5°	6

Switches		
6-12065 or 6-81949	O48 Left Remote or O48 Left Remote & Command	2
6-12066 or 6-81948	O48 Right Remote or O48 Right Remote & Command	1
6-12057 or 6-81951	O60 Left Remote or O60 Left Remote & Command	2
6-12058 or 6-81950	O60 Right Remote or O60 Right Remote & Command	3

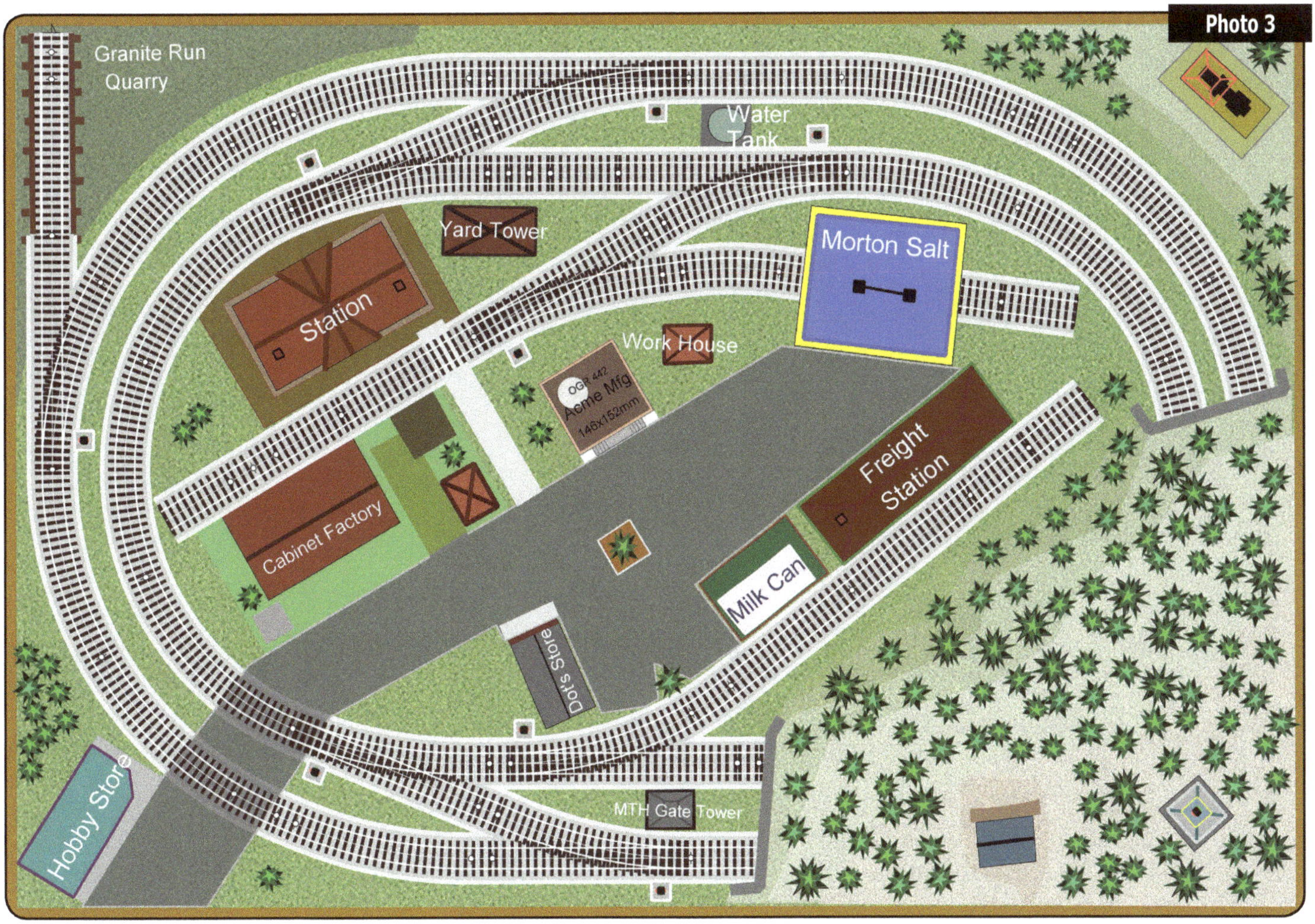

Scenery and Operations

Scenery includes a mountain with two tunnels at the lower right, topped with a rotating beacon and a small shack. At the upper right is a hillside with an oil derrick. At the upper left is the Granite Run Quarry, which can be served by the aforementioned Granite Run Quarry Set, which includes a dockside switcher, four short dumping gondolas, and a work caboose. Position a loader and dump truck in the mine area to load the gondolas.

Operation is mostly by imagination, but some switching is in order with three tracks plus the quarry. The track below the station is interesting, as it also provides access to the Morton Salt track. The 22" long space between the switch points and the bumper on the 5" lighted buffer track section will allow a short locomotive like the 0-6-0 shown here, to pull a car in or out of the Morton Salt track.

Structures

The layout plan here shows structures from a variety of manufacturers: animated structures from Lionel include the Freight Station; Oil Derrick with **nodding donkey** oil pump; Milk Can Unloader; and the Rotating Beacon; plus the Work House, which includes sound. Also from Lionel is the Yard Tower.

The Morton Salt tower and Cabinet Factory are from Menard's. The Hobby Store and Gate Tower are from MTH. OGR's Ameri-Towne line provides Acme Machine Shop and Dotty's Store.

There is a small shack or cabin on the mountain, which could be from Woodland Scenics or could even be scratch built.

Lionel Granite Run Quarry
LionChief Plus 2.0 Set
Item No. 2022010

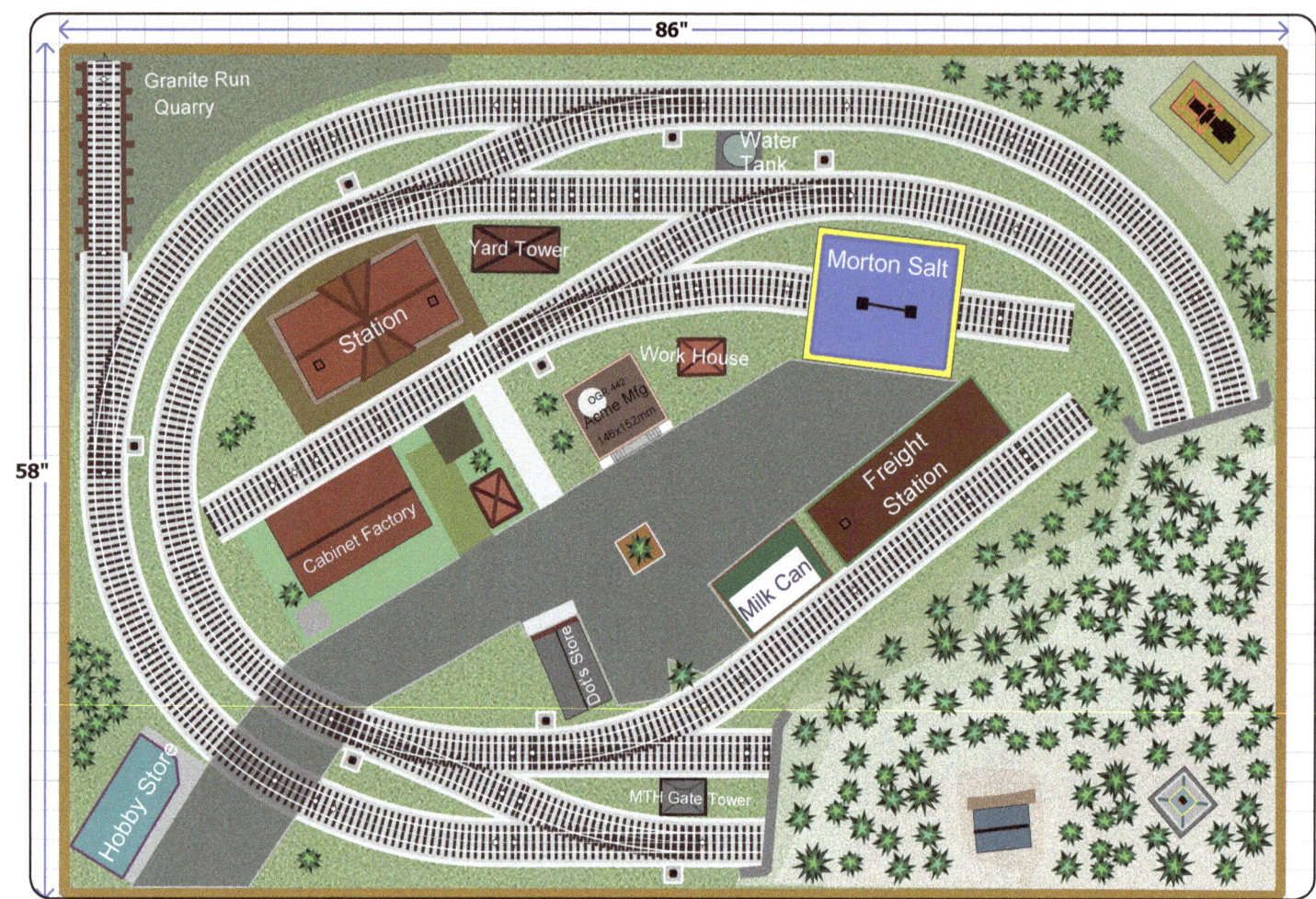

Menards, Woodland Scenics, and Walthers all make a small depot, and various manufactures provide small water tanks for topping-off steam locomotive tenders. An option is an animated operating water tank with sounds from Broadway Limited, which fits between the two ovals at the top of the plan.

Wiring and Control

The two loops should be electrically isolated for conventional transformer control by removing the jumper wire on the 1-3/8" section between the switch pairs forming the crossovers. Each track should have the inside rail isolated, with the track itself being powered with an on/off switch. For command control, the power supply can connect to both loops, allowing command locomotives to run anywhere.

The Lionel Train Table layout

This Lionel Train Table layout is an excellent first layout or kid's layout, providing a good amount of action with two-train operation, some switching capability, animated accessories, a two-track tunnel, and a granite quarry. Children and adults alike will enjoy hours of pleasure with this compact layout.

Happy Railroading!

Lionel FasTrack Layout for a Spare Room
FasTrack Operations for Two Trains

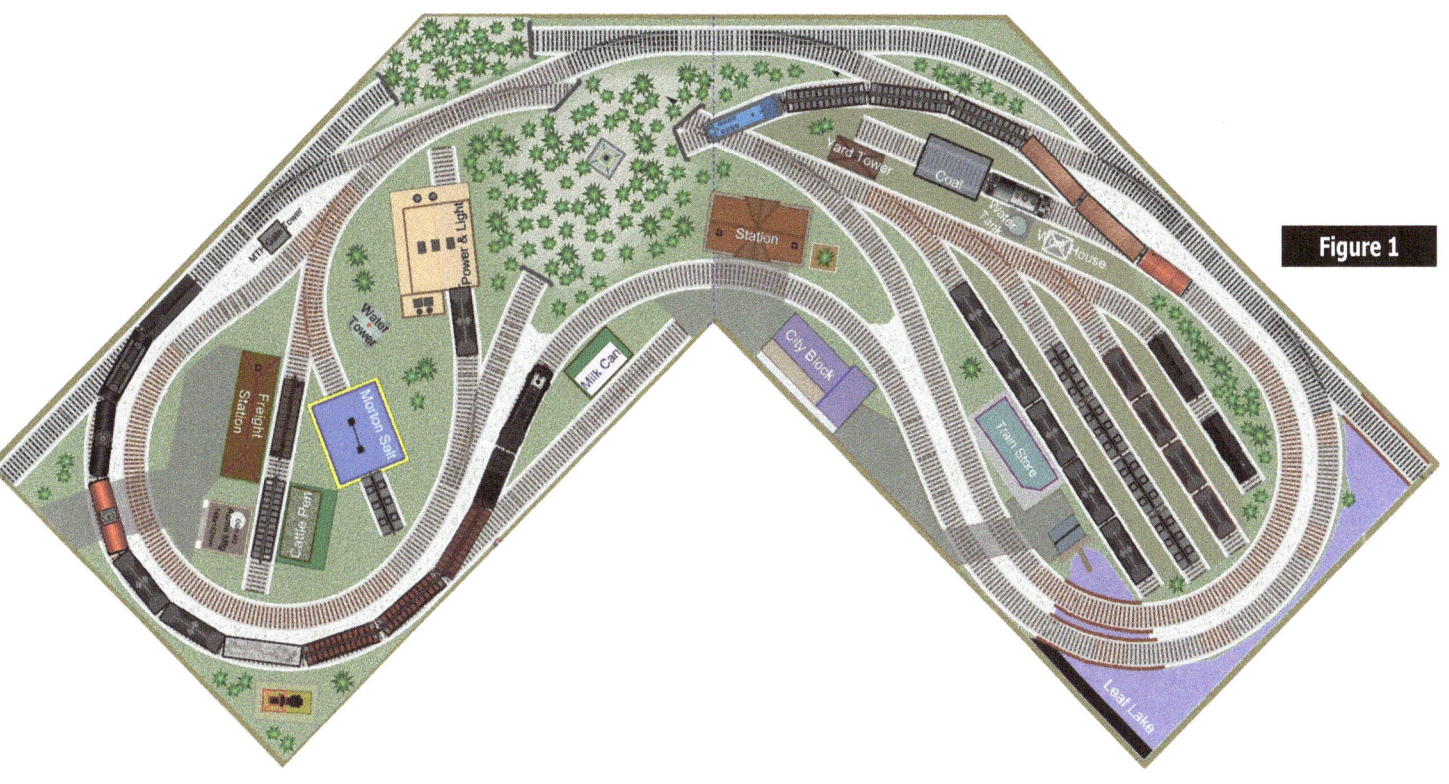

Figure 1

Two trimmed 4x8 plywood sheets make up this compact layout (Figure 1) that fits conveniently in a typical small bedroom or spare room, yet offers two-train operation with a small yard and some industry switching.

The layout features a lake shore paralleling the main lines with a fishing shack and dock, two mountains with tunnels, a crossing in the middle of the layout, and train route variety via changing main lines and reversing direction. The railroad makes a connection with a continuing main line running along the outside edge of the layout. That line originates, and is also the destination for, passenger and freight traffic.

The two 4x8 plywood sheets are trimmed to a point to fit together to make the L shape. The layout easily transports to another room or site when the two tables are constructed so that they fit together.

The Track Plan

The outside loop is an O44.5 compound minimum diameter route (assembled with O48 sections interleaved with short quarter-sections of O36 that are highlighted in red) running around the perimeter of the *L* shape. These curves will handle most O42 equipment. There are two crossovers to the inside route, which allow trains to switch main lines and also to reverse direction. The outside main line has two optional O48 switches that create the continuing main line connecting off-layout at either end of the layout. These could be replaced with O48 curves if desired.

The inside main line is a bent figure-8 with O36 minimum curves at each layout end, which pretty much restricts the inside main line to O36 and smaller minimum diameter equipment.

The Spare Room Layout
FasTrack Bill of Materials

Straights

Part #	Description	Qty
6-12042	Straight 30"	2
6-12014	Straight 10"	12
6-12024	Straight 5"	4
6-12025	Straight 4-1/2"	8
6-12026	Straight 1-3/4"	21
6-12073	Straight 1-3/8"	13
6-12054	Remote Operating Track 10"	2
6-12035	Lighted Bumper 5"	9
6-12020	Uncoupling Track	7
6-12051	45° Crossing 10"	1

Curves

Part #	Description	Qty
6-12015	O36 Curve, angle 45°	8
6-12022	O36 Curve, angle 22.5°	1
6-12023	O36 Curve, angle 11.25°	9
6-12043	O48 Curve, angle 30°	6
6-16834	O48 Curve, angle 15°	8
6-16835	O48 Curve, angle 7.5°	7
6-12056	O60 Curve, angle 22.5°	9
6-12041	O72 Curve, angle 22.5°	1
6-12055	O72 Curve, angle 11.25°	5
6-12061	O84 Curve, angle 11.25°	1
6-81250	O96 Curve, angle 11.25°	1

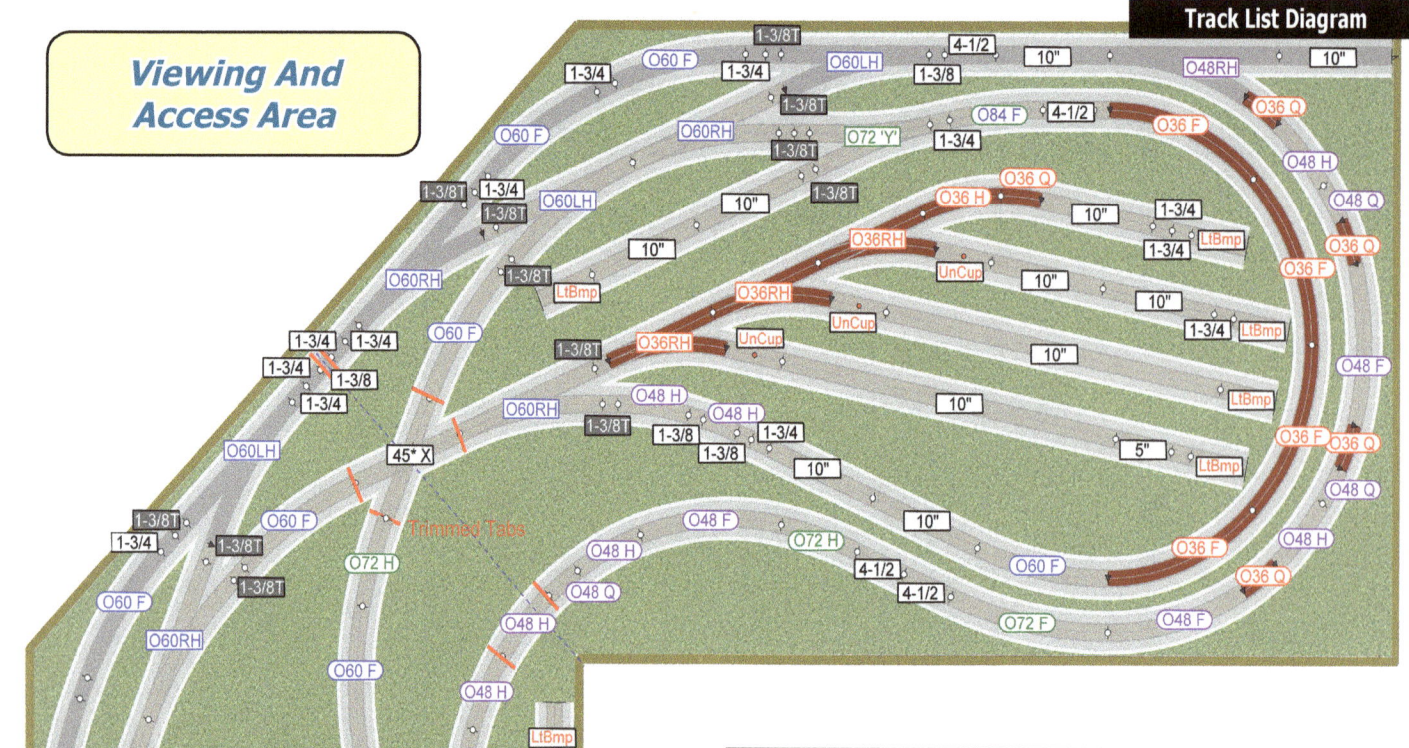

Track List Diagram — Viewing And Access Area

FasTrack Layout for a Spare Room

Switches		
6-12045 or 6-81947	O36 Left Remote or O36 Left Remote & Command	2
6-12046 or 6-81946	O36 Right Remote or O36 Right Remote & Command	3
6-12065 or 6-81949	O48 Left Remote or O48 Left Remote & Command	1
6-12066 or 6-81948	O48 Right Remote or O48 Right Remote & Command	1
6-12057 or 6-81951	O60 Left Remote or O60 Left Remote & Command	5
6-12058 or 6-81950	O60 Right Remote or O60 Right Remote & Command	5
6-12047 or 6-81954	O72 Wye Remote or O72 Wye Remote & Command	1
6-12048 or 6-81953	O72 Left Remote or O72 Left Remote & Command	1

The layout uses switches of O36, O48, O60, and O72 curvature. There is a small four-track yard in the upper-right sheet with O36 switches. The lower-left sheet has two industry switches of O36 curvature. The cross-overs between mains are all O60 switches. The upper right sheet has one O72 Wye switch, while the lower-left sheet has one O72 left-hand switch. In the center of the layout is a 45-degree crossing.

The layout includes two FasTrack accessory activation tracks for Lionel's animated milk can unloader and the cattle or horse pen. FasTrack remote uncoupler track sections are included for switching and servicing the industries. Though locomotives with remote couplers may not need all of these uncoupling sections, they may still come in handy. The tracks are terminated with FasTrack lighted bumpers, adding a bit more nighttime lighting and color to the layout.

In order to build two main lines within a 48" overall dimension with O36 as the minimum diameter, the O44-1/2 compound main line creates minimum track center spacing of 4-1/4", which is tight, but generous for traditional O gauge locomotives and rolling stock.

Scenery

One of the scenic highlights of the layout is Leaf Lake in the upper right, with three trestle bridges carrying the tracks across the water. Under the trestles, toward the yard, is a fishing shack with a dock, including a good place to moor a fishing boat or canoe. The lake can be excavated to an inch or so of depth, with the shore and bottom first detailed and painted before liquid water is poured for the lake itself.

The trestles supporting the FasTrack over the water can be scratchbuilt; and if desired, the edges of the FasTrack over the piers can be detailed and the roadbed disguised or enclosed.

Just off the center of the layout are two mountains that rise steeply to about 10" in height and include a tunnel.

Table Construction

The two 4x8 sheets are trimmed to fit at 45-degree angles to a point in order to create the L-shape layout. If constructed as two stand-alone tables, these trimmed sheets can be made to separate, making the layout movable and modular. These tables could also have removable legs to facilitate transport.

The table tops are supported with 1x4 sides, with 2x2 or 2x3 runners supporting the table surface. The outside frames can reach above the layout surface as much as one half inch—the height of the FasTrack railhead—to ensure clearance.

The FasTrack sections that span the joint between the tables can be made to more easily disconnect from the track fixed to the tables by trimming the plastic tabs that assure a tight grip holding each section tightly to the next. A small trimmer or saw can be used to cut off the tabs at the joints indicated on the Labeled Track Section illustration. This makes the 45-degree crossing, one 1-3/8" straight section, and one O48 half-curve—all of which span the joint between tables—easier to loosen when the tables are being disconnected.

Wiring and Control

Wiring for command control is easy, with power drops at the ends of each curve. Power drops to each siding should be controlled with an on-off switch for the center rail to allow a locomotive or powered unit to be powered down when not in use.

If Lionel's TMCC or Legacy command control systems are used with FasTrack command control switches, the switches can be controlled from the remote with no additional wiring needed for switch controllers. Switch power would then be supplied by the command control capability.

Conventional wiring suggests two blocks for each main line, creating four power blocks supporting two-train operation.

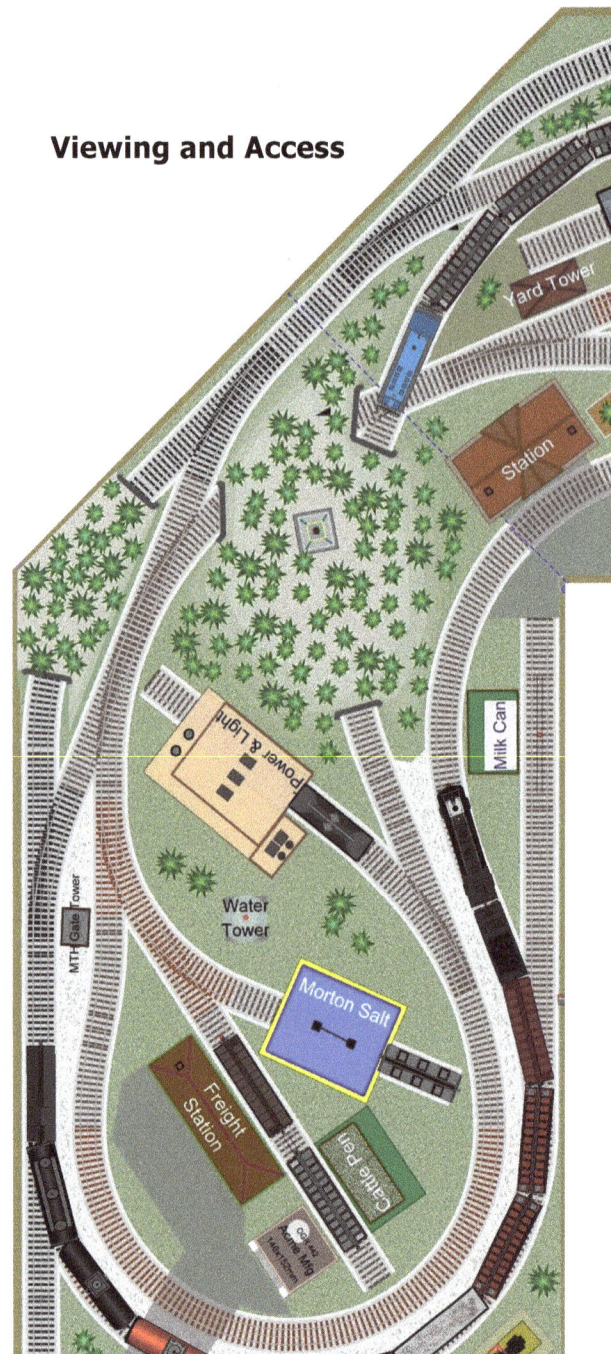

Viewing and Access

Structures

The layout includes a nice set of structures and industries to service, running loads from the yard to the industries, and then interchanging with the connecting railroad. There are two accessory tracks for Lionel's operating cattle pen and milk can unloader.

The coal loader and rotating beacon on top of the mountain are also operating Lionel accessories, as is the Work House with Sound. OGR's Acme Machine Shop and Lionel's Animated Freight Station share a siding. The Morton Salt, Power and Light, and City Block lighted structures are Menard's products. MTH provides the Gate Tower (used here as a switch tower) and the Train Store. The station is a Walthers product. Also included on the layout is a water tower, water tank, and fishing shack—products that are available from several manufacturers.

Wrapping Up

This movable 10x10 FasTrack layout provides plenty of railroading action in a small space, considering that it is constructed with just two 4x8 sheets of plywood as its base. Construction, maintenance reach, and access are facilitated by the convenience of the movable layout halves that would also allow this layout to move with you as you change residences, or just move as your space needs evolve. With its switching and main line running routes, this plan is the basis for an excellent first or second layout that will provide good train-watching opportunities combined with some realistic operations.

Happy Railroading!

Locomotives and Rolling Stock

The O44.5 outside route will allow most O42 locomotives and cars to run that route; but the rest of the layout is, as noted earlier, O36 minimum diameter. Traditional equipment will be at home here, including LionChief and MTH RailKing items. The LionChief+ SD60M is a large and scale-size locomotive rated at O36 minimum diameter, and it would look best running the outside main line. You will need to be careful if you want to run very very cars and locomotives on the outside O44-1/2 main line preferably, due to the tight center rail spacing minimum of 4-1/4" and large overhang.

Railroad Action at Bellows Falls, Vermont
An Action-Packed 4'x 8' Layout

The Boston & Maine (B&M) Railroad crossed the Connecticut River at Bellows Falls, Vermont, where a canal had been dug to bypass the falls on the Connecticut River, allowing barge traffic to proceed upriver. The canal was completed in 1802, with a 52-foot change in water level elevation. This created the industrial town of Bellows Falls as an island between the canal and the river. The town thrived on the barge traffic and light water-powered industry, and then again, after the railroad came to town in 1849. Bellows Falls is a small town with a population a bit more than 3,000. The Rutland Railroad also connected at Bellows Falls; and the town is currently home to the Green Mountain Railroad, a small Class III freight railroad.

Track Plan

This layout is a compact 4x8 with a 1'x 2' extension (which could be made longer) using Lionel FasTrack with O36 minimum curves and O36 switches. The track plan consists of a loop with extras, including two B&M connections: one continuing across the Connecticut River at the top right of the layout, and the other across the canal to the layout extension at the bottom of the layout.

The layout loop with a passing siding at the bottom and one reversing connection running through the middle of the layout plan also serve industries within Bellows Falls.

The railroad has a lot of action for a 4x8, with the passing siding and reverse loop, plus two connections and the extension with two tracks at the bottom. The extension can be made longer, as space allows.

This is a great layout for industrial buildings to populate Bellows Falls. There are sufficient operating possibilities to keep two engineers busy with short trains, using the passing track and reverse-loop connections to service the five tracks in town and the connections to the rest of the B&M (three more tracks). These tracks can be used to set out cars to be picked up by passing freights. A trolley could also run through and around town, if desired.

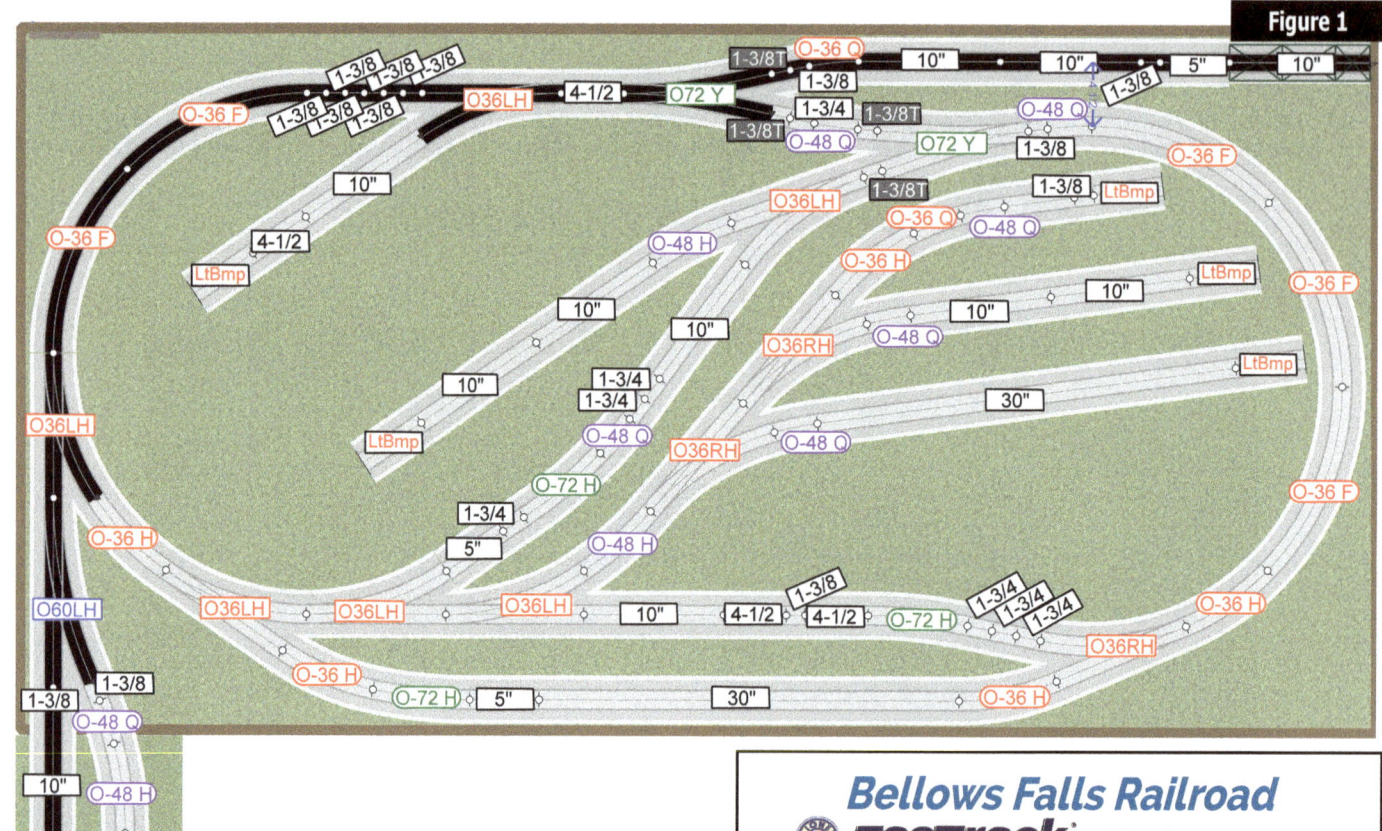

Figure 1

Water Features: River, Canal and Locks

The canal connects the river from left to right, with the Connecticut River also continuing off-layout around the top and right edges of the layout. There are two locks on the canal connecting to the river, one each on the left and right sides of the layout. The layout craftsman will have interesting opportunities to create water features: the river, locks, and the canal itself, as well as four railroad bridges crossing the water.

Layout Construction

Construction can be simple as a sheet of 4x8 plywood or 2" thick foam, with a fascia of 1x4 around the layout. A sturdy framework makes the layout quite movable if the various structures have been removed from the town. The curves are mostly O36, but with a few sections of O48, and two short half-sections of O72 as part of the passing track. There are nine O36 switches, one O48 right-hand switch leading to the extension, and two O72 wye switches at the top of the layout.

Bellows Falls Railroad Lionel FasTrack Bill of Materials

	Straights	
6-12073	Straight 1 3/8"	14
6-12026	Straight 1 ¾"	10
6-12025	Straight 4 ½"	4
6-12024	Straight 5"	4
6-12014	Straight 10"	13
6-12042	Straight 30"	2
	Curves	
6-12023	O36 Curve, angle 11.25°	2
6-12022	O36 Curve, angle 22.5°	5
6-12015	O36 Curve, angle 45° (O36)	5
6-16835	O48 Curve, angle 7.5°	7
6-16834	O48 Curve, angle 15°	3
6-12055	O72 Curve, angle 11.25°	3
6-12035	Lighted Bumper 5"	6
	Switches	
6-12045 or 6-81947	O36 Left Remote or O36 Left Remote & Command	6
6-12046 or 6-81946	O36 Right Remote or O36 Right Remote & Command	3
6-12057 or 6-81951	O60 Left Remote or O60 Left Remote & Command	1
6-12047 or 6-81954	O72 Wye Remote or O72 Wye Remote & Command	2

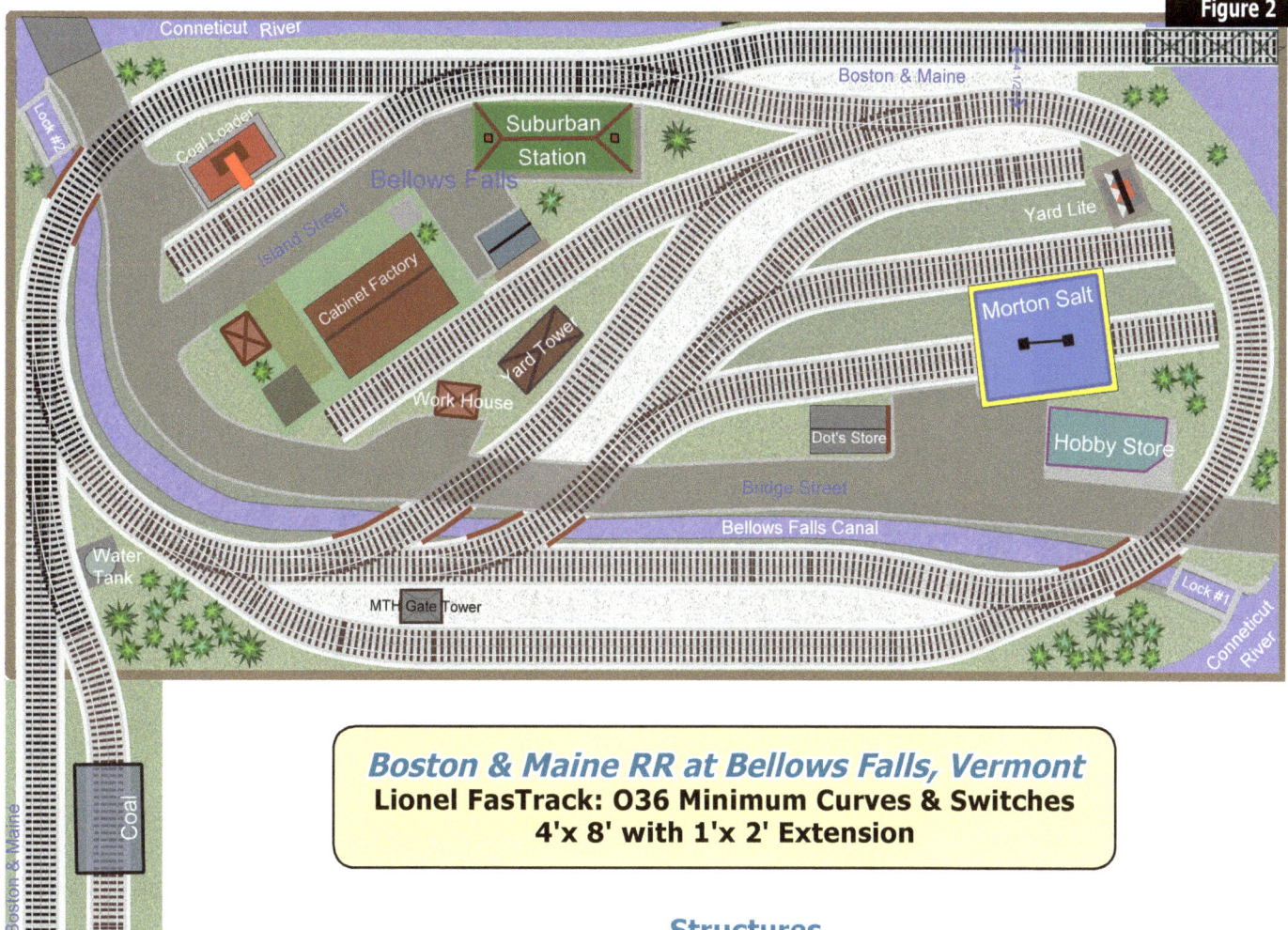

Boston & Maine RR at Bellows Falls, Vermont
Lionel FasTrack: O36 Minimum Curves & Switches
4'x 8' with 1'x 2' Extension

Scenery Construction

There are numerous scenic elements to build, with sections of the Connecticut River, the canal, structures in town, and the four railroad bridges. There also is a highway bridge at the upper left, providing access to the town. Only a few trees are needed, along with some small sections of grass and turf ground cover.

A road passes through the town; and the locks themselves can be complex or simple, but they will be interesting features either way. Put a few small boats and a barge on the river and in the canal, and include a fisherman and some boys playing in and around the water.

If not experienced with one of the scenic water systems, start small by isolating the canal into sections, with a hidden *dam* underneath each of the four railroad bridges. This creates smaller canal sections that can be poured as a continuous layer, and then each layer can be built up with multiple pours to create the water depth.

Structures

As shown, the layout has two Lionel operating accessories: the coal loader in the upper right and the coaling tower on the layout extension. Other Lionel accessories include the Work House with Sound and the Yard Light Tower. Menard's Cabinet Factory is a nice complex served by a track on the left, with the eye-catching Menard's Morton Salt tower on the right. Lionel's Suburban Station or any number of others could serve as the town's station. The illustration also shows a water tank on the lower left, a yard tower in the center, Ameri-Towne's Dotty's Store, and a gate tower from MTH between the passing track and main at the bottom.

A Small 4x8 Layout

The B&M and Green Mountain Railroad at Bellows Falls is a nice first layout, with operating possibilities and some cool scenery. There are industries, a passing track, reversing track, and layout track extension for some fun switching activity. The water features add an interesting visual element and scenic challenge.

Happy Railroading!

O Gauge Railroading
Digital Edition Subscription!

- Extra content in each digital issue
- Access to more than 50 Years of Back Issues
- Access the OGR Video Library
- Premium Membership in the OGR Forum
- Get your issues earlier

Visit ogaugerr.com/subscribe For Current Pricing and Special Offers! or call 1-800-980-6477 for more info

OGR Publishing, Inc.
1310 Eastside Centre Court, Ste. 6
Mountain Home, AR 72653

A Room Full of Operating Fun
An 8'x 10' Lionel FasTrack Layout

This interesting layout is for two trains and two engineers and uses Lionel FasTrack on an 8'x10' base. The layout features many different routes that will keep operations varied, exciting, and interesting. In addition, there are tracks to switch, a number of operating accessories, plus a four-track yard with engine servicing facilities and caboose/locomotive storage.

This layout is easy to build on a flat base, and is especially appropriate for a first layout, particularly if built in stages as described below. The layout will keep a family busy building and operating trains for years of good, shared fun.

Overview of the Track Plan

The layout curves are O36 minimum diameter, except where noted. O48 switches and curves are indicated in blue. O60 switches and 1-3/8" roadbed-trimmed sections are illustrated in green. There also are two sections of O96 in yellow, located near the Morton Salt tower.

There are several routing options that can be used in a number of combinations, thus providing a whole lot of fun, particularly with two trains and two engineers. There are four primary routes and return-loops incorporated in this track plan:

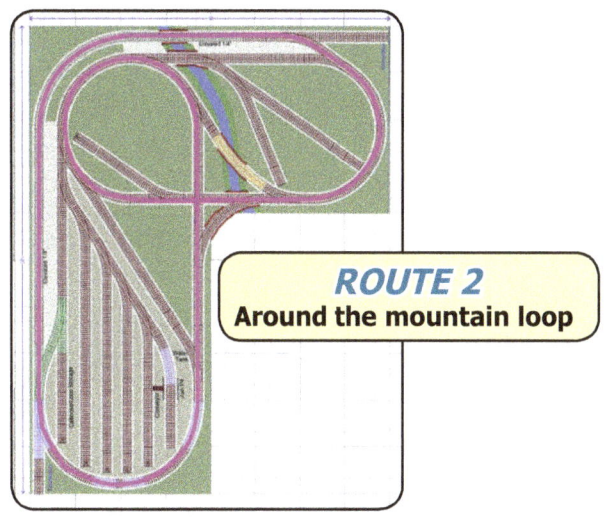

ROUTE 2
Around the mountain loop

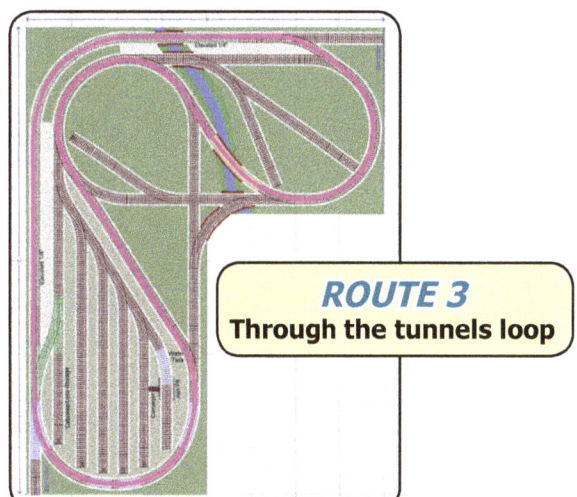

ROUTE 3
Through the tunnels loop

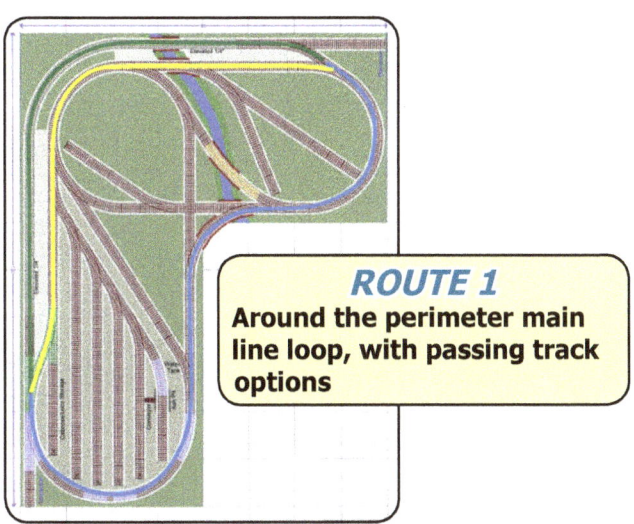

ROUTE 1
Around the perimeter main line loop, with passing track options

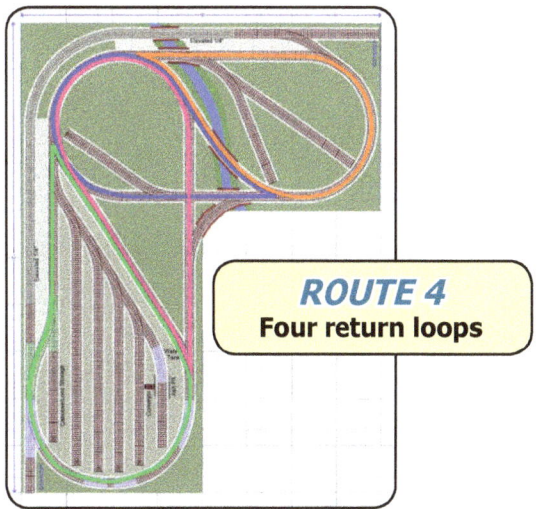

ROUTE 4
Four return loops

A Room Full of Operating Fun

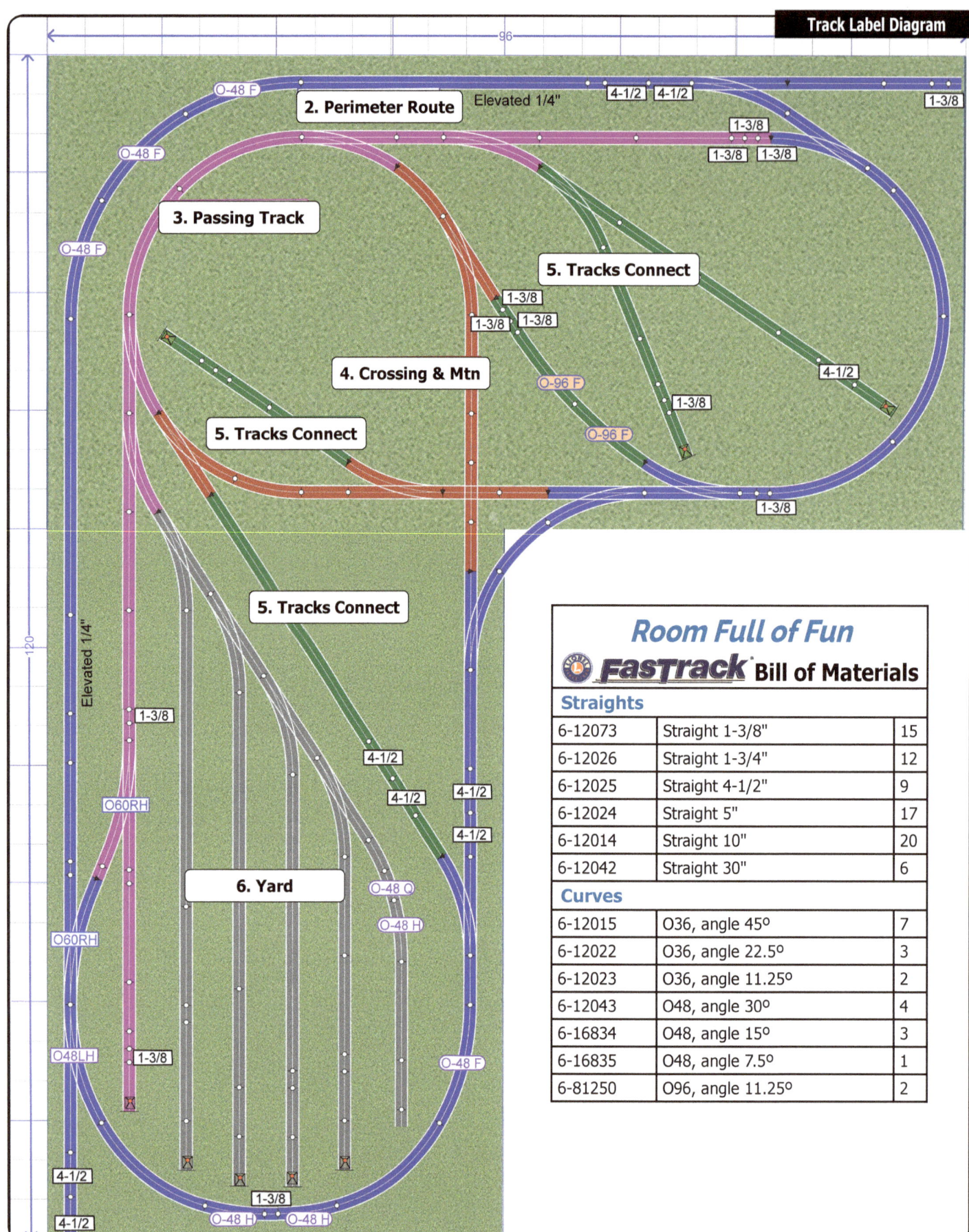

Room Full of Fun
FasTrack Bill of Materials

Switches		
6-12045 or 6-81947	O36 Left Remote or O36 Left Remote & Command	6
6-12046 or 6-81946	O36 Right Remote or O36 Right Remote & Command	12
6-12058 or 6-81950	O60 Right Remote or O60 Right Remote & Command	2
6-12065 or 6-81949	O48 Left Remote or O48 Left Remote & Command	1
Other Track Items		
6-12019	90° Crossing, 6"	1
6-12035	Lighted Bumper, 5"	8

The return loops allow trains to turn; but they also create multiple return-loop-to-return-loop routes, including green loop to orange loop, and blue loop around the outside perimeter to rose loop.

The only reverse curve is with the two O60 right-hand switches, separated by a 1-3/8" roadbed-trimmed section, which is very smooth for O36-capable locomotives and equipment.

A connecting railroad with shared trackage is shown with a gray strip. Imagining a connection with another railroad adds operating possibilities with trains envisioned to arrive from, and depart to, this connecting road, and with cars exchanged in the yard.

The layout includes a steam locomotive servicing facility in the lower section, and it includes a water tower with two pipes to reach both the locomotive track and the main line (for use when a passenger train pulls into the station, which would allow the locomotive to take on water while passengers are boarding). Also included is an ash pit with a conveyor to fill a hopper on the adjacent track, and a coaling tower. Locomotives can be parked here and across the lower section on a track that will accommodate locomotives and cabooses.

Construction

The foundation for the layout can be created with a conventional plywood top, with supporting legs. Or, as an alternative, lightweight 2"-thick foam board might be considered. The foam board could simply be placed loose on tables, possibly even three folding tables.

Lionel's FasTrack is a fairly noisy system when attached directly to a wood platform, so I recommend that a vinyl grass mat or some other sound reducing material be used between the track and the table top. Check the **OGR Online Forum** (ogrforum.ogaugerr.com) for various threads from that have discussed sound-reducing techniques for FasTrack and other O gauge track systems.

If you build this on top of 2" foam board, the FasTrack layout is considerably quieter.

This layout is flat, and it can be constructed that way. But for visual interest, you may choose to elevate the outside main line at the left and top by 1/4" for a more interesting look. This can be done with 1 foot of 2% grade at each end of the elevated section. Prototype railroads occasionally can be seen with a main line that is slightly higher than a parallel passing track. This visual scenic idea is easy to do and may be a variation well worth considering. This is also a simple way for you to construct your first layout grade.

Build-Out over Time

This layout, with its many routing options, includes a good number of switches, which raises the cost to build it. For this reason, you could build the layout in stages. The stages are listed here with details on track sections you'll need for each stage. To spread out the cost, which primarily involves the cost of switches, you may choose to substitute straight or curved sections of track for O36 switches on a temporary basis, with plans to reuse those temporary sections elsewhere on the layout in the future. Substitute either a 10" straight section or a 1/4 O36 and 1/2 O36 curved sections, depending on the direction taken through the switch. Do not secure those yet in order to to allow for some wiggle room.

The Build-Out and Track Label diagrams identify the track with different colors for each build phase. Track curves and switch track sections that are not O36 are labeled, as are the straight sections that are not easy to differentiate: 4.5" and 1-3/8". The 5" and 1-3/4" sections are not labeled.

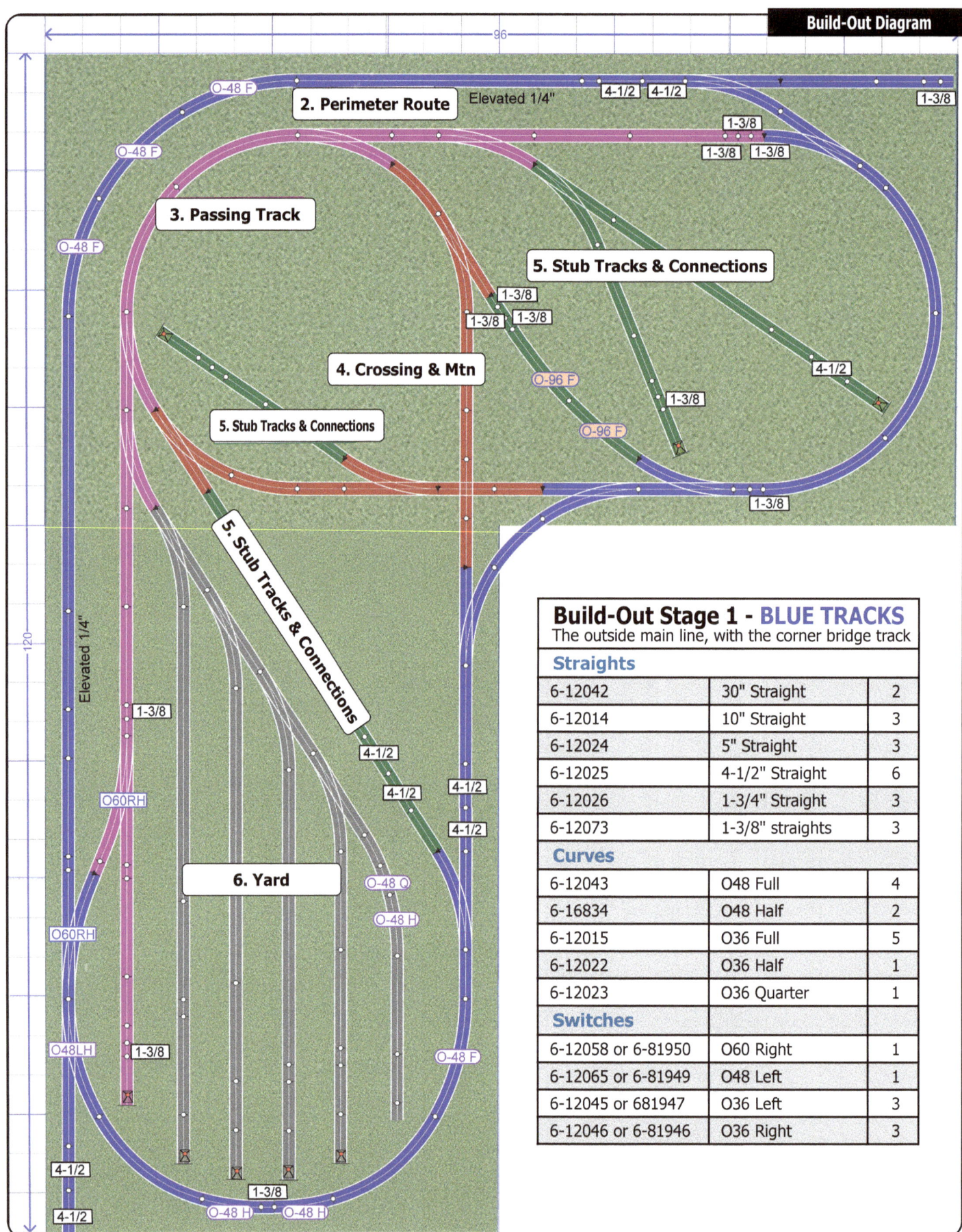

Build-Out Stage 2 - PURPLE TRACKS
Inside passing track and stub tracks

Straights

6-12014	10" Straight	5
6-12024	5" Straight	2
6-12026	1-3/4" Straight	2
6-12073	1-3/8" Straight	5
6-12035	5" Lighted Bumper	1

Curves

6-12015	O36 Full	2

Switches

6-12058 or 6-81950	O60 Right	1
6-12045 or 6-81947	O36 Left	2
6-12046 or 6-81946	O36 Right	2

Build-Out Stage 3 - RED TRACKS
Loop around the mountain with crossing

Straights

6-12014	10" Straight	1
6-12019	90° Crossing	1

Curves

6-12022	O36 Half	2

Switches

6-12045 or 6-81947	O36 Left	1
6-12046 or 6-81946	O36 Right	2

Build-Out Stage 4 - GREEN TRACKS
Stub Tracks and Connections

Straights

6-12042	30" Straight	1
6-12014	10" Straight	4
6-12024	5" Straight	3
6-12025	4-1/2" Straight	3
6-12026	1-3/4" Straight	3
6-12073	1-3/8" straights	4
6-12035	5" Lighted Bumper	3

Curves

6-81250	O96 Curve	2

Switches

6-12046 or 6-81946	O36 Right	1

Build-Out Stage 5 - GRAY TRACKS
The Yard

Straights

6-12042	30" Straight	3
6-12014	10" Straight	4
6-12024	5" Straight	4
6-12026	1-3/4" Straight	4
6-12035	5" Lighted Bumper	4

Curves

6-16834	O48 Half	1
6-16835	O48 Quarter	1
6-12023	O36 Quarter	1

Switches

6-12046 or 6-81946	O36 Right	4

Layout Control Systems

This plan can be constructed using conventional blocks and toggle switches, but due to the large number of blocks required to build and the complexity, this is the not optimal way to run this layout. In addition, a large number of blocks requires a lot of tedious block power wiring.

Instead, LionChief, TMCC, Legacy, and even MTH DCS command control systems are recommended, so two trains can run on the layout without tracking and flipping block assignment controls frequently. Engineers can then focus on managing the switches to dispatch their trains in the correct route.

As noted, this plan uses a great many FasTrack switches. How to control this many switches is your decision. I would suggest three options:

1) Some switches can be manual if they are within reach of the layout edge, with the rest remote-controlled, which requires a switch control panel or remote switch controllers mounted on the layout fascia.

2) Another idea is to use manual, push-pull controls in the fascia with all manual switches to save cost, and with controls positioned so they are easy to access and use by two engineers. But this would require a lot of time installing and fine-tuning switch control rods and knobs.

3) Yet another option is to use command control switches, and then operate them using command control. The cost to build using command-control switches is considerably more, but switch wiring time and expense is avoided. The switches draw power from the track, supported by the transformer.

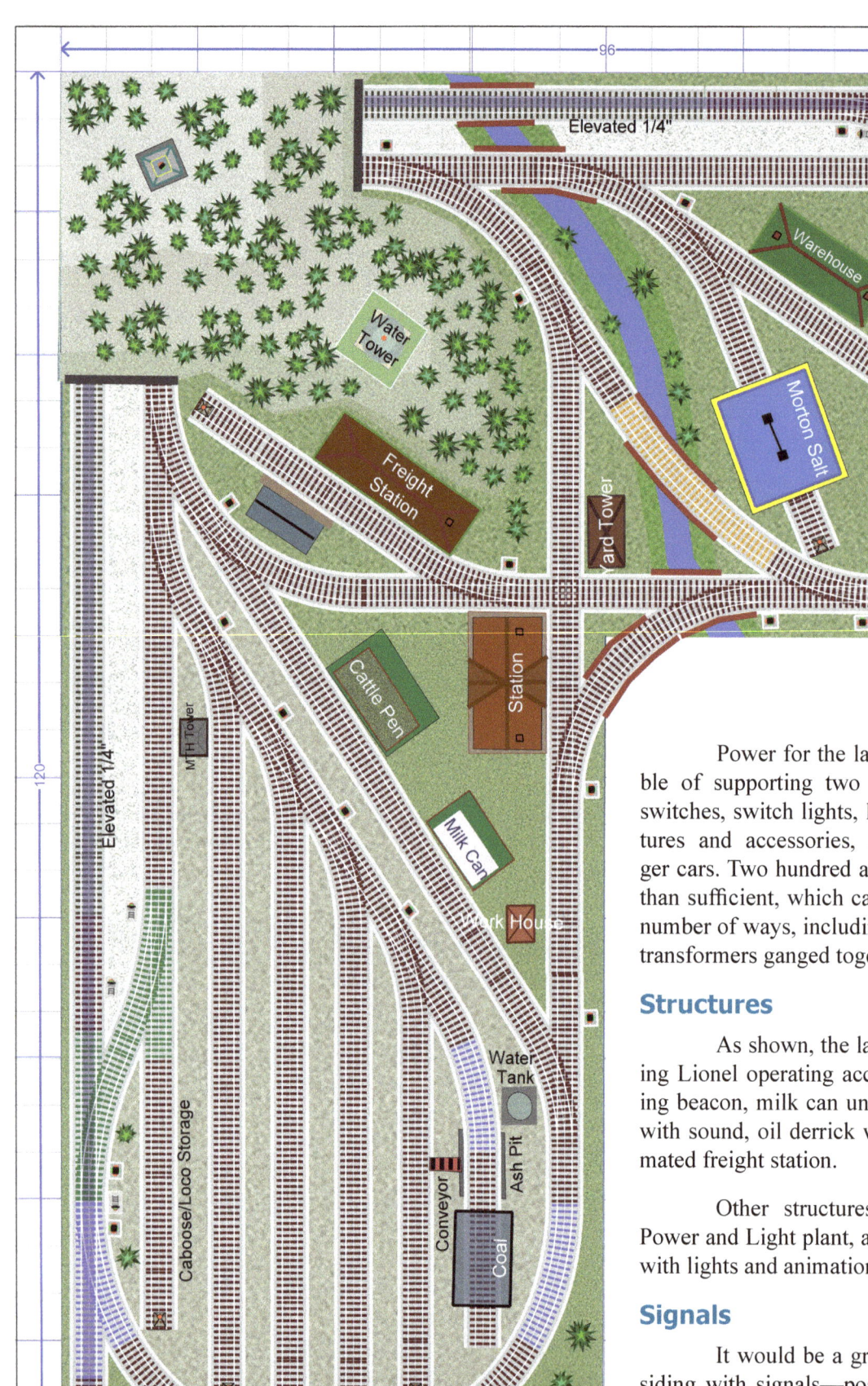

Power for the layout needs to be robust, capable of supporting two running locomotives, remote switches, switch lights, lighted bumpers, lighted structures and accessories, and possibly lighted passenger cars. Two hundred and forty watts should be more than sufficient, which can be obtained inexpensively a number of ways, including with three CW80 or similar transformers ganged together.

Structures

As shown, the layout plan includes the following Lionel operating accessories: coaling tower, rotating beacon, milk can unloader, cattle pen, work house with sound, oil derrick with ***nodding donkey***, and animated freight station.

Other structures indicated include Menards Power and Light plant, and Menards Morton Salt plant with lights and animation.

Signals

It would be a great idea to protect the passing siding with signals—possibly with two overhead signal bridges—so engineers can watch for the appropriate permissions.

Scenery

There are three scenic elements included in this plan: the previously mentioned optional elevation of the main line around the left and top, the mountain, and the stream. The mountain and stream should be constructed only after all the track is laid and secured so disruptions as new sections are built do not interfere with the scenery. A variety of modern techniques and materials, such as those described in scenery manuals from Woodland Scenics and other print and online sources, can be consulted for useful scenery-building ideas.

The bridges over the river might be modeled with flexible wood or plastic wrapped around the edges of the track and then detailed and painted to look like a steel bridge.

Finally, the layout should be decorated with your choices for trees and bushes. The grass mat foundation, if used, can be detailed and colored to suggest different types of ground cover.

Light Show

In a darkened room for nighttime operations, this layout will provide a striking view if fitted with the incredible number of lighting possibilities, including the animated signage on the power plant and Morton Salt tower, a rotating beacon, blinking light on the water tower, structure lights, yard lighting, lighted switches, and lighted bumpers. Plus, the headlights and other lights of operating trains will certainly enhance the effect.

Expansion Possibilities

This layout easily expands to the right or left, with additional switches to extend either or both loops. In addition, a turntable could be added within the upper-right loop, replacing the industry tracks. This is not necessary for operation since the four reverse loops allow locomotives and trains to easily reverse direction, but who doesn't like having a turntable?

Conclusion

During construction, you and your kids can show visitors the build-out plans for the complete layout, and discuss and show where planned features will be added. The complete layout will be a blast to operate with two trains, with many routes and operating possibilities!

Happy Railroading!

www.ogaugerr.com

Your source for 2-Rail and 3-Rail Modeling Online

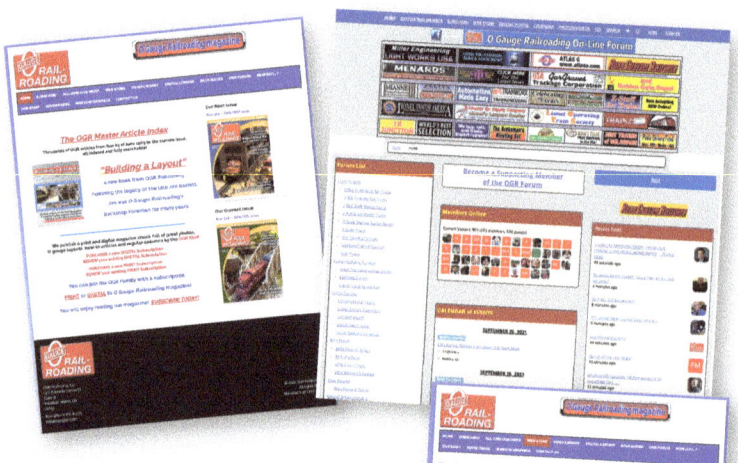

What You'll find at ogaugerr.com

- *OGR* Forum
- Find Local *OGR* Dealers
- Find Local Train Meets
- Order from the *OGR* Online Store
- Subscribe/Renew your Subscription
- Much, Much More!

Visit ogaugerr.com or call 800-980-6477

OGR Publishing, Inc.
1310 Eastside Centre Court, Ste. 6
Mountain Home, AR 72653

Summit Canyon RR on a Shelf
A 2'4"x 14' Lionel FasTrack Layout

The Summit Canyon Railroad is a short switchback railroad on a 2'4" wide shelf, that uses a switchback at 5% grade to travel from Glenwood Springs at 0 elevation to the town of Summit at 6-3/8" elevation.

You can switch cars and build short trains to move freight and passengers between the flatland at Glenwood Springs to the elevated Summit, servicing the industries and the mine.

There is a connecting main line that runs through Glenwood Springs and pierces the mountains at the right below the elevated tracks of Summit.

This layout also boasts two hidden storage tracks under Summit, and a car transfer *cassette* to rotate cars (and locos if desired) on and off the layout at the left.

The design of a switchback layout starts with the length of the switchback leads, here set at 35", which will allow a locomotive and two to three cars to make the climb. The second design aspect is creating a switchback grade of sufficient length to climb to the elevated terrain. For the Summit Canyon RR, the grade percentage is 5%, and the elevation at Summit is 6.4". The overall length of the layout then must accommodate two switchback leads, one at each end, and two grades of sufficient length to make the desired elevation at the desired grade. The two switchback leads (one at each end), one grade, and the length of two switches set the overall length of the layout at 14'.

The minimum curve diameter is O60, allowing O54 and smaller diameter equipment to work the layout.

Construction and Grades

The layout is constructed with two 7' long and 2'4" wide shelves attached to and supported by brackets on a 14'-long wall. Plywood or 2"-thick foam lengths can be used for the shelves. A notch in the shelf at the left allows for a removable module so a rolling car-loading cassette can be plugged into the layout.

The grade is based on Woodland Scenics inclines for a 5% grade. Woodland Scenics uses an 8' length (96") for their grades, so their grades are calculated based on a rise over 96" rather than 100". Consequently, the Woodland Scenics inclines are a bit steeper. Woodland Scenics offers inclines of 2%, 3%, and 4%, which are easy to use and curve to match the curvature of the tracks. To create a 5% incline, it is simple to glue a 2% and 3% incline directly on top of each other (I suggest regular white glue or another foam-safe glue). The precise grade of Woodland Scenics 5% inclines is 5.2%.

Determining the height of the layout shelf starts with the height of the car-loading cassette, and the platform to support the car tracks on the top of the cassette.

Car-Loading Cassette

The car-loading cassette is 35" long, with four tracks of that length. The cassette plugs into the layout as shown, replacing the lift-out module to connect to two tracks on the level layout at the left. Cars can then move onto and off the layout manually, or be moved by a locomotive. The cassette is reversible, so the four tracks can be used to hold cars by rotating the cassette to have two tracks connect at a time. The cassette is constructed on top of a wheeled tool caddy, with storage shelves for tools, parts, and more cars and locomotives.

A variety of tool caddy carts are available; choose one less than or equal to the 35" length that will support a shelf with four tracks. Build and secure a top to hold the tracks, adding elevation and additional shelves, if desired, to reach the intended layout height above the floor. Moving and rotating the car-loading cassette is easy if it sits on a flat floor without a carpet. For a carpeted floor, the construction adds one additional consideration because the vertical alignment of the car tracks may not precisely match the layout height after rolling and rotating the cart around. Adding thumb screws to adjust the height of the top surface by a small amount will facilitate matching the height of the layout and cart for cars to roll on an off without problems.

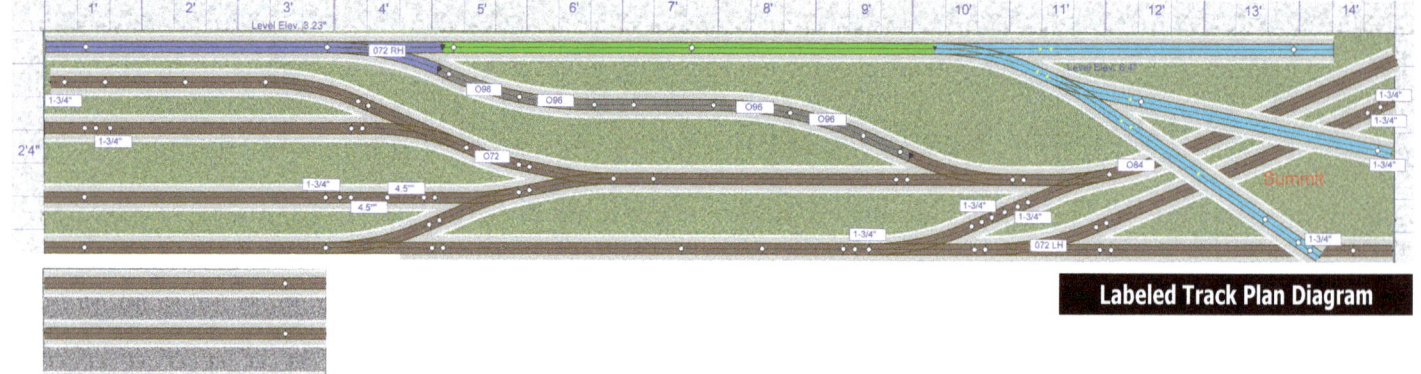

Labeled Track Plan Diagram

Summit Canyon RR
Lionel FasTrack Bill of Materials

Straights		
6-12042	Straight 30"	16
6-12014	Straight 10"	10
6-12024	Straight 5"	13
6-12025	Straight 4-1/2"	1
6-12026	Straight 1-3/4"	10
6-12035	Bumper (Lighted) 5"	5
6-12073	Straight 1-3/8"	6
Trimmed roadbed 1-3/8" straights (also are included with switches)		19
Curves		
6-81250	O96 Curve	4
6-12061	O84 Curve	1
6-12055	O72 Half Curve	1
6-12056	O60 Curve	1
Switches		
6-12048 or 6-81953	O72 Left	1
6-12049 or 6-81952	O72 Right	1
6-12057 or 6-81951	O60 Left	3
6-12058 or 6-81950	O60 Right	2
6-12047 or 6-81954	O72 Wye	4

Operations on the Summit Canyon Railroad

Many different operating schemes and switching plans can be devised for operational fun. A wide variety of loads with different intended destinations is facilitated by the flexibility of having the car-loading cassette with four tracks of cars. The layout also has two hidden tracks, which can be used to stage a short train or locomotive; or alternatively, each can hold hidden cars. On the main line through Glenwood Springs, cars can enter and leave the layout, and switching can be variable with the added consideration of setting out cars for interchange with the main line.

Conventional control can be used, with either manual or remote switches. One idea to consider is the use of FasTrack command control switches and the Legacy system (full Legacy or Legacy Lite) to control switches and set routes from the handheld. Legacy and TMCC locomotives designed for up to O54 diameter can be used, as well as LionChief+ locomotives with remote couplers.

Additional remote uncoupler tracks can be added, if desired, so you can break a cut of cars in two. A suggestion would be to have one remote uncoupler on each of the industry tracks, and one mounted between the stations on the passing track. Remote uncouplers are not needed on the switchback leads, the locomotive service track, or on the hidden tracks beneath Summit.

Scenery Construction and Structures

Scenery is based on the switchback grade inclines; the level tracks at Summit, with the main line and hidden tracks beneath; and a tall Flatiron Mountain in the middle of the layout, pierced by two switchback grades. Lay out the level tracks first, then build the switchback grades. Then add the flat, elevated shelf for the tracks at Summit. Fill in the terrain around the switchback grades, and finally work on Flatiron Mountain. Populate the layout with trees while adding structures.

An example set of structures are shown, using Lionel's Suburban Station and Animated Freight Station in the center. The layout also shows the use of Lionel's operating cattle pen, milk can platform, coal loader, and rotating beacon. A mine, station, and an industry of some type should be selected for Summit. Other structures can be added as desired.

Build-Out Diagram

Labeled Track Plan Diagram

On the Labeled Track Plan Diagram, switches are left-hand and right-hand O60 and O72 wye. Two O72 switches are labeled. You can choose the manual/remote or command-controlled switches. FasTrack switches are packaged with the 1-3/8" trimmed roadbed straights.

There is one O60 curve in the loco service track; otherwise, the O72, O84, and O96 curves are labeled.

The small section 1-3/4" straights are labeled; the other short sections are 1-3/8". The half section sized 4-1/2" sections are labeled. Unlabeled are 5", 10", and 30" straight sections.

Summing Up the Summit Canyon RR

The Summit Canyon Railroad is a fun layout in a small space that will fit along a wall without requiring the width needed to turn trains around in a circle, which would otherwise need about 64" minimum for O60 turn-around curves. The plan has an attractive look, with the layout divided into three scenes, the tracks at the left where the cassette plugs in; the runaround track in front of Flatiron Mountain in the center; and the elevated tracks and industries at Summit, with the main line and staging beneath. Many operating schemes and car-load variability will keep you engaged for hours with switching and planning train movements, in addition to running the switchback.

Happy Railroading!

Anaconda Mining Railroad
A Compact Lionel FasTrack Layout

Photo 1

The Anaconda RR is a switchback 4x8 plan using Lionel O gauge FasTrack, with two trains for two engineers. The railroad basically has an oval of track, connected to two switchback curves at 4% to reach 6" elevation at the mine on the upper level. The main line plunges beneath the mine though a tunnel, with modest grades of 2% to make the descent. This is a good beginner's layout plan that will provide a lot of good fun and develop experience with train operation planning, simple grades, and scenery with elevations and a tunnel.

Layout Plan and Operation

This railroad moves ore from the elevated mine in small ore cars led by a Lionel Dockside locomotive. The train moves down the switchback to a destination in the lower right consisting of either a bridge to a connection beyond the layout, or to a car ferry that would shuttle cars across the bay (which is off-layout and not shown here). Two trains can pass each other on the lower pair of tracks on the switchback. Each train should be just long enough to fit on those lower tracks.

Shown in Photo 1 is the Lionel Granite Run Quarry train set with a Docksider, four ore cars, a shorty tank car, and a bobber caboose. The short tank car carries water that can be used to extinguish any line-side fires started by cinders from the steam locomotives, and it is also used to spray down the surface of the ore loads to reduce the possibility of ore dust coating any line-side scenery and structures. Miners can hitch a ride on the caboose from the station to their work at the mine. You can use whatever locomotives and cars you have available and are certainly not limited to the Lionel Granite Run Quarry sets.

Operation includes some interesting features as trains shuttle up and down the switchback grades, with locos sometimes pushing the train uphill or leading the train downhill.

Trains must back into the mine at the upper left, so ore cars are spotted beneath the mine for loading. There are two tracks on grade at the mine, for both loads and empties, with the tracks at the very end of the tracks level. The engine is available to shuttle cars from one track to another as they are filled.

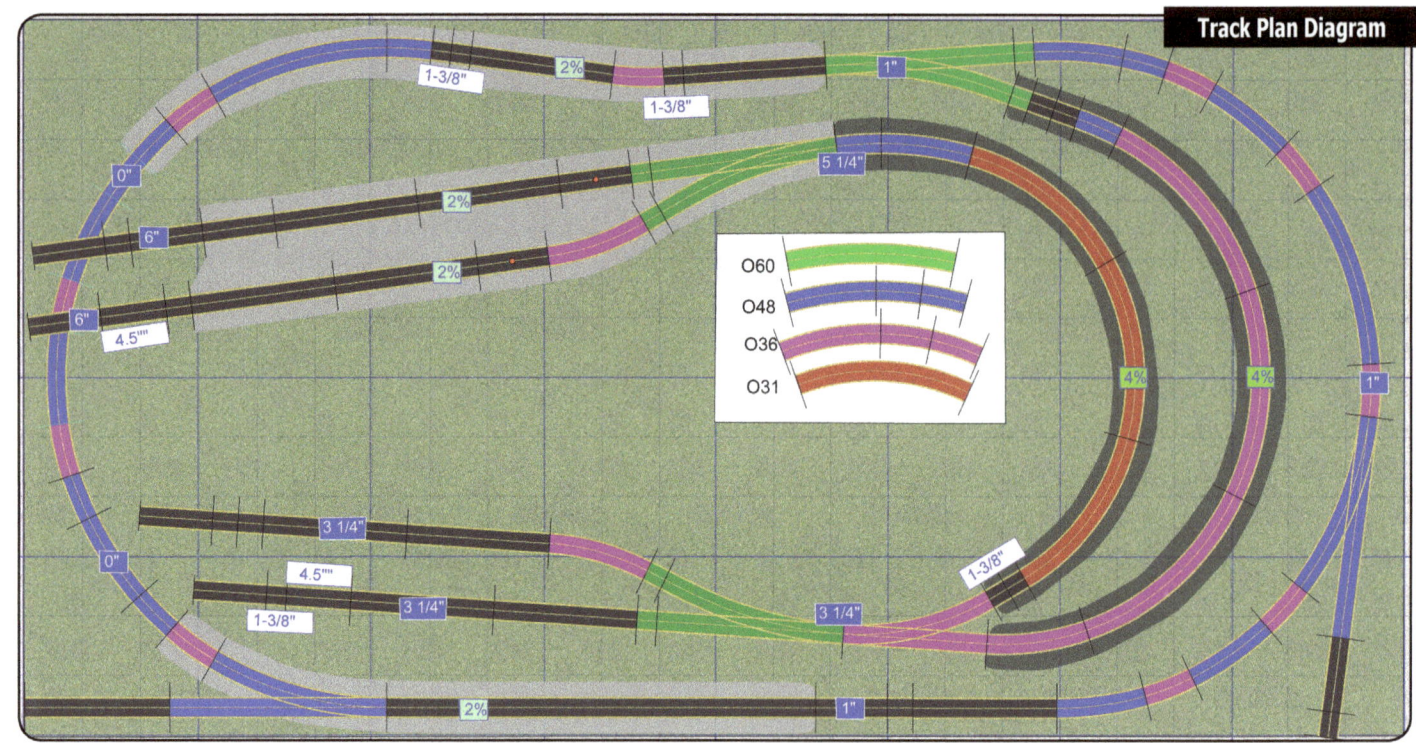

Track Plan Diagram

At the midlevel tracks, one train must wait for the other to arrive so they can pass each other, faced nose in toward the lighted bumpers. These tracks are level, so there is no risk of cars running downhill in the event of a coupler disconnect or a knuckle break.

At the bottom of the hill is the loop for continuous running, with a track at the lower right that connects to the ore destination. The destination is shown as a removable 30" straight FasTrack section, which can be connected for operation (sticking out from the layout), and then disconnected when the layout is not in use. This destination track can be supported on a narrow folding table or a folding sawhorse, as seen in Photo 2 (plastic or steel are available) with the track on top, set level with the layout.

Photo 2

At the lower level, the locomotive must use the oval to run around the train in order to push the cars onto the destination track. Alternatively, the track on the lower left of the loop with the Acme Machine Shop building can connect to an off-layout destination for ore and can also be used for a main line connection to another railroad to generate

Anaconda Mining Railroad
Lionel FasTrack Bill of Materials

Straights		
6-12042	Straight 30"	2
6-12014	Straight 10"	12
6-12024	Straight 5"	4
6-12025	Straight 4-1/2"	2
6-12026	Straight 1-3/4"	8
6-12073	Straight 1-3/8"	6*
* The 1-3/8" Straights are included with the switches		
6-12020	Uncoupling track	2
6-12035	Lighted Bumper	4
Curves		
6-37103	O31 Curve, angle 45°	3
6-12015	O36 Curve, angle 45°	3
6-12022	O36 Curve, angle 22.5°	1
6-12023	O36 Curve, angle 11.25°	10
6-12043	O48 Curve, angle 30°	2
6-16834	O48 Curve, angle 15°	8
6-16835	O48 Curve, angle 7.5°	8
Switches		
6-12045 or 6-81947	O36 Left	1
6-12066 or 6-81948	O48 Right	2
6-12057 or 6-81951	O60 Left	1
6-12058 or 6-81950	O60 Right	2

traffic. This track can also be a convenient connection for further layout expansion. And if the equivalent O48 curve at the top left is replaced by another switch, a passing track can be added to the left, allowing for more layout expansion.

Layout Construction

Any preferred method may be used to support a simple 4x8 sheet of plywood or 2"-thick 4x8 sheet of extruded Polystyrene foam. The layout as shown is faced with 1x4s, but these are optional.

As noted earlier, the ore destination is a 30" section of FasTrack. This is removable, as it otherwise sticks out from the layout. To facilitate easy connection and disconnection from the main layout, the ball of the ball-and-socket of each end of both sections of FasTrack at this joint should be filed down a bit. This is easy to do since the plastic FasTrack base is workable plastic. Modifying this joint tension will not affect track alignment or electrical conductivity.

Sections, Grades, and Elevations

The Track Plan Diagram shows that curves of O31, O36, and O48 are used in the track plan, and each is highlighted with a different color. The widest O48 curves are in the lowest-level main line loop. O36 is used to make the first switchback curve, and O31 is used for the final highest switchback curve to the mine tracks. The O60 switches come with 1-3/8" straight sections with roadbed trimmed, which are also highlighted with the O60 switches themselves. In the illustration, 1-3/8" and 4.5" short straight sections are labeled, while 1-3/4" and 5" short sections are not.

The illustration also shows the five grades incorporated in the plan. Two grades are 4%, and three are 2%. Each grade is outlined with light (2%) or darker (4%) gray. Track that is not outlined is level, but at different flat levels, as indicated. Of note are the two 2% grades at the top and bottom of the main line oval in light gray, which allow the line to descend one inch to pass beneath the mine above at 6" through a tunnel, with easy vertical clearance within. If it is desired to have the entire main line loop at one consistent level, the switchback curves must be at a steeper 5% grade to make the top. Grades less than or no greater than 6% are recommended.

Making the grades is easy if using Woodland Scenics inclines and risers, which come in 2% and 4% inclines (Photo 3). These are foam lengths in an accordion-cut shape, which can be easily curved to follow the track. The inclines can be used to directly support the tracks, or used simply as guides to get the elevations right. Woodland Scenics inclines and risers are 3" wide, while FasTrack is 3-1/2" wide, so plan to add some outside support posts against the foam risers to support the track width at each section joint.

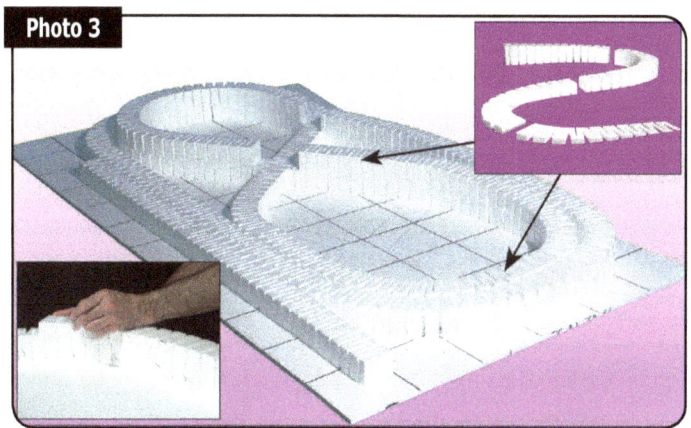

Power and Control

The Lionel Dockside sets are controlled with Lion-Chief Plus 2.0 wireless command control, which simplifies the layout for operating two trains on the same lines. Power need only be run to the layout, without the use of insulated track joints. It is recommended that one power drop be connected to the middle of each of the three curves on the right to feed power consistently to the entire layout.

Conventional wiring with block control may also be used, with four blocks:

1) The main level loop and the lowest level switchback curve should be individual blocks.
2) Each midlevel passing track must have its own block (two blocks).
3) The final switchback curve and the two tracks to the mine can all be one block.

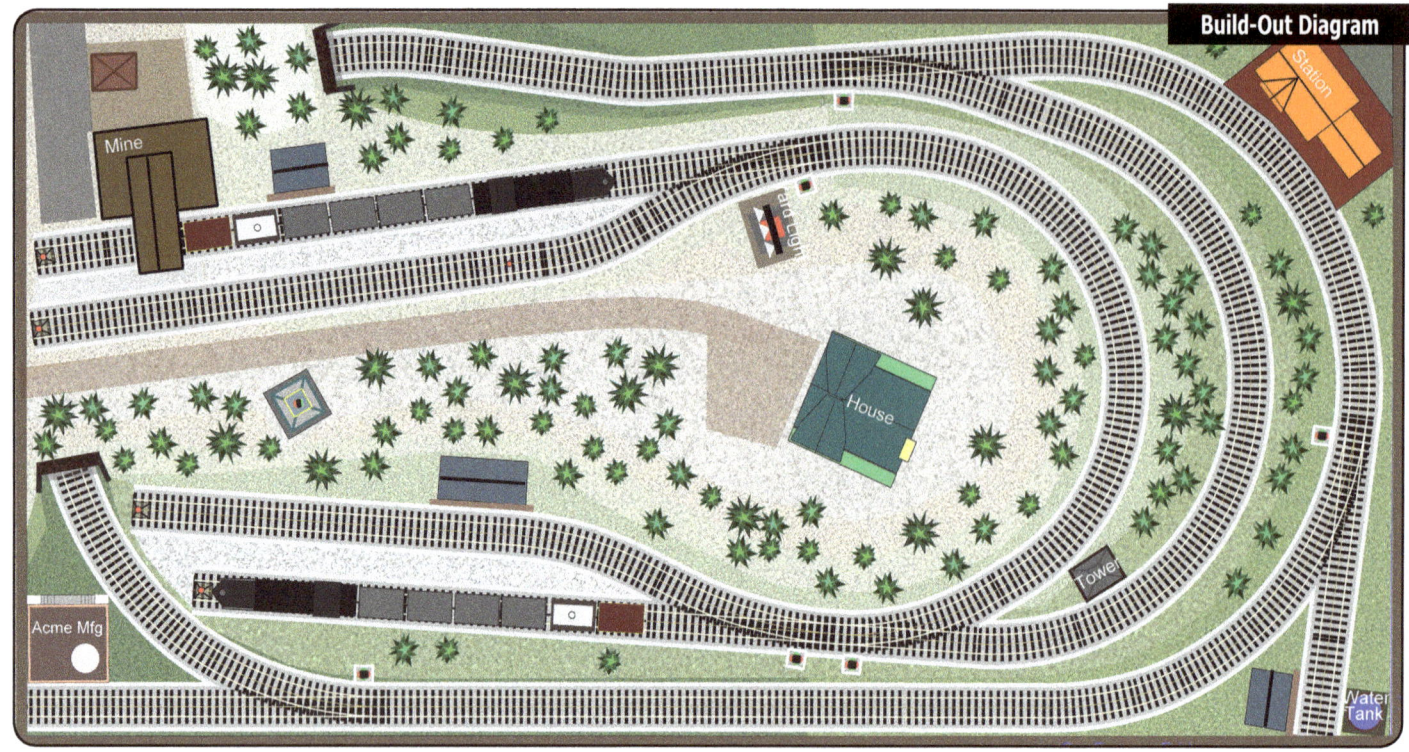

Switches and Wiring

This small layout has a total of six FasTrack switches: three O60, two O48, and one O36. If the layout allows access to three sides, all switches can be easily reached using manual switches. If this small layout table is on casters or wheels, the layout can be pulled out for operation and access to manual switches.

Remote switches can also be used, requiring that the switch controllers be wired with wires running beneath the layout to switch controllers placed along the front edge of the layout (not shown). Alternatively, command-control switches can be used with Lionel TMCC/Legacy, powered by the track, so no additional wiring at all would be needed to the switches. This would certainly simplify layout construction (but at an increased cost for each switch).

Scenery and Structures

As you can see in the Build-Out Diagram, building the scenery on this layout is fun, with the mountain rising up the middle of the layout and the switchbacks curving around the slopes. Once the tracks are down and supported on their risers and grades, the mountain can be filled in between the tracks and then colored and decorated. The different levels of tracks will add an attractive and interesting look to the layout. The mountain rises above the level of the mine tracks to provide more of a visual separation between the two long sides of the layout, with the house in the middle of the mountain above the switchback curves. You can place trees around the layout as you desire.

Structures include:

- Lionel Rotating Beacon Tower
- Lionel Work House with sound
- Lionel Yard Light
- Ameri-Towne No. 442 Acme Machine Shop
- Woodland Scenics Station

Other structures can be included from various manufacturers or scratchbuilt, including the mine, a warehouse, a small switch tower, a shack by the track at the ore destination, a water tower for the locomotives, and the shorty tank car.

A Fun and Easy First Two-Train Layout Plan

The Anaconda Mining RR is compact and easy-to-build on a simple 4x8 platform and will provide hours of fun operating two trains up and down the switchbacks, passing at the midlevel tracks. The construction of the mountain and grades, with one tunnel, are a good initial challenge for the beginning railroader.

Happy Railroading!

The Easy-A Railroad
Dual Layout Possibilities Using Atlas O Track

The Easy-A Railroad is an O54/O45 easy-access layout designed as either a 10x10 corner layout or a 6x12 along-the-wall pike. Track components for this layout are all Atlas O.

In either the corner version or along-the-wall configuration, the Easy-A RR is designed for two-train operation with track diameters of O54 and O45. The railroad uses both Atlas O sectional track and Atlas O Flex-Track (cut sections of straight can be substituted for the Flex-Track).

Either arrangement provides good reach and access around the layout, with reverse loops, two crossings, crossovers between the concentric loops, a small yard with a steam locomotive service track, and a few industry tracks.

The outside loop of O54 has a passing siding and an industry track or two. The inside O45 loop allows O42 and smaller equipment to run anywhere on the layout, with reverse-loops, tracks, and a small yard.

Both configurations have two 40" lift-out bridges that allow access to the center access and operating area.

Construction and Access

The layout base can be constructed as either a single 6x12 table, or in two sections as an L-shaped 10x10. Access and reach are very good as a 6x12, with two corner access areas requiring either an under-table access to either or both corner-access areas.

The 10x10 corner configuration has good access from two centered access areas, with the back area reached by rolling under the main table.

The 10x10 is actually a bit less than that full measure, coming in at 9'9" by 9'9". There are no S curves on the main lines; and all connections and tracks curve in a single direction, with the exception of the locomotive service track, through a left-hand and right-hand O45 switch. Switches are O54 and O45, with two No. 5 switches in the corner arrangement. Track center spacing is 4.5" minimum. The Flex-Track sections are all straight and all curves are sectional track. Straight sections of 40" fixed track can be cut to length instead of using Flex-Track.

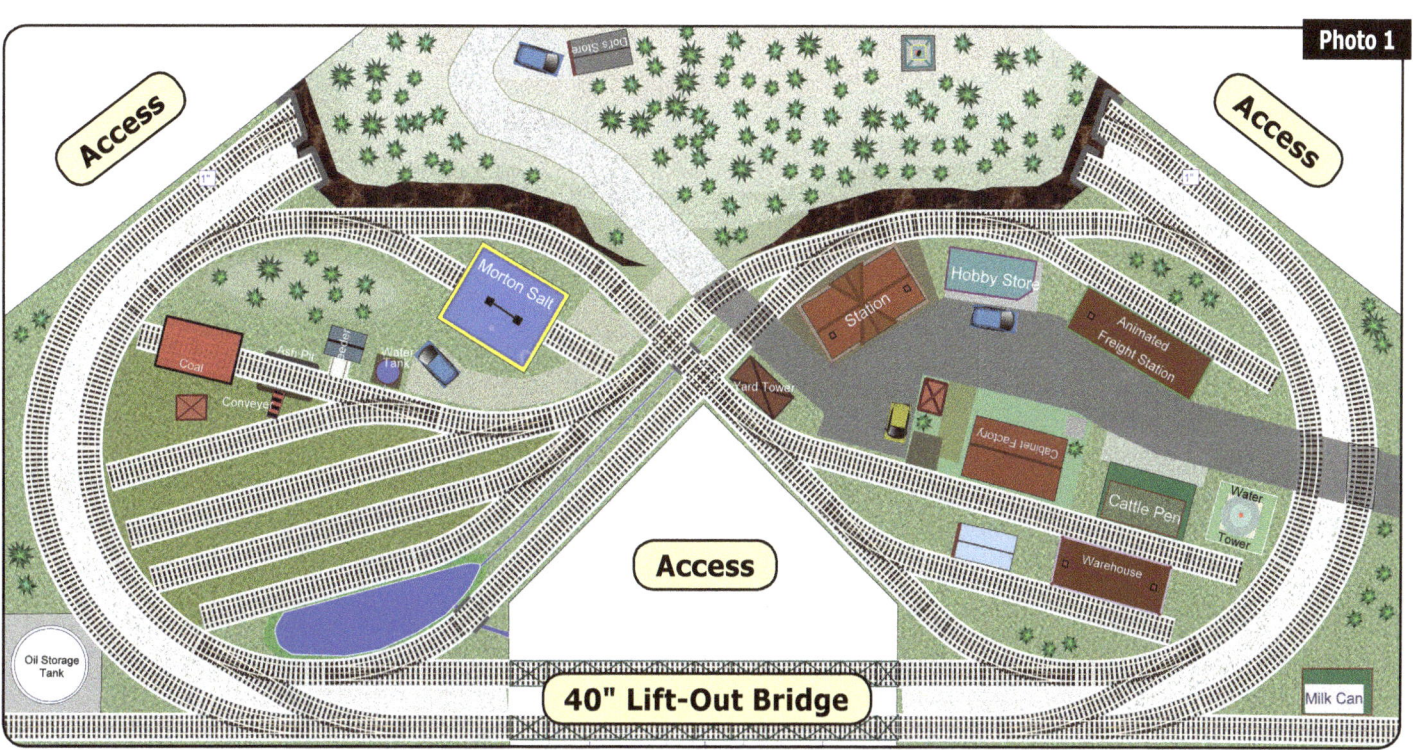

Photo 1

The front of the layout has two 40" lift-out bridges as single sections of Atlas O 40" straight track. These could, alternatively, be assembled as one double-track lift-out bridge. If you are comfortable with a duck-under, the double-track bridges could be constructed as fixed rather than lift-out.

Terrain

The layout in either configuration is mostly flat, with a mountain with tunnels hiding the O54 passing track and the back leg of the O45 loop. For a visual interest option, the O54 rises with a slope of 1.5% from the loop crossovers to the mountain entrance, continuing under the mountain at 1" in height. The layout can be constructed entirely flat if you wish. There are water features of a small pond with streams.

The front face of the mountain is shown as a rock face, which can be created with rock molds or by carving plaster or foam. The ceiling of the tunnels is 7" above the layout base to accommodate the grade and the 1" elevation of the outside loops. If constructed without the grade, the tunnel ceiling can be at 6".

Operation

The layout has two concentric loops (O54 and O45), with the interior O45 loop having a figure-eight embedded, thus allowing reverse loops and train direction reversing. The two loops are connected with smooth crossovers. There is a small four-track yard, with a yard lead that can be operated without interfering with the interior O45 route, only precluding the inside O45 figure-eight while switching. Both layout configurations have a connection to another railroad or branch, so cars can be interchanged and staged in the hidden passing-track under the mountain. Three trains can be on the layout, with one staged and taking turns running the layout and switching.

A local train can leave the yard and circle the loops, then switch the industries of the inside O45 loop. One or two industries can be added as tracks off the outside O54 main line loop. Two trains can run the loops without intervention for solo train-watching. A typical out-and-back run from the yard through the inside and outside loops would involve servicing industries and then reversing through one of the reverse-loops of the inside O45 main line to loop in the other direction, and then return to the yard.

Wiring and Control

The Easy-A can be wired using conventional block control, with four blocks for each loop (left-hand, right-hand, front straight section, and back straight section). The passing track could constitute a ninth block. Yard tracks should each have an on/off switch to shut off power in the track in order to park an engine.

The layout is at its best running command control, such as LionChief, MTH DCS, and/or Lionel TMCC/Legacy. This avoids the hassle of wiring blocks and switching block toggles while running trains.

With just two trains, and a third train waiting in staging, power requirements are modest and would be handled by two Lionel CW80 or MTH Z-1000 transformers for conventional block control wiring, which can then be ganged together with a power strip to power the entire layout in command control. A single wire and toggle switch can connect the black terminal of the transformers, allowing them to run independently for block control, or ganged together for command control, as desired. You can then choose to run your treasured conventional locomotives along with modern command control engines.

As a minimum, the two loops should be wired as separate blocks, with a third block being the passing track. This provides options for both conventional and command control with a minimum of block wiring to the tracks.

The Atlas O switches can also be controlled under TMCC/Legacy using Z-Stuff for Trains (www.z-stuff.net) DZ-2500 slow-speed switch machines (above-table or under-table) connected to the Command Base through a single-wire data buss from a DZ-2001, which is wired to the transformers.

Structures

As shown, the layout has the Morton Salt Tower, Station, Hobby Store, and Cabinet Factory from Menards. Lionel items include the Animated Freight Station, Rotary Beacon, Cattle Pen, Milk Can Unloader, Water Tower, Yard Tower, Coaling Tower, Oil Storage Tank, and one Workhouse with sound. OGR's Ameri-Towne line gives us Dotty's Store. Other manufacturers can provide items such as the speeder shack and a couple of warehouses.

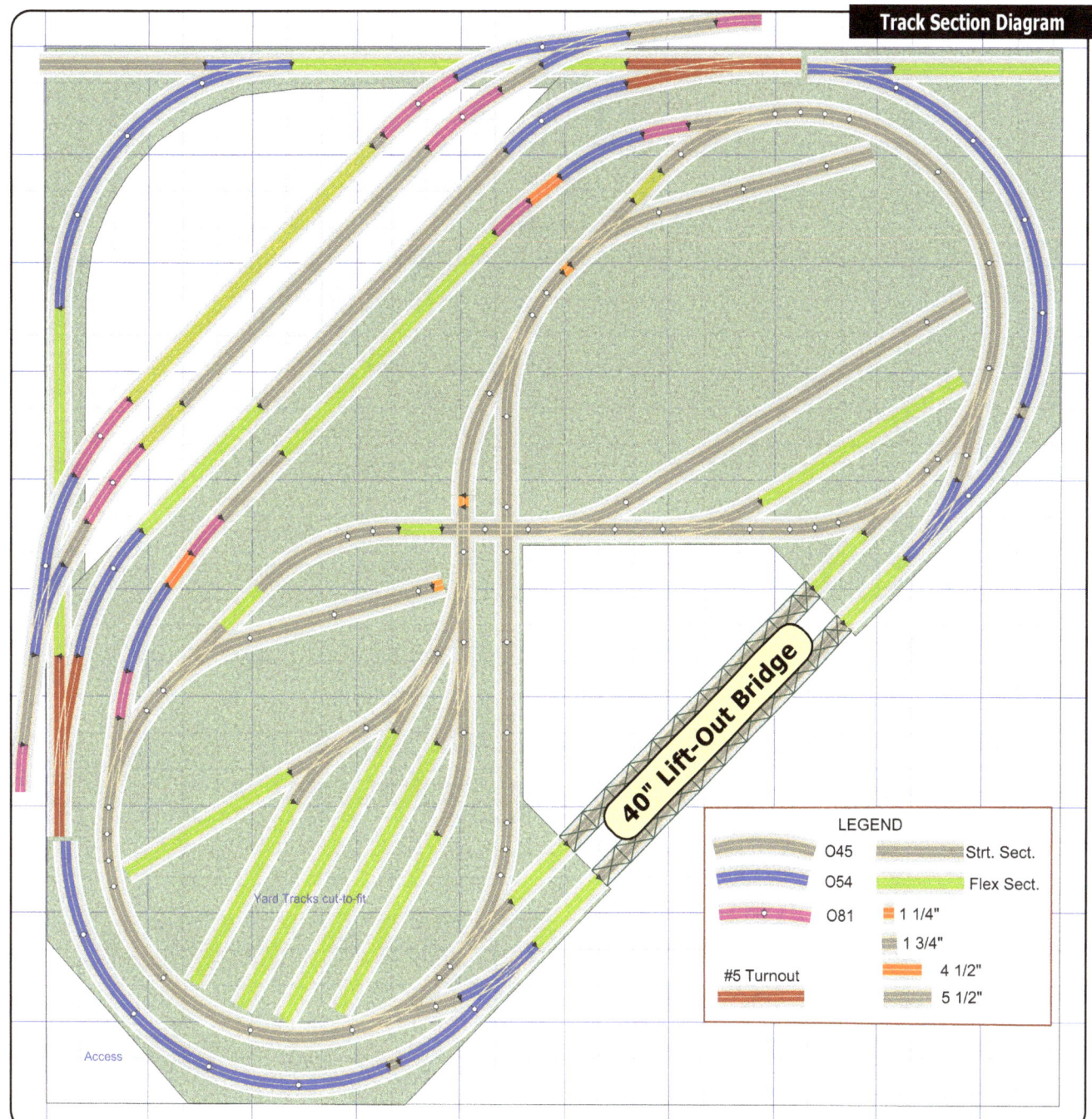

Track Section Diagram

The Easy-A RR Track Section Diagram above shows the sections needed by color. There are three curve diameters used, O45, O54, and O81. Short straight sections are hard to differentiate: 1-1/4" and 4-1/2" are highlighted with color, while 1-3/4" and 5-1/2" are the background straight and O45 color. The two No. 5 switches are highlighted with RED.

Flex-Track sections are highlighted with their own color. These are all straight sections; all curves in the layout are sectional to assure perfect alignment. Cut sections of straight track can be used instead of flex, which will ensure that these tangent (straight) sections are perfectly straight.

A Flexible Plan for a Modest-Size Layout

The Easy-A RR provides good fun in either configuration, hosting two engineers and trains, with a third train in hidden staging. Two trains can run the loops for solo train-watching. Train-routing operations keep things interesting, with the crossovers, inside figure-eight, reverse-loops, and some industries to service. With its good reach and access, construction and maintenance will be straightforward and pleasurable, with few hard-to-reach derailments to deal with. The Easy-A RR is an excellent first or second layout, or family layout, providing O gauge fun and excitement for years to come.

Happy Railroading!

The Easy-A Railroad

The Easy-A Railroad
Bill of Materials

	TRACK ITEM	BOTH BUILDS	ADD FOR CORNER 10X10	ADD FOR 6X12
Curves				
6012	O81 Curve, angle 7.5°	4	0	10
6060	O54 Curve, angle 22.5°	13	5	2
6061	O54 Curve, angle 11.25°	0	2	0
6045	O45 Curve, angle 30°	9	0	0
6046	O45 Curve, angle 7.5°	20	0	0
Straights				
6015	Straight 1 -1/4"	5	0	0
6052	Straight 1 -3/4"	4	0	0
6051	Straight 4 -1/2"	7	0	0
6053	Straight 5 -1/2"	3	0	2
6050	Straight 10"	9	0	2
6058	Straight 40"	3	1	1
6056	Flex or Straight 40" Cut to fit	19	2	1
6080	Crossing 90°	2	0	0
Switches				
6085	O45 Left switch	7	0	0
6086	O45 Right switch	8	0	0
6070	O54 Left switch	1	1	1
6071	O54 Right switch	2	0	1
6024	No. 5 Left switch	0	1	0
6025	No. 5 Right	0	1	0

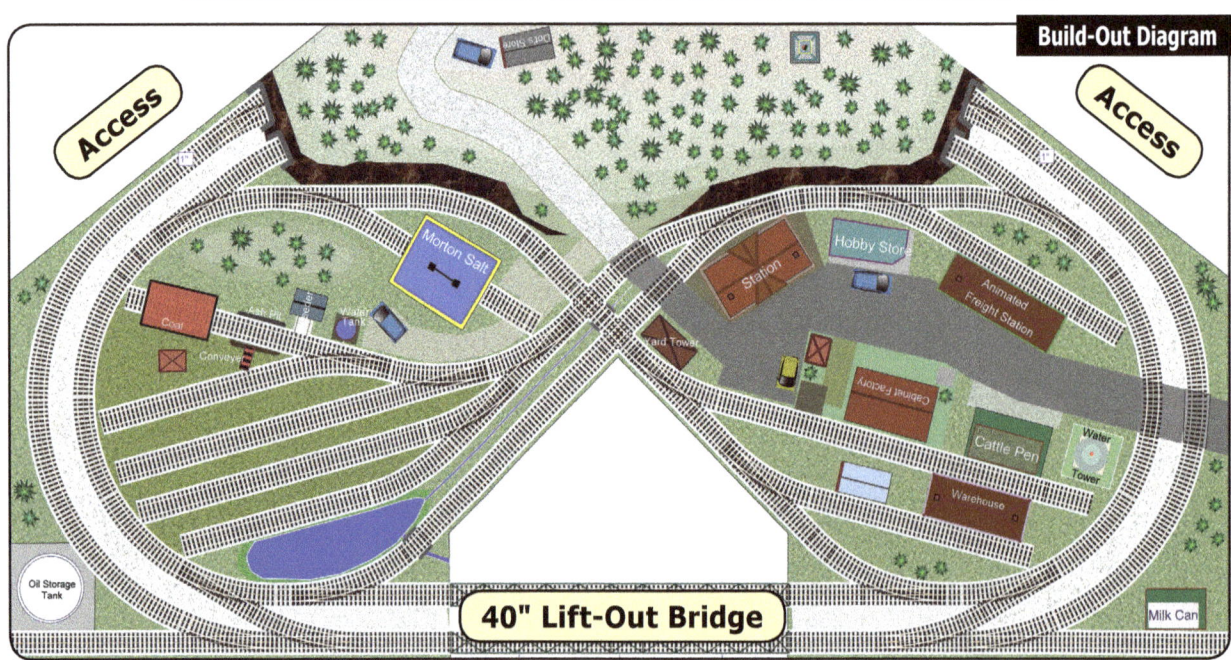

Build-Out Diagram

40" Lift-Out Bridge

The Great Valley Western RR in 4x8
Track Plan for a Sheet of Plywood

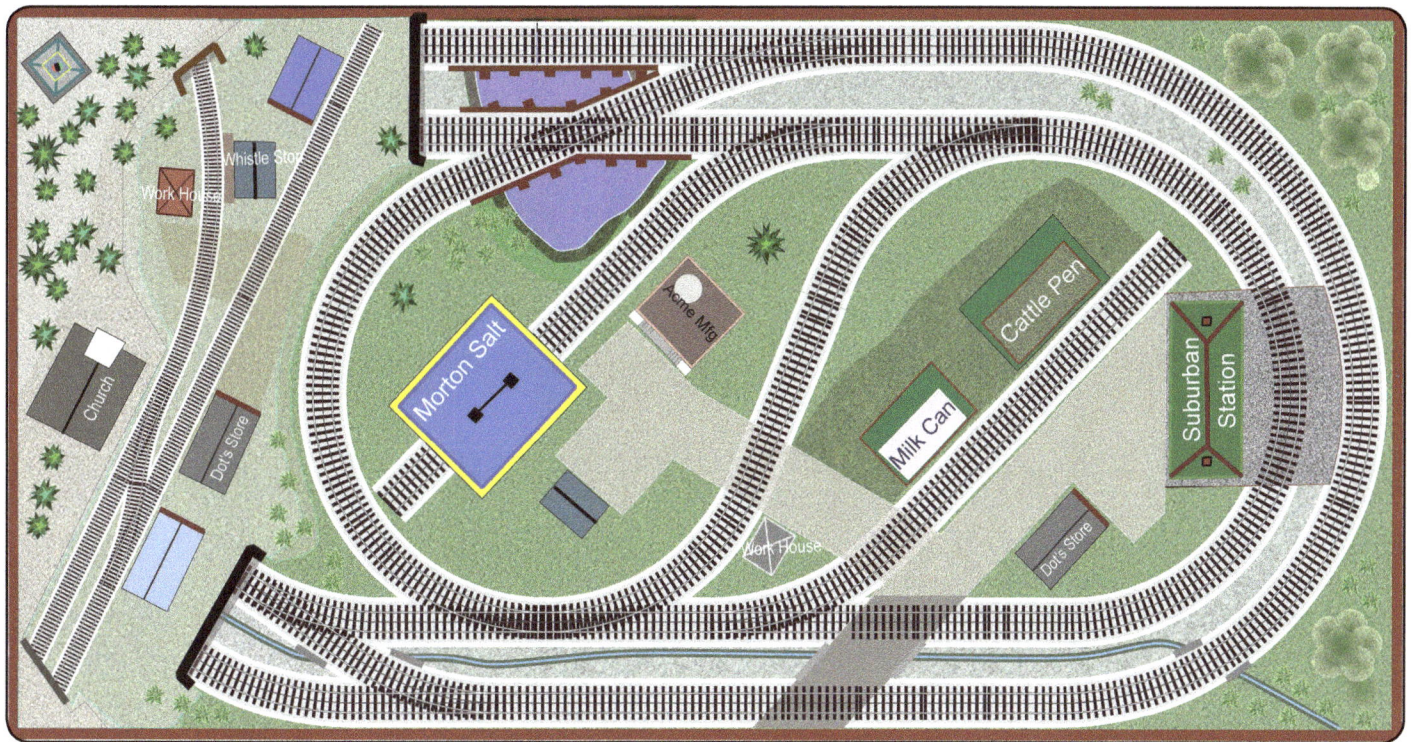

The Great Valley Western RR is a double-loop plan designed for Lionel FasTrack in 4'x 8' and mounted on a table framed with 1"x 4" lumber. The inside loop is all O31 track sections, and a mix of O36 and O48 is used to build the outside loop. This layout is a good two-train layout for beginning operators and can also host a third On30 narrow-gauge train on the mountain.

But besides the two-loop, double-track lines, there is also a twice-around route traversing the crossing at the center top and the crossover between the loops at the bottom left. When running the twice-around, the outside left curve under the mountain is not traversed, so it can hold a short train as a hidden staging track. Trains can then take turns running a few laps around this circuit.

There is also a reversing curve through the middle that allows trains to switch direction from counterclockwise to clockwise running. Reversing direction back to counterclockwise requires a backing move through this reversing curve.

Trains should be traditional trainset, properly sized for this small 4x8 layout that is limited with O31 curves on the inside loop route.

The On30 tracks at the left—atop the mountain—are for fun and interest, adding some eye-catching details with an old-time steam locomotive and car as a working tourist line. It is designed here with excellent and easy-to-use Kato Unitrack that snaps together with integrated roadbed, as FasTrack does. A locomotive can be set to be shuttled back and forth automatically with a timer delay as a third running train. This On30 line is optional, as is the mountain it runs across.

Construction in Phases

Phase 1: The first tracks to go down are the inside loop, along with the switches. With six switches, this phase is the largest expense. The FasTrack sections snap together very tightly in perfect alignment, so a little planning in the order of assembly might be needed. Start by connecting the crossing and switch to the left, then connect the reverse curve to the main line with the switch to the crossing, and then the rest will assemble easily.

Phase 2: The outside loop is next and will snap together without difficulty. This main line includes only two switches, an O72 left-hand and an O36 right-hand.

Phase 3: The optional terrain features of the pond and the mountain with tunnel are next. The pond is below-grade and should be painted with details added, such as rocks or logs, before the pond water is poured. The tracks cross the pond on simple trestles, constructed with small lengths of wood and supporting posts that will descend below the pond waterline.

The mountain is about six inches high or more, sufficient to allow clearance for the trains passing beneath. A variety of techniques can be tried, but plan to leave the left side open for access inside the tunnel. Towering above the layout on the mountain top height is Lionel's Rotating Beacon.

Phase 4: Optionally, add the On30 line. As noted earlier, Kato Unitrack is fun and easy to work with; and Bachmann offers a line of On30 locomotives and cars at modest expense, with optional sound and DCC decoders installed. The On30 arrives and departs the layout scene through tunnels, and five inches of clearance inside these tunnels will work well for On30 equipment.

Great Valley Western Railroad FasTrack Bill of Materials

Part No.	Description	Inner	Outer	Total
Straights				
6-12014	Straight 10"	5	3	8
6-12024	Straight 5"	1	2	3
6-12025	Straight 4-1/2"	2	3	5
6-12026	Straight 1-3/4"	4	7	11
6-12073	Straight 1-3/8"	7	1	8
6-12035	Lighted Bumper	2	0	2
6-12050	22.5° Crossing	1	0	1
Roadbed Trimmed 1 3/8" (with O72 switch and 22.5 crossing)		3	2	5
Curves				
6-81662	O31 Curve, angle 11.25°	8	0	8
6-37103	O31 Curve, angle 45°	6	0	6
6-12023	O36 Curve, angle 11.25°	0	10	10
6-12022	O36 Curve, angle 22.5°	0	4	4
6-12015	O36 Curve, angle 45°	0	1	1
6-16835	O48 Curve, angle 7.5°	0	5	5
6-16834	O48 Curve, angle 15°	0	5	5
6-12043	O48 Curve, angle 30°	0	0	6
Switches				
6-81253	O31 Right	1	0	1
6-81254	O31 Left	2	0	2
6-81947	O36 Left	3	0	3
6-81946	O36 Right	0	1	1
6-81953	O72 Left	0	1	1

Bill of Materials - Kato HO Scale Unitrack

Part No.	Description	Total
2-130	Straight 6-7/8"	1
2-150	Straight 9-3/4"	1
2-180	Straight 14-1/2"	3
2-250	31-1/8" Radius Curve, 22.5°	2
2-851	(EP550R), HO Kato Unitrack, Right switch 7-9/32"	2

The Great Valley Western Railroad

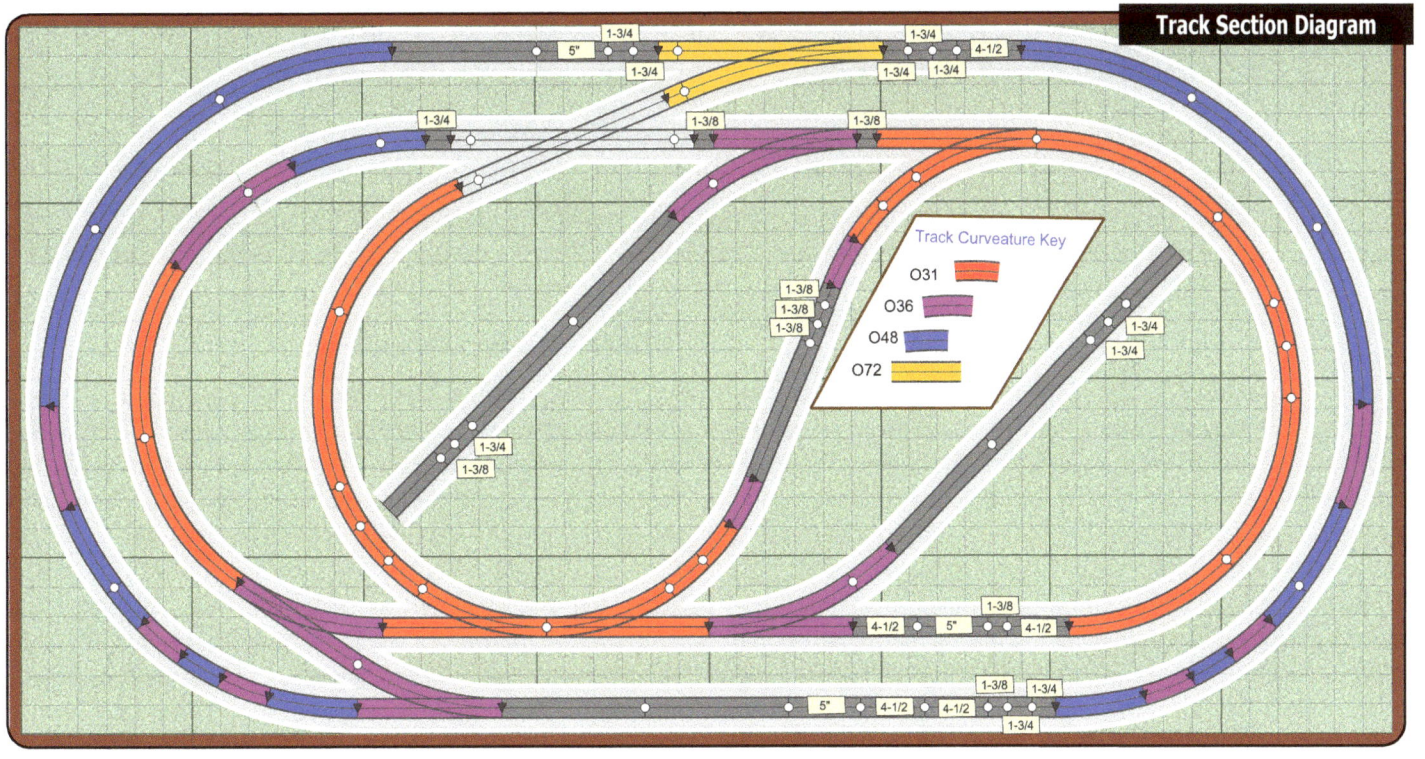

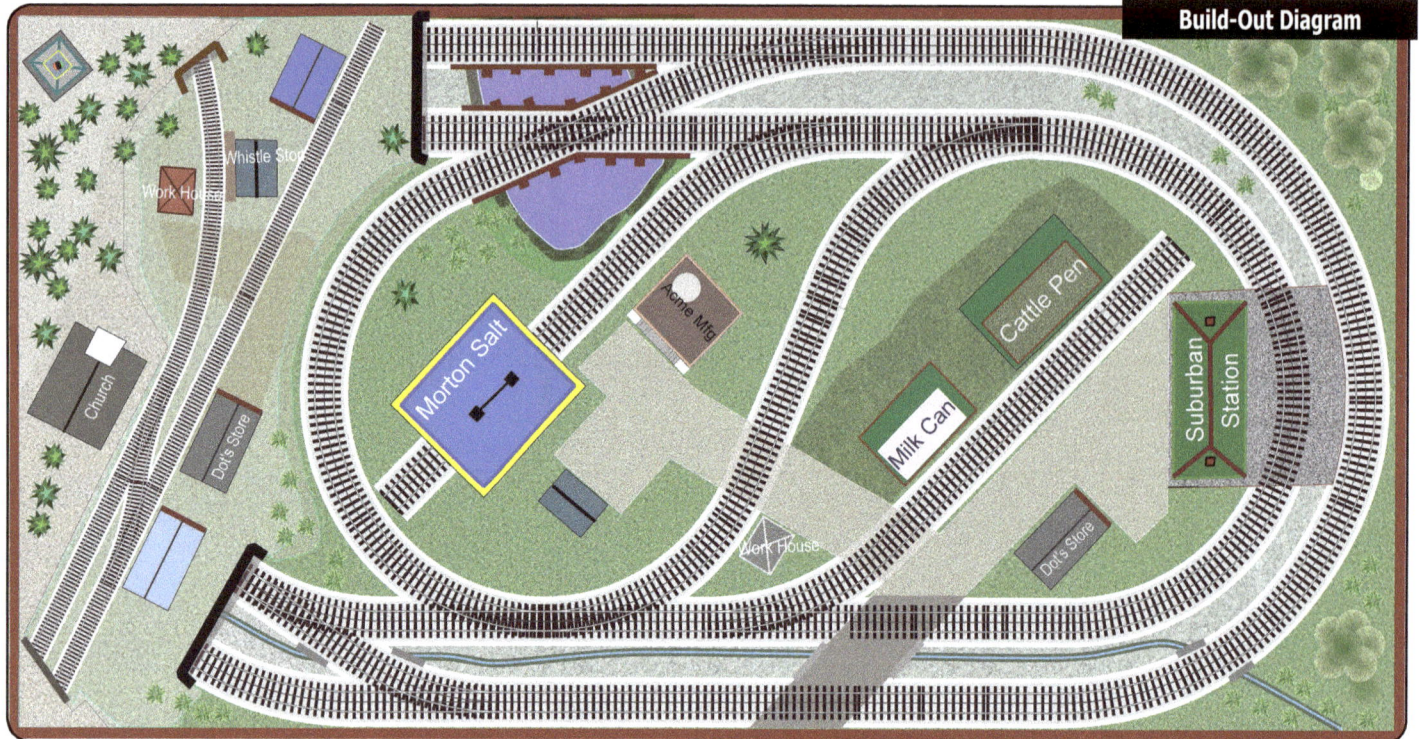

Structures

At the layout's right side is Lionel's Suburban Station, with a paved surface for travelers to reach a waiting train on either track. Nearby is Dotty's Store, from the OGR Ameri-Towne line. Moving left to the first industry track, at the switch is Lionel's Work House with Sound and two of Lionel's classic operating accessories: the Milk Can Unloader, and the Cattle Pen for exercising livestock. Lionel has produced several versions of these accessories, and there is space to accommodate the footprint of any version.

On the other side of the reverse track is the second industry track, shown with Menards Morton Salt Tower, with a track running through. Menards makes a variety of industries where the track runs though the structure, and a number of alternatives will fit in this space. Nearby is the OGR Ameri-Towne Acme Manufacturing structure and also a shack or small structure, or possibly a scratchbuilt shed.

On the mountain with the On30 line there are a variety of structures one can chose from various manufactures, including a church, a store, another Lionel Work House with Sound, and a small whistle stop station.

Power and Electrical

The O gauge layout needs adequate power for two-train operation, as well as for accessories and lighted buildings. Two Lionel train set CW-80s will be sufficient, and they should be ganged together on a power strip. This small layout can be operated with conventional control and can be divided at the switches for separate power blocks. It is suggested that each half of each oval be a separate block (four blocks total), and the two inside curves also be separate blocks. Power on/off switches for the tracks allow a locomotive to be parked on either. The layout can also be very conveniently operated using LionChief locomotives and command control.

This small layout could use manual switches if the layout can be pulled out to access around three sides (top, bottom, and right side). Otherwise, remote or command switches can be mixed in for convenience. Two of the tracks might be manual, as if a brakeman has to step off the locomotive to throw the switches.

The Great Valley Western RR layout plan is a great start as a first layout, requiring just a 4x8 space to work with while running two traditional O gauge trains, with opportunities for some fun operation. The layout is easy to build in stages, yet still makes for an exciting train-running layout that will entertain kids and visitors of all ages.

Happy Railroading!

The Southern & Pacific Railroad

Long Run Operation in 4-1/2'x 16'

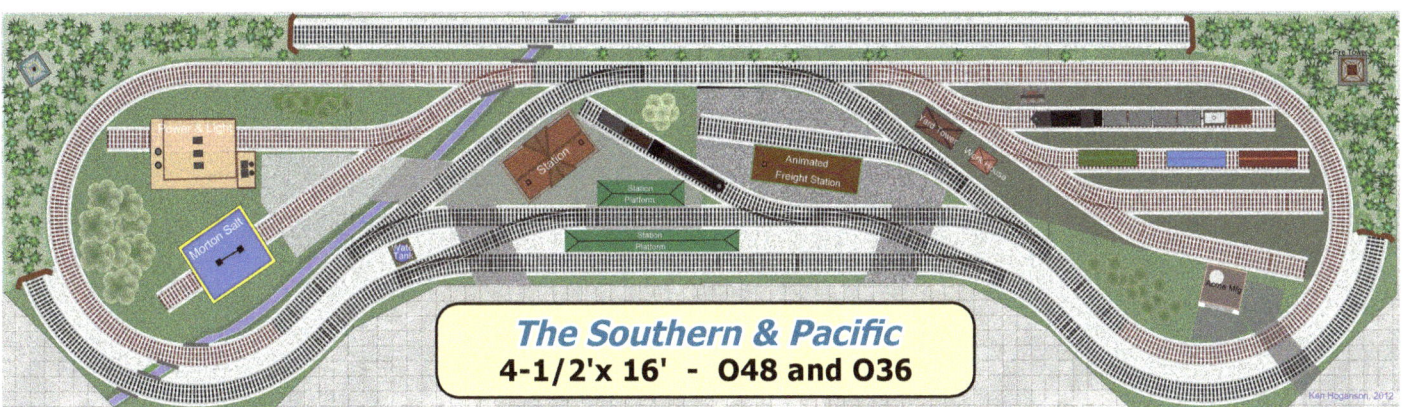

The Southern & Pacific
4-1/2'x 16' - O48 and O36

The Southern & Pacific Railroad Layout is a 4-1/2'x 16' design that uses two 4x8 sheets of layout foundation surface, with an O48 FasTrack minimum route (the outside loop) to run larger equipment beautifully, including scale trains requiring O36, and even the (somewhat rare) O42 equipment offered by Lionel.

Layout Base Construction

A first consideration: the O48 reverse loop at the end of the layout requires a minimum of 48" for the center-rail diameter FasTrack plus the 3-3/8" width of the track, and thus requires a minimum of 51-3/8" of total width.

With some space between the FasTrack and the layout surface, a minimum of 52" of width (4'4") might be needed to lay out a reverse loop. This layout design allows for a 4'6" width of layout surface at each end for the reverse curves, and it needs two identical sections. The surface can be trimmed to more closely follow the track.

The two 4x8 sheets are each cut at 4'6" to create the layout-end reverse curves sections, leaving two sections of material that are 4' long and 3'5" in width. These two sections comprise the middle sections of the layout (see Fig. 1). This shape creates an inside access indent area for easier reach across the layout and a space to operate the layout from. This basic form can be trimmed a bit to fit the track plan.

The framework for the layout can use any variety of structural support, but you might think about making the layout on two separate table-halves for possible future transport. Building the layout on a long, ridged table of 16' is also possible, rolling on casters or wheels to easily provide access to the back of the layout.

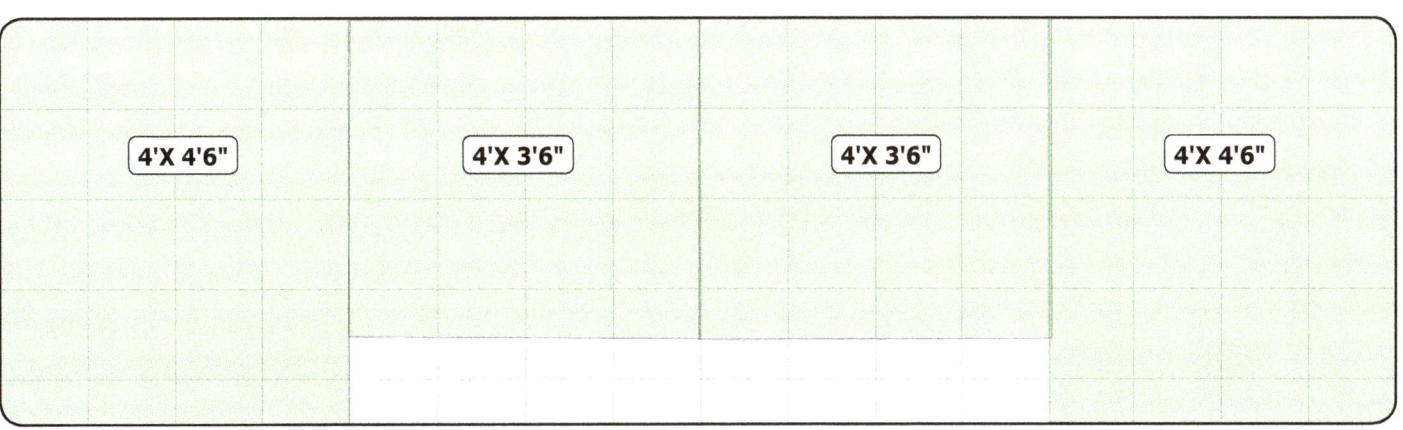

The Southern & Pacific Railroad

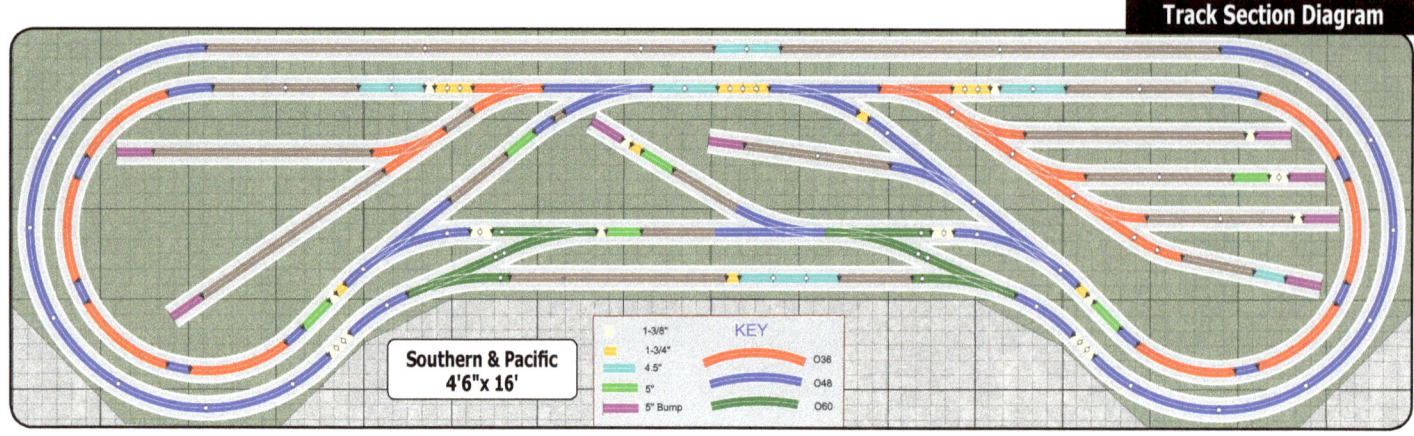

The Track Plan

The track plan is basically a dogbone shape with two routes. The outside route is O48 minimum, while the inside route is O36 with some O48 sections to widen the inside reverse curves to 38", thus bringing the two main lines closer together for better appearance. This also provides more interior space for the layout inside the main lines and increases the length of the inside loop run a bit.

The track plan has a pair of O60 crossovers linking the two main line loops together at a 6" center-rail spacing, which varies down to 5" at the closest. The inside main line also has two connections creating return loops so the inside main can reverse train direction, but also run as a loop-to-loop route. Trains on the outside main line can cross over to the inside main to change direction.

The plan features some industrial tracks, an engine set-out track negotiable by O42 locomotives in the center, and a small yard using O36 switches.

The long length of the railroad, at 16 feet, allows for some excellent views of trains running the layout while negotiating smooth curves, and of long high-speed trains running straight in the back. With the crossovers and two reverse loops, a huge amount of train-running fun is in the offing!

The Southern & Pacific Railroad
Lionel FasTrack Bill of Materials

Straights		
6-12042	Straight 30"	8
6-12014	Straight 10"	16
6-12024	Straight 5"	7
6-12025	Straight 4 ½"	12
6-12026	Straight 1 ¾"	19
6-12073	Straight 1 3/8"	18
6-12035	Lighted Bumper	7
Curves		
6-12043	O48, angle 30°	14
6-16834	O48 Curve, angle 15°	6
6-16835	O48 Curve, angle 7.5°	16
6-12015	O36 Curve, angle 45°	8
Switches		
6-12057 or 6-81951	O60 Left	2
6-12058 or 6-81950	O60 Right	2
6-12065 or 6-81949	O48 Left	3
6-12066 or 6-81948	O48 Right	3
6-12045 or 6-81947	O36 Left	4
6-12046 or 6-81946	O36 Right	2
Six Lionel O36 Curves, angle 11.25° are included with the switches. Only TWO are used.		

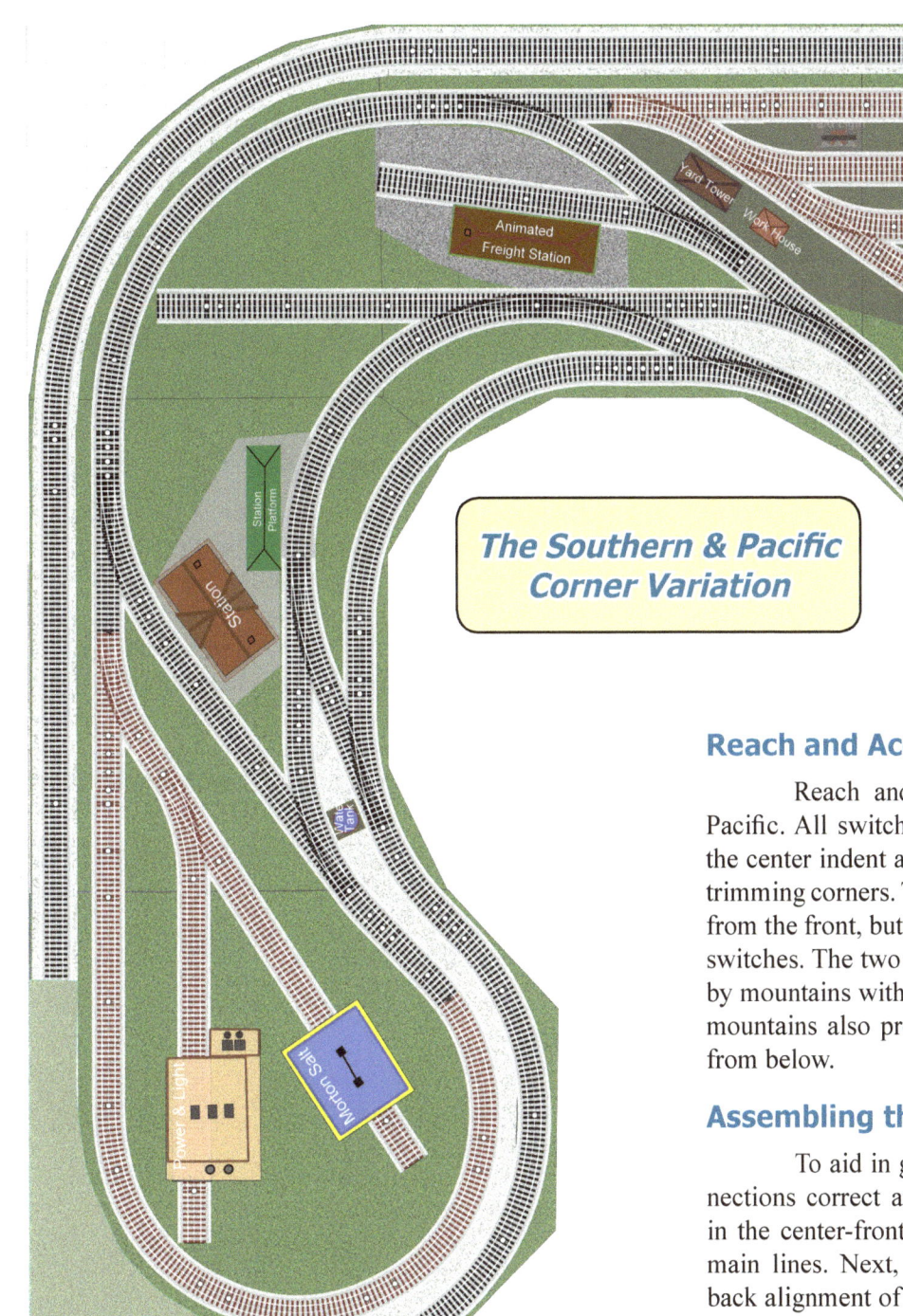

The Corner Variation

The Southern & Pacific Corner Variation

The Southern & Pacific Corner Variation

This track plan can also be converted to fit in a corner, creating a beautiful and engaging layout that can fill a small bedroom, requiring 11'4" on each side. Separating the return loops in the middle, a set of 90-degree curves is inserted, varying from O48 to O72 in curvature. The length of the main line runs is stretched with this idea, and more center space is created for more structures and scenery. A third 4x8 sheet of layout base material will be needed to span the corner space thus created.

Reach and Access

Reach and access are good on the Southern & Pacific. All switches are within a comfortable reach from the center indent and operating section. Access is eased by trimming corners. The outside back main line is a long reach from the front, but fortunately it is all straight track with no switches. The two back side corners of the layout are filled by mountains with tunnels for enhanced scenic beauty. The mountains also provide access (although not ideal) inside from below.

Assembling the Track

To aid in getting all FasTrack alignments and connections correct and tight, assembly of track should start in the center-front with the double-crossover between the main lines. Next, add the return-loop connections to the back alignment of the inside main. Then add the rest of the track, with tracks and the big curve-back loops of track.

Raising the Rear Straight for Visual Effect

The rear alignment of the outside main line can be optionally elevated. This happens frequently on prototype railroads, with parallel tracks at different heights. For this model railroad, elevating the back main line enhances the look of the railroad with a variation of track heights, and also serves as a commonly employed theatrical technique to have the rear of the layout rise in accordance with the angle of viewing from the operators and spectators as they look further back into the layout. A modest height increase of 1/4" to 1" will produce pleasant visuals and highlight the operation of trains on the long straight rear alignment.

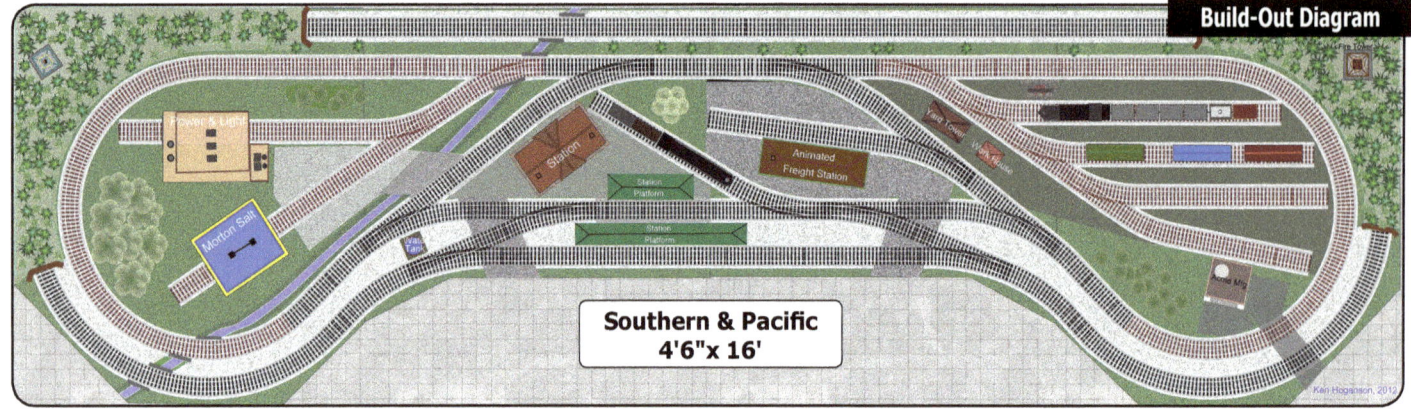

Alternatively, this long outside main line run between the crossover switches could be a place to use a trestle set to climb to a bridge in the center back, and then descend again back to level.

Wiring and Electrical

Two 80-watt power supplies, like Lionel's CW-80, should be sufficient to power the layout. But the length of the main line runs means that each main line needs multiple power connections. At a minimum, each section of track isolated by switches should have a power connection.

The outside main line should have four power connections: one in the middle of each reverse curve, one in the middle or the far back straight alignment, and one in the front between the crossover switches.

The inside main line similarly needs four power connections as well, in the same locations. Then, each track might have an on/off power toggle switch.

For conventional operation, each main line needs four blocks at a minimum: one between the crossover switch, and three dividing the long main lines into two curved blocks and a long straight block.

Command and LionChief control make things easier, but still require the eight main line power connections to the track.

All switches are within reach of the front indent and access area, and the close-in switches could be operated manually, if desired, and to save cost. But at least the back switches of the inside main line should be remote or command-controlled, as reaching across trains and scenery to these far switches will become tiresome.

Buildings and Structures

A Menards station is in the town center area, along with two platforms. One is from Lionel, while the narrow platform that runs between the parallel tracks at 6" center-rail spacing may need to be scratchbuilt. Also in the center area is Lionel's Animated Freight Station. To the left of the station, between the tracks, is a water tank, which could be from any manufacturer. To the right of the center area is the yard with Lionel's Yard Tower, Yard Light, and Work House with Sound. At the far right is Acme Manufacturing, from OGR's Ameri-Towne series. At the left is the industrial area, with two large, striking structures from Menards: the power plant and Morton Salt Tower.

Scenery

Scenery as shown is basic:

- Two corner tunnels over the outside main line
- One stream embedded into the layout about 3/4"
- An outside main line, raised in the back and ballasted
- Detailing with trees shrubs, weeds, and grasses
- A few short roads with level crossings over the tracks
- A road bridge over the stream

Conclusion

The Southern & Pacific layout offers excellent train-running and watching fun, with two independent main lines, return loops, and crossovers to maintain operating interest with a variety of routes. The wider O48 curves will enhance the look of trains running the layout, and the long main line runs will allow trains to **stretch out** on this long layout.

If you have a small room to dedicate to trains, consider the corner variation of the Southern & Pacific for even longer main lines and more space for structures and scenery.

Happy Railroading!

Twice the Fun on the Cisco RR
Two-Train Operation on a 4' x 8' Platform

Named for the real whistle-stop town of Cisco, Georgia, just four miles from the Tennessee border in the foothills of the Appalachian Mountains, the Cisco RR track plan is a great way to expand a Lionel FasTrack train set into a two-train empire in a limited space.

My fictional Cisco RR serves the small town of Cisco with its one store, two industries, water tower, and station platform at the edge of town along a gravel road that leads around the hill to a coal-loading facility. With your choice of terrain and vegetation, the railroad could be located in just about any region. The track plan accommodates modest-size steam or diesel power pulling freight and passenger trains. Any equipment that is happy with the Lionel O36 FasTrack curves included in the firm's starter sets will run just fine on this layout.

For ease in construction and a small footprint, the plan fits two independent O36 FasTrack routes on a single 4x8 sheet of plywood or, in this case, a 4x8 sheet of extruded polystyrene foam board available at home and building supply stores. The layout is ideal for conventional operation of traditional-size trains (typical train set equipment) and works great with Lionel's new LionChief and LionChief Plus trains.

The Concept

The plan consists of two independent routes linked by two short connecting tracks (Photo 1 and Figure A). Trains can run on each route without conflict or switching so two kids can run trains at the same time without tension or the need to throw switches or block toggles to get the trains past each other. The two independent routes also allow two-train continuous running without intervention, allowing you to kick back and enjoy watching the trains go.

The FasTrack O36 diameter curves included in Lionel train sets are the minimum diameter curves used in this layout. Lionel and nearly all other traditional train set engines and cars will negotiate these curves flawlessly and look good doing so. In addition to the minimum diameter of O36, each route includes easements leading from straight to curved, allowing trains to ease into the curves (Figure B). While only minimally improving operation for model trains, the prototypical wider-curve easements are aesthetically pleasing, leading the eye to see the curves as less sharp with trains gliding smoothly around the layout. See Figure C for the full list of track components.

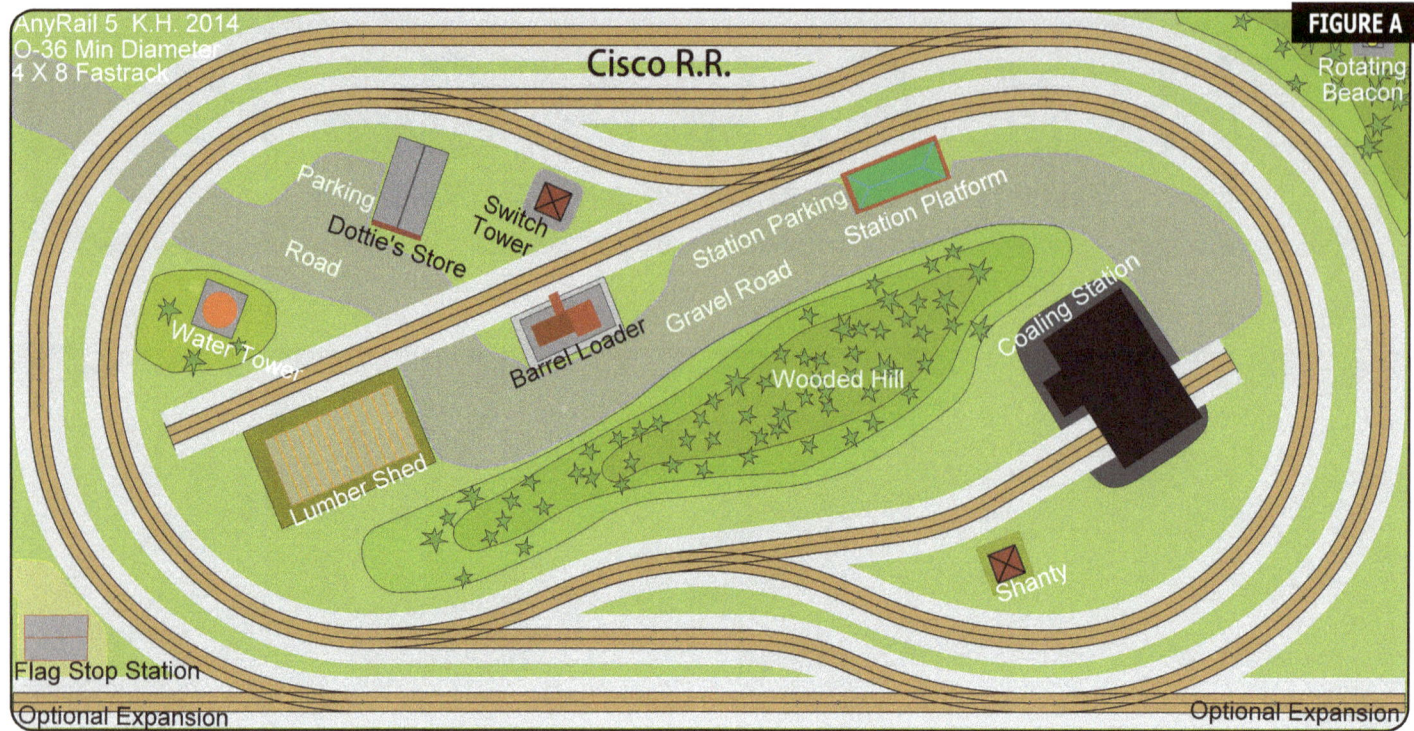

FIGURE A

The outer loop is O36 minimum diameter with the transition from straight to curve eased by O48 diameter curves. Also shown in Figure A are the optional O48 switches and layout expansion tracks leading off the edge of the layout. These may be included to connect the Cisco RR to the class 1 railroad of your choice, justifying the use of your favorite railroad locomotives as run-through power.

The inner route is a butterfly or hourglass shape with O36 minimum diameter curves and O60 switches easing into each curve. The waist of the hourglass is comprised of O48 switches and O48 curves. The inner route also includes two tracks to serve industry: one the town of Cisco and the other the Lionel coal loader facility.

The layout adheres to strong design guidelines for small layouts: minimum diameter O36 curves (as opposed to O27 or O31). All curves have easements from straight track, and switches are all wider than the minimum curve diameter. Even the S curves of the loop connecting tracks are made of a generous O60 switch with a short section of O36. These are good design rules to follow for any scale leading to a reliable and enjoyable layout.

The track plan also features more closely spaced parallel tracks for better viewing. The track spacing is 4-1/4" at its tightest points and about 5" at its widest, giving a more prototypical spacing with more than adequate room to allow O gauge trains to pass on the curves (the O48 and O60 easements help here). See Photo 2 of two trains at the closest spacing, with two steamers on parallel tracks.

Each Lionel O60 switch comes with two small 1-3/8" fitter tracks without roadbed on one side, designed to fit into the switch (see short section at top of Photo 3). These fitters are not needed if you trim a piece of FasTrack to match. Trimming a small section from the plastic roadbed is not hard and can be done with a hand tool or power tool. The Cisco track plan needs two pieces of O36, 22.5-degree curves with one edge trimmed.

LionChief or Command Control

For command control, wire the entire layout from a single power source without any power toggles with recommended two power drops in the middle of each loop semi-circle (four total). This will ensure that all trains will see strong power voltages across the entire layout.

Photo 2

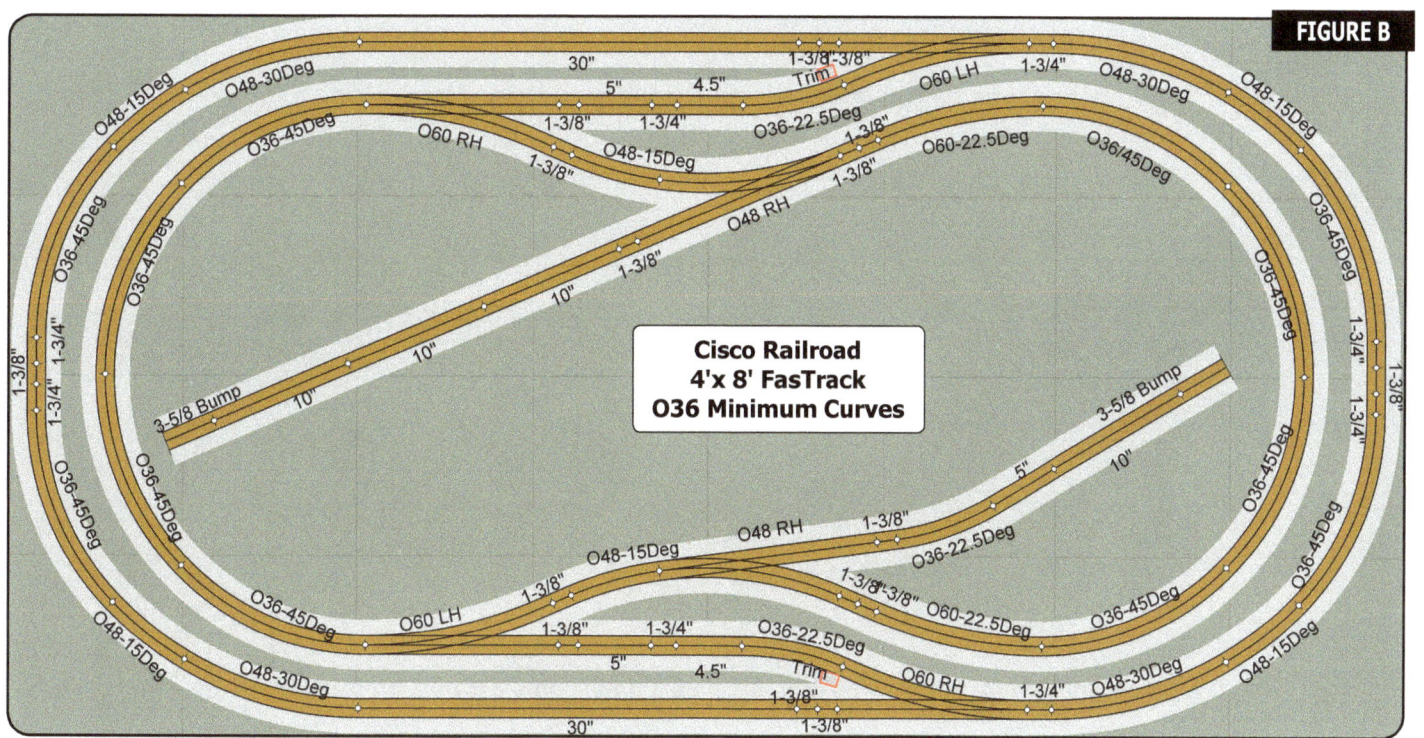

FIGURE B

Cisco Railroad
4'x 8' FasTrack
O36 Minimum Curves

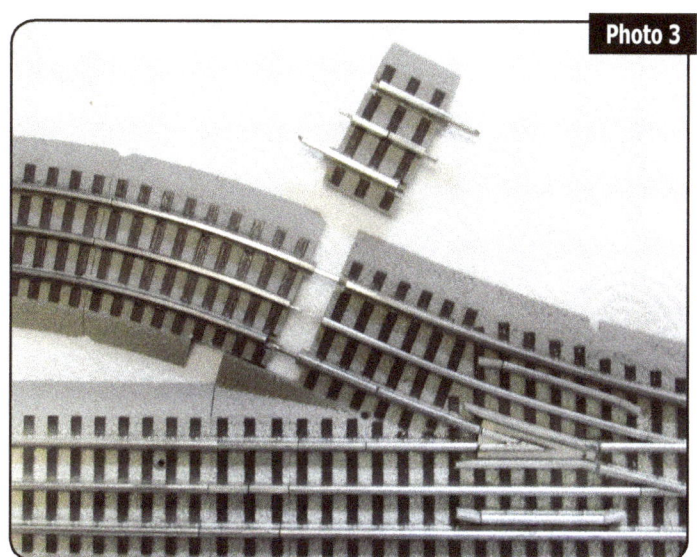

Photo 3

Conventional Transformer Control

Though this is a perfect layout for Lionel's Lion-Chief locomotives or another command control system, many engineers still prefer conventional transformer control. To run conventional control, wire each of the two loops to separate transformers with a shared common on the outside rails and the center rails from each route wired to a different transformer. One transformer will control the outer loop route, and the other will control the inner hourglass route.

The two short connecting tracks that connect the two loops should have isolated center rails, each wired to a single-pole, double-throw toggle. Each toggle connects its siding's center rail to either transformer thereby facilitating trains changing loops. This allows the dispatcher to electrically assign the connecting track to either the inside or the outside route. The two industry tracks should each have center rail on/off toggles to allow a parked locomotive to sit isolated on either track.

Constructing the Cisco

Cisco RR construction philosophy involves simplicity and ease in building for the new O-gauger who may be assembling a first layout. The layout could be constructed on traditional plywood, but I elected to use a 2-inch thick sheet of 4'x 8' foam insulation board (extruded polystyrene) for the platform (Photo 4). The foam sheet is rigid, light-weight, and portable. It can rest on a bed, kitchen table, dining table, or upon one or two folding tables (also portable of course). If your home building supply store does not stock the 2-inch thick foam, you can make do with three sheets of 1-inch thick foam board glued together.

1) The foam plus a grass mat covering results in a layout base quiet enough to listen to TV in an adjacent room at normal volume.
2) Wrap the edges of the foam sheet with Duct Tape to protect them from erosion while handling and to improve overall appearance (Photo 5).
3) Roll out the grass mat on the smoothest side of the foam sheet. The grass mats are sold larger than a 4x8, so trim one side and one edge to fit (Photo 6).

Photo 4

Photo 5

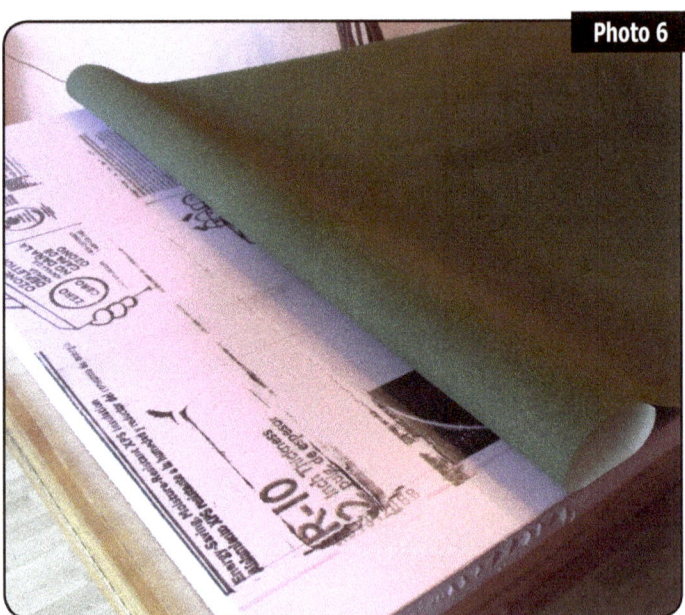

Photo 6

4) Working around the layout, glue one edge of the grass mat to the foam board using Gorilla Glue. Glue from the edge to about 4″ in—the interior of the grass mat should not be glued at this time. After applying the glue, place weights on the glued area (the glue behaves a bit like expanding foam and will rise up creating a hump without the weights). Allow about two hours to bond to 90 percent of its strength.

5) Now lay out and connect the FasTrack sections following the track diagram and then place the buildings. The structures and accessories I used are listed in Figure D. Do not fasten anything down at this point.

The Cisco RR runs all wires for power for track and buildings underneath the grass mat and above the foam foundation. This technique is very easy. It involves no crawling under the layout; the bottom of the foam board stays smooth and unobstructed; changes are easy to make; and mistakes are easily covered up. The foam board is easily compressed using thumb pressure alone to create a trough for the wires. All that's needed is one 50' roll of 22-gauge solid-core two-conductor wire (or two 25' rolls of different colors for track power and accessory power), a sharp hobby knife, and the transformer(s) or power sources of your choice (Photo 7). You will need two runs of wires: one for train power and a second for building and accessory power.

Cisco RailRoad Lionel FasTrack Bill of Materials

FIGURE C

(Without optional layout expansion connections)

Part No.	Description	Qty
Switches		
6-12057 or 6-81951	O60 Left Remote Only or O60 Left Remote & Command	2
6-12058 or 6-81950	O60 Right Remote Only or O60 Right Remote & Command	2
6-12066 or 6-81948	O48 Right Remote Only or O48 Right Remote & Command	2
Curves		
6-12056	O60 22.5-degree	2
6-12043	O48 30-degree	4
6-16834	O48 15-degree	6
6-12015	O36 45-degree	12
6-12022	O36 22.5-degree	3
Straights		
6-12042	30" Straight	2
6-12014	10" Straight	6
6-12024	5" Straight	3
6-12025	4.5" Straight	2
6-12026	1-3/4" Straight	8
6-12073	1-3/8" with roadbed both sides	6
Included in switch	1-3/8" with roadbed one side	6
6-12035	3-3/4" Lighted Bumpers	2

Cisco Railroad List of Buildings and Structures

FIGURE D

Part No	Description	Size
Lionel 6-37102	Watchman Shanty (lighted)	2-1/4 X 2-1/2
Lionel 6-81629	Lumber Shed	6-1/8 X 3-1/8
Lionel 6-81017	Barrel Loading Building (lighted)	5-3/4 X 3 X 3
Lionel 6-81016	Coaling Station (lighted)	13 X 9-7/8
Lionel 6-37166	Crossing Shanty (lighted)	2-1/3 X 2-1/2
Lionel 6-37807	Station Platform	5-3/4 X 2-7/8
Ameri-Towne	Dotty's Store Kit	6 X 3
Ameri-Towne	Flag Stop Station	3 X 4
RMT	Water Tower (lighted)	3 X 3 X 12
RMT	Rotating Beacon (lighted)	3 X 3 X 12

The Cisco RR runs LionChief locomotives, greatly simplifying locomotive power wiring. Power enters the layout at one corner where wires dive beneath the grass mat and provide power to each of the loops nearby. A wire pair also runs beneath the outer route track to the other end of the layout. This run will connect to a track section within each train route. Power connects at four places on the layout: two connections at each end of the loops.

Power for the lighted buildings is routed from the transformer to the nearest building and then runs in turn to the next and the next working from one end of the layout to the other. Underneath each building will be access for wires to provide power.

1) Begin where your power will enter the layout. Here a single CW-80 transformer on one corner of my layout provides all power for trains and accessories. Create a flap in the grass mat, using a hobby knife, positioned to allow the wires from the power supply to dive under the grass mat.
2) Make an X in the grass mat beneath the four track sections that will connect train power. Flip back the four sides of the mat to allow access beneath.
3) Cut a length of two-conductor power wire to run from the power supply to each of the two track sections that will connect power, allowing extra length. Remove insulation from each wire end.
4) Push the wires beneath the grass mat from the power supply flap over to each track access flap.
5) Connect the wires at the transformer and to two track sections. Test connectivity. Reconnect track sections and test a locomotive on each loop.
6) Push down using thumb pressure to indent the foam board so it accepts the wires running beneath the grass mat.

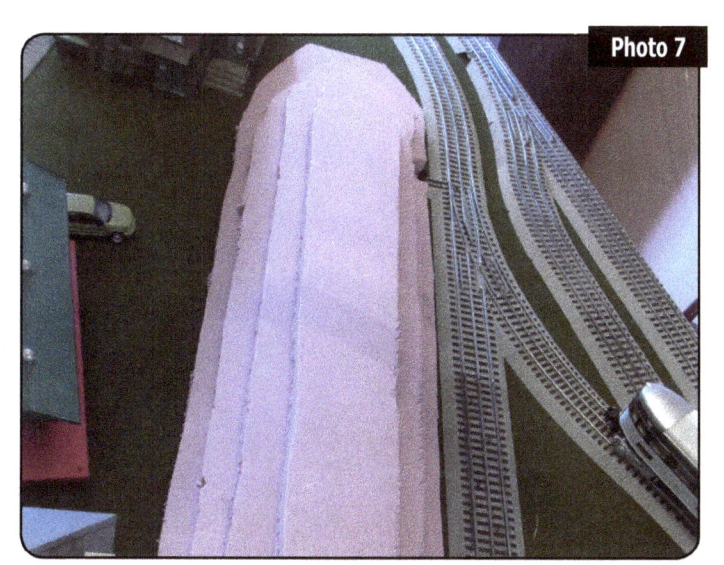

Photo 7

The Cisco Railroad

7) Run a length of two-conductor wire from the power supply to an access hole beneath the outer track route. This wire runs beneath the track and above the mat all the way to the far end of the layout where it will provide power to the far end of the layout.
8) Connect power to each track route and test with a locomotive. Trains should be able to circle the layout without problems.
9) Run accessory and building lighting wires from the transformer to the first structure, feeding beneath the grass mat. Each structure will be joined in turn working from one end of the layout to the other. Test that power reaches each structure as you progress and that the building lights properly.

Create a Scenic Feature

As a simple and possibly first layout, the Cisco uses lightweight modern foam materials to construct a single, long, thin, wooded hill and commercially available trees.

Scenery Materials

Half of a 4x8 sheet of 1-inch thick foam to be cut into layers to build up the hill
A sharp hobby knife and one hacksaw The hacksaw will make a mess but leaves natural-looking rough surfaces and eroded shapes.
One 16 oz tub of Woodland Scenics Foam Putty used to fill and smooth the hillsides as desired
Tan and green spray paints
Assorted trees and foliage

1) Cut the rough hill shapes. Using the hobby knife, cut four foam layers to shape the hill, checking the shape on the layout (Photo 8).
2) Glue the layers using either white glue or Gorilla Glue sandwiched between boards with weight on top and allow to dry overnight.
3) Shape the hill with the knife and hacksaw accepting the inevitable mess and clean-up. Have fun shaping the terrain to your liking (Photo 9).
4) Use Foam Putty to fill and smooth your hill as you like. It's okay to experiment; the foam putty remains flexible and removable (Photo 10).
5) Repeat steps 3 and 4 until satisfied with hill shape and texture.
6) Spray the hill with tan or earth-colored paint in an outside or well-ventilated area using newspapers to protect overspray areas.
7) Using green spray paint, spray the top surfaces of the hill. Grass, moss, and vegetation will cling more to the horizontal surfaces, but steep-angled hillsides should also receive some green. Be creative and experiment. An optional step at this point is to add commercial grass sprinkled onto the paint while still wet.
8) After the paint is thoroughly dry, plant trees and vegetation using white glue (Photo 11).

Photo 9

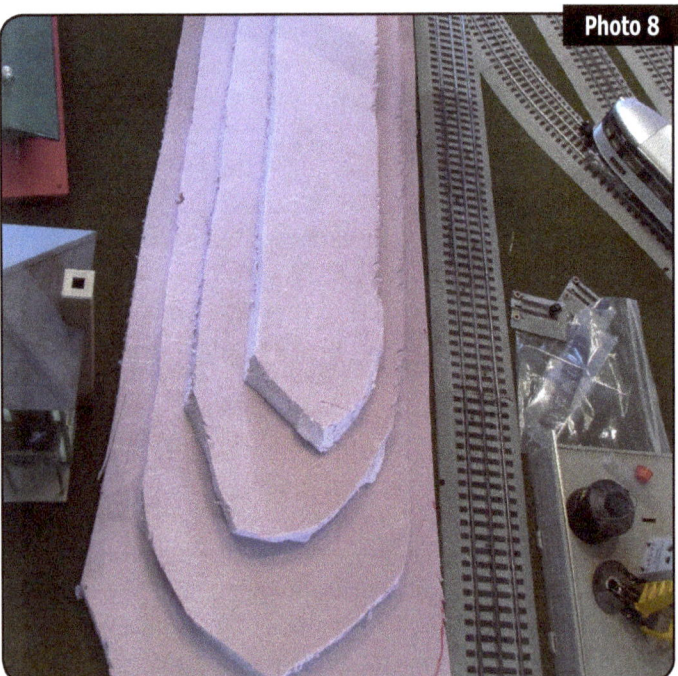

Photo 8

Photo 10

Secure the Track

The Cisco road construction is intended to be lightweight and portable. Moving the layout requires first removing the trains, vehicles, and some scenic details, but the FasTrack needs to be secure.

1) I used screw-type hollow-core door and drywall anchors to secure the track with screws that can be removed to access the underside of the track or to move or add track. You'll need a total of 50 anchors, 50 No. 6 x 1″ sheet-metal screws and a Phillips-head screwdriver (Photo 12). Note that the screws packaged with the anchors have round heads that project above the roadbed while the replacement No. 6 sheet-metal screws seat flush.
2) Doing a section of the layout at a time, use a nail or small screwdriver to push through the FasTrack mounting holes to puncture the grass mat and foam below thus marking the location for the anchors. Most track sections will need only one anchor.
3) Remove the track sections. Using the screwdriver, widen each hole a bit by inserting with a single thrust.
4) Insert a large drop of Gorilla Glue into each hole.
5) Insert and screw an anchor into each hole so the anchor is flush with the foam top (Photos 13 and 14).
6) Repeat steps 1 through 4 for the entire layout. Allow the glue to set at least two hours.
7) Screw each FasTrack section into the anchors.
8) Each switch accepts two screws. Take care to ensure that the screws don't interfere with movement of the switch points.

Road Building

Road Building Materials
HO scale cork roadbed, 9´
HO scale cork sheets, 3´ for parking areas
Krylon Natural Stone textured paint, your color choice or Granite color
Brads 3/4" to 1" long and thin with a small head for securing the cork roadbed to the foam

Photo 15

Roads are constructed easily and inexpensively using HO scale cork roadbed.

1) Paint the roadbed in a well-ventilated area separating about half of it into sides, each with a beveled edge. Do not try for a perfectly painted surface, but allow the cork texture and color to show through for a more natural look.

2) Lay out the road where you would like it to run. A beveled-edge roadbed section forms each road side with a center section of roadbed not yet separated. Use a sharp hobby knife to slice sections. Push brads through the roadbed into the foam to hold it in place (Photo 15).

3) Use Foam Putty to fill in cracks and edges and to create a simple grade crossing.

4) Touch up with textured spray paint. Careful application can be done to the assembled roads on the layout with barriers for overspray. Alternatively, spray into the inside of the can top and use a brush to dab and paint the roadbed and Foam Putty filler.

Once you've reached this point, all that's really left to do is the fine detailing. Add an assortment of vehicles, people and animal figures, benches, trash, parts, lumber, mailboxes, etc. around the layout to suit your tastes.

This completes an action-packed, 4'x 8' starter layout that supports operation of two trains, conventional or with command control (Photo 16). This railroad will provide fun and easy operation in a compact space with attractive scenery and train-watching views and with plenty of options for future expansion.

Happy Railroading!

Photo 16

www.ingramcontent.com/pod-product-compliance
Lightning Source LLC
Chambersburg PA
CBHW051307110526
44589CB00025B/2968